T0369261

POINT OF SORROW

- -

AYERSVILLE PILOTS FOOTBALL
From the Playground to Playing in the
Ohio High School State Championship

Andrew P. Groll
with Lynn F. Groll

Order this book online at www.trafford.com
or email orders@trafford.com

Most Trafford titles are also available at major online book retailers.

© Copyright 2010 Andrew P. Groll with Lynn F. Groll.
All rights reserved. No part of this publication may be reproduced, stored in a retrieval system,
or transmitted, in any form or by any means, electronic, mechanical, photocopying, recording,
or otherwise, without the written prior permission of the author.

You may contact the author by e-mail groll@frontiernet.net

Printed in Victoria, BC, Canada.

ISBN: 978-1-4269-2401-9 (sc)

*Our mission is to efficiently provide the world's finest, most comprehensive book publishing
service, enabling every author to experience success. To find out how to publish your book,
your way, and have it available worldwide, visit us online at www.trafford.com*

Trafford rev. 1/6/2010

www.trafford.com

North America & international
toll-free: 1 888 232 4444 (USA & Canada)
phone: 250 383 6864 ♦ fax: 812 355 4082

DEDICATION

For my parents, Gary and Pat Groll, who asked for
so little and gave so much. By attending 242 of my
school sporting events, you were the true Champions.

Winners do things losers don't like to do.

-Coach Craig McCord

CONTENTS

PART III: The Playoffs

ACKNOWLEDGEMENTS

There are many people that I would like to thank for helping me write this book. Without them, it would not have been possible. The abundance of help offered, when I asked for something, was overwhelming.

My wife Lana for supporting me and being so understanding while I spent most of my time at the computer, on the phone, or buried in game film. You were always there for me. For being there to bring me whatever I needed and for listening to me ramble on about the different ideas I had. For giving me that smile whenever I started to complain about the technical details of the book. You are the best!

My parents Gary and Pat Groll, they have always been supportive, and without them, none of this would have been possible. Also for keeping so many things from my playing days, it made it much easier knowing I had so much information in a box you saved for me.

My five children (Brie, Carly, Greg, Billy, and Austin) for always wanting to know what I was doing and when I would be done with the book.

My Brother Lynn Groll for all of his help with this project, the endless editing, grammar corrections and unique writing style he brought to the book. Without him, I could not have done it. Also for getting me permission to use the photos from *The Crescent News*, you made it happen.

William B Evans, author of *"Growing Up Green"*, for his help with auto shapes, advice on publishing a book, and help getting started with this project.

Coach Craig McCord for leading our team, showing us the right way to play, giving us the skills to not only succeed in football, but in life as well. For the use of his plays, formations and other contributions, you have always been there for all of us.

Rob Giesige for his input, contributions, help locating different players, pictures and the use of his scrapbooks.

Jeff Okuly, who gave me his time, and for all of his contributions, including pizza, beverages, cookies, pictures and the use of his scrapbook.

Hope Okuly for being a computer whiz, scanning, formatting and sending Jeff's pictures directly to my computer, which was a huge help, while Jeff and I reminisced.

Missy (McCord) Weyrich for making my scrapbook, I had so much information right at my fingertips.

Steve Deitrick for going beyond anything I asked of him and putting so many great details in e-mails. Steve also contributed some pictures, including the cover photo.

The Crescent News for covering our games and the use of their pictures.

Susan Johnston for taking pictures for me at the state final and welcome home, I used two of them in the book.

I would like to thank all of these individuals for the memories and contributions they made to the book. Jerry Carnahan, Chris Schlachter, Denny Martin, Shelby Dawson, John Finn, Tim Boals, Mike Wilson, Eric Burket, Marv Andrews, Aaron Roth, George Schaffer, Kim (McCord) Engel, Amy (Shinabery) Snyder, Kristen (Bell) Warren, Coach Don Hammersmith, Coach Norman Beck, Coach Jeff Maag, Coach Bill Ondrus, Teresa Weddelman, Mark Weddelman, Doug Johnston, Tolly Hanna, Todd Hanna, Jaime Briseno and Johnny Armes.

AUTHORS NOTE

The following is a depiction of the events of the 1986 Ayersville High School football season, and the events that preceded that magical season. This is a true story and every precaution was taken in trying to provide a true and accurate account of the details involved.

Even with all of the resources available, certain events may be remembered differently by those involved because a lot of the story is based on the memories of me and the individuals that could remember certain details.

I used game film to give an accurate account of each of the games played in 1986. Newspaper articles were also used to gain knowledge of our opponents each week.

Nothing in this story is meant to offend anyone in any way. This is the way it was remembered and no facts were skewed in my quest to depict the events as they happened.

Some of the accounts in this story were either written or told to me by the individual credited with the information provided. I have no way of validating the information and present it to the reader as it was provided to me. In an effort to provide the most accurate story possible, I tried to get at least two accounts of the same story for validity sake.

To help the reader better understand formations, plays, and even the school ground layout, I inserted diagrams at the back of the book that will enable the reader to get a better understanding of the technical aspects of the book.

I took opponents names, height, weight and grade, right from the game programs provided on the night of the game. In no way would a spelling error or numerical error be intended in my account of these details.

Some of the records contained in this book may no longer be accurate. The story is meant to be an accurate depiction of the year 1986 and before.

Sit back, and follow along, as a group of young men, women, coaches and a whole community, create a lifetime of memories and allow the reader to be a part of it in "Point of Sorrow". I hope you find the reading enjoyable.

PROLOGUE

Everyone else had left the locker room, but still I sat there in my familiar place, directly in front of my locker. I was in street clothes, but my helmet was on, buckled tightly. The smell of powder and an entire season's worth of sweat still lingered. Only a few lights were on, creating a dim and peaceful atmosphere.

We had just returned to the locker room to gather our belongings after a welcome home assembly in our gymnasium. The place was packed with hundreds of screaming fans and children waving their support. We had not been victors, but still the jubilation in the gymnasium would have made you think otherwise. We had just culminated our season in a one-point heartbreaking loss in the Division V Ohio High School Football State Championship to Newark Catholic. Yet, we were welcomed home as if we were victorious.

I sat there in front of my locker, unable to move, helmet still on, tears under both eyes and the big arm of our standout tackle, Jeff Okuly, draped across my back. He had stayed behind, not allowing anyone to be left behind.

"Groll, we have to go, Coach needs to lock up," he pleaded.

"Give me a few more minutes, I am enjoying the view," I replied.

The view being face mask bars, the warrior mode, when the helmet went on and we were ready for battle. Anyone who played football can remember that view, it was priceless.

His words came again, "Groll, come on, we really have to go."

I replied, "I can't seem to leave Oak (his nickname), we will never be sitting here again, I will never wear this helmet again."

He whispered dejectedly, "I know, we had a great year, we had four good years. It was a great time of our lives. We lost, but it's time we got out of here, everyone is taking this loss hard."

Still I sat there. It wasn't the loss that was keeping me in front of the locker with my helmet on. Even if we had won the game, I still would have been sitting there in the same exact way. It was over, the AYERSVILLE FOOTBALL experience. The view I enjoyed for four years was gone.

We finally made our way out of the locker room. When we walked by the coaches office, Coach Craig McCord was sitting in a chair, his hat off, and his head in his hands. All of the memories came over us; he was our leader, the man responsible for all of those memories. He was literally the cornerstone of AYERSVILLE FOOTBALL.

We did not disturb him because he needed his moment as much as we needed ours. We closed the door and reluctantly trudged our way in silence to the parking lot.

The following will explain my journey to that moment in time, just hours after our heartbreaking loss in the Division V state championship. It was not a journey I would walk alone, it would be OUR journey.

INTRODUCTION

The peaceful and quaint town of Ayersville is located just outside of Defiance, Ohio on the corner of Highland Center Road and Ayersville Road. I don't think you could really even say there is a downtown area. The school, gas station, firehouse, Ayersville Telephone Company and the D&G's Dairy Bar were the only attractions during the time frame of this story. The school district consists mainly of rural farm homes. There is the occasional warm and friendly sub-division here and there, and of course the strips of homes that line the streets right around the Ayersville School, but most of the students come from the flat, crop-growing outlying areas. The district consists of the region south of the Maumee River, which stretches to Putnam County, and from the city of Defiance, all the way to Henry County.

The school building lays in an L-shape, consisting of the elementary on the north end, the middle school in the middle, and the high school on the south edge. The two-story building is made of brick, and delights the eye as its contours and sprawling grounds take shape in the viewer's mind.

Behind the school lies the vast area of a playground, grass practice fields, six baseball and softball diamonds, two tennis courts, and in the far northeast corner, a state-of-the-art track encircles a perfectly manicured football field. On the edge of the school property stands a water tower with the letters AYERSVILLE painted on it. The tower can be seen from miles and has been welcoming and beckoning our opponents for years. There could be many stories written about the history of the Ayersville School, but there is only one that I would be interested in writing about, and that is football.

Ayersville football began in the fall of 1974. In the initial year of the program, the team played three freshmen games. The following year in 1975, the team grew and completed an eight-game reserve schedule. The team continued to grow, and by 1976, Ayersville football was on the map.

The first year of varsity football at Ayersville occurred in the autumn of 1976 under the direction of head coach Craig McCord, who had been the original coach when the team began to take shape back in 1974. The 1976 team did not win a single game, eight games resulted in a loss, and the game against Tinora resulted in a 0-0 tie.

However, the first gridiron team ever at Ayersville was never forgotten. Coach McCord would make reference to them each and every year, about how those players were against all odds, but they never ever gave up. It was obvious to anyone that played for Coach McCord, even though this team never won a game, they would always hold a special place in his heart. This team paved the way for future teams and the success of the program.

In 1977, the team went 7-3 and Coach McCord had started a tradition and winning program in the short span of four years. The 1978 team finished at 5-5, narrowly escaping a losing season. The juniors of that team went on to work hard, and finished with an impressive 8-2 record the following year in 1979. The 1980 team continued the winning ways and achieved a 7-3 record. In 1981, the team once again rebounded to 8-2 before falling back to 6-3-1 in 1982.

This brought the overall record of Ayersville and Coach McCord to 41-26-2 going into the 1983 season. Coach McCord had taken a non-existent program and turned it into an annual winner.

Would the winning ways continue? Would Coach McCord ever suffer a losing season again? Would Ayersville ever win a conference championship? Would a team ever go 10-0? Was playoff football on the horizon?

All of those questions would be answered in the next four years. I was blessed with the opportunity to be there for those years, the seasons of 1983 through 1986. It was a special time, filled with highs, lows, laughter, sadness, friends, and especially memories. The memories of football, but especially the memories of the times we shared.

Part I:
Before 1986

CHILDHOOD

I grew up just outside of Defiance, Ohio and went to the Ayersville School from kindergarten until the time I graduated. I was raised in a nice farmhouse where we farmed, raised vegetables, made cider, raised beef steers, fished and hunted. You could say I grew up country. I have an older brother, two older sisters and a younger brother. My family was a huge part of my life and they all played a part in my football career.

My Mom, Pat, did so many little things that went unnoticed at the time. I can't believe she put up with it. She washed all of my clothes. She made sure I was well fed, always had an encouraging word, and supported me through everything. She never ever missed a single game I played in. She was a cheerleader on Ayersville's 1957 state champion basketball team. Going to their 25-year reunion celebration gave me my first taste of what it was like to be on a magnificent team.

My Dad, Gary, was an inspiration to me; he too never missed a single game. It was his never-say-die-attitude, which inspired me to never give up. After he broke his leg and couldn't even walk, he would still sit in a chair and throw footballs to me.

My oldest brother, Darrel, enjoyed some fine success on the baseball field at Ayersville. By watching him play, and by going to all of his games, I became interested in team sports. I also experienced the magic in a playoff run, as his team advanced to the regional baseball tournament in 1976.

My next oldest sibling is my sister Teresa. She took me to my first Ayersville High School football game in 1977. She took me to lots of games. She would take me everywhere with her and I am in debt to her for treating me so nicely when I was just a little kid tagging along.

My next oldest sister, Tammy, took me to the games after Teresa graduated. She would even pick me up after practice sometimes when I was in junior high. She would also blast the song "I Ran So Far Away" by A Flock of Seagulls on her cassette deck while we drove home in her infamous Audi.

My youngest brother, Lynn, was my most feared opponent. He was in kindergarten during my senior year, but that didn't stop us from playing a lot of football together. I would get down on my knees and we would play full tackle football right on our dining room floor if we couldn't go outside. We kept score and he always won.

I remember when I first got the football bug, and it must have been something fierce when I did get it. It was around 1975 when I pulled my first football card out of a loaf of Wonder Bread. The pads and helmet just drew me in. The next day, I was outside in the snow becoming a football player.

Growing up, we didn't have any access to pee-wee football or anything else of that nature, so until we got in the seventh-grade, there would be no organized football. If we did have it, my Mom surely kept it a secret, so as not to draw too much interest from me. I think deep down, she was always hesitant about me playing.

Getting equipment was my next desire. I wanted a helmet and all of the pads. This was a time when we didn't get just everything we wanted. Money was tight, so a young boy's football equipment would have to wait.

That Christmas, I did get a helmet. It was the most awesome helmet in the world to me. It was cheap, plastic and white with a blue stripe; a piece of crap by today's standards. I really didn't care what it looked like, it had a face mask and chin strap. *Wow, how cool would I feel wearing an actual football helmet?*

Even though I didn't get the shoulder pads and other stuff, I could improvise. An old lifejacket under a big shirt became my shoulder pads. How many other people have used a lifejacket or something similar for football pads? I wadded up socks, and anything else I could find, and stuck them in my pants for pads.

Next was the absolute most essential item of my football ensemble. I had a football card of Carl Eller, the Minnesota Vikings' ferocious defensive end at the time. He looked liked the meanest guy I had ever seen and he was wearing these terrifying black gloves. I needed the gloves, so I got a pair of my Dad's brown jersey gloves, stuffed them full of paper towels, and on my small hands, they looked like Carl's massive black gloves.

I was ready for some football. I went outside to take on my opponent. Once outside, just off our driveway, there they were. Some were big, some were small, but all of them were tall, that's for sure. They may have all been taller than me, but not a one was faster. I was looking at the woods beside our driveway. That's right, my opponents on that day were trees.

My parents and siblings used to laugh so hard at me. "Look at that idiot out there trying to tackle a tree," they'd say. "He is going to kill himself. How dumb do you have to be to run into trees?"

I didn't care, they were very worthy opponents and they never talked smack when they got the best of me. The smaller saplings would even bend when I would run into them; sometimes I would run right over them. The bigger trees wouldn't budge and I would have to hit and spin off of them. I played out there for hours. I was Dallas Cowboys' Hall of Fame running back Tony Dorsett on offense and Carl Eller on defense. Maybe it was crazy playing football with a bunch of trees, but they were not trees to me. They were lead blockers, halfbacks, nose guards and linebackers.

After a while, I got tired of the trees just standing in one place and came up with an ingenious idea. I thought, *what if I took one of those old tires behind the barn, tied a rope to it, and hung it from the bar that hung between two trees out in front of our house?* Before my time, there used to be a rope that hung from the bar that my parents and older siblings would use to swing out over the steep hill above our pond and drop into the water below. It had to be about a 40-foot drop. I always thought, *they must have been crazy, and who were they to call me dumb for tackling trees?*

The tire was a formidable opponent. Once in place, I would get the tire swinging mightily, run up, and meet it for a bone-jarring hit. I would alternate wrapping it up and making a tackle, meeting it in the hole to take on a lead blocker, to it trying to tackle me while I was carrying the ball.

Sometimes, I would run into one of the big trees beside the swinging tire, bounce off, spin, and try to stay on my feet when the tire hit me. It made for some great practice and simulated taking and delivering a hit quite well.

One day, I was feeling like I needed something more. I was putting the hurt to that old tire and needed a new challenge. I could stop it dead when I simulated taking on a lead blocker.

For my next bright idea, I decided to load the inside of the tire with a few big rocks. I now had a lead blocker like, monster-mashing machine swinging back and forth. I thought at the time, *it was now or never, I am going to blast this big pile of rubber and rocks.*

I always liked to hit the tire with the front of my helmet, because on good hits, it would leave a cool black mark on my helmet. I timed it perfectly; as I ran forward, the tire was on its downward swing. It was collision time!

The tire blasted me and I swear it nearly ripped my head clean off. Not only that, but my awesome helmet's chin strap was busted to pieces. I was lying there half-knocked out, and thinking, *you have to be quite stupid to run into a swinging tire filled with 100 pounds of rocks.* My head hurt for a long time, I probably had a concussion, but I wasn't going to say anything. I knew what would be said back to me by my family, "We told you that you would get hurt running into those trees and that tire, that's just stupid."

> "We would all stand in front of the window and watch," explained my sister Teresa. "We couldn't believe anybody would be so stupid. You were out there for hours at a time running into those trees and that tire. The tire would be swinging really hard and you would run into it and it would knock you flat. It was so funny when it would clobber you. We would say, 'Oh that one hurt, he isn't getting up this time.' You would sometimes have trouble getting up, but you always got up. When you came inside,

we would all act very busy so that you didn't know we had been watching. Then you would sit there with the scratches from the tree branches all over you. You wouldn't even wipe the blood off because you thought it looked cool."[1]

Teresa took me to my very first football game. It was to an Ayersville High School game in 1977. I remember getting there early and just throwing a nerf football around in the grass before the game started.

When the players came out of the locker room, they just looked huge with all of those pads on. They were in lines, holding hands and had these fierce and intense looks on their faces.

I had never seen anything like it. I thought, *oh how I long to be one of them when I grew up.* A lot of kids just horsed around at the games in the grass behind the home stands. I couldn't, I had to watch the game. It was all completely fascinating to me. At the time, Ayersville didn't have lights, so the games were played on Saturday afternoons. After the games, I would go home and play football by myself for hours.

The first time I can remember playing in a real tackle football game was at Steve Thieroff's birthday party. I must have been about eight or nine-years-old. He was a year older, but we played youth baseball together and grew up in the same church. Plus, he only lived about three miles away. There will be more about Steve later on, as he had a huge influence on my football career.

We were all in the front yard playing tackle football without any sort of equipment or pads and Kevin Cooper, another kid I played youth baseball against, was carrying the ball. I came up and hit him with my forehead right in his stomach. He went down hard and sat out the rest of the day.

Now, Coop wasn't a very big kid and I hope this didn't end his football career since he never played for Ayersville, but I always felt bad about that hit. Coop ended up being a real good baseball player and we enjoyed many successful seasons together on the diamond.

My cousin, Shelby Dawson, who was a year younger than me, and would later play an integral part on our 1986 team, lived next door to me. We played quite a bit of football in the yard while we were growing up. My dad, my brother, or my uncle, Jack Dunbar, would throw one of us passes while the other defended.

There were many pass patterns drawn up with a stick, but my favorite was when my Uncle Jack would say, "Run a fly pattern."

A fly pattern meant that we would just run straight down the field. He would then just throw the ball out there and if we could get a step on the defender, we would catch the long bomb just over the small ditch that was our goalline. We played out there for hours at a time in the crisp fall Ohio weather. This was my favorite time of the year, the leaves were falling, the temperature was cool, and all of the aspects of fall scream out, "Its football season".

> "I would throw that football out there as far as I could," explained my father of those days in the yard. "Back then when I was younger, I could throw it pretty far. It always amazed me that you could run under it and make the catch."[2]

I also played some completely unorthodox football. We had a pond in front of our house, and once it turned cold enough, we would lace up the ice skates and play down there as much as we could. I wasn't really into hockey, and I loved football, so it wasn't long before my Dad and brother were throwing passes with footballs, instead of sliding pucks with a hockey stick as I skated down the ice. Everyone got into it, and it wasn't long before we were playing some actual games. My Dad would even have some guys come over from where he worked so that we could challenge them.

My uncles, Craig Becher and Jack Dunbar, would be there all the time playing around. My cousins and other family members would filter in and out as well, so we had plenty of bodies to at least have a quarterback, receiver and defender.

On ice skates, football was quite challenging and dangerous, as we would find out. As the games grew and time became an issue, my Dad and brother put up flood lights all over the hillside next to the pond so we could play when darkness struck. There was just something about playing football, or any other kind of ball for that matter, under the lights. I felt like this was my very first taste of what it was like to play before a big stage. When those lights were on, and the ball was floating into your awaiting hands, it was just magical. Especially on the nights when there was a light snow falling.

When the ball was in the air, and I was looking up into the night air illuminated by the lights, while the snow flakes floated and danced around the ball, there was no better feeling. Soon the ball would plummet out of the sky and through the glowing snowflakes like it was a falling meteor into my awaiting hands. That was pure football, and I still have those vivid images in my mind.

Then one day, tragedy struck. We had advanced to the stage where we were even utilizing the kicking game on the ice. We were playing an afternoon pick-up game, when my dad skated forward to kick the ball off of the tee to get the game underway, and his skate caught in the ice. He went down hard and the result was an ice-football season-ending broken leg. He was out for the year and we didn't play as much after that.

His leg healed and there was much anticipation in the off-season that he would be back at full strength for the next winter season. It was always more fun when Dad played, and he was so much fun to be around.

The next year rolled around and indeed my Dad was back on the ice ready to go. We started a football game up immediately upon his return to the ice.

Once again, tragedy struck. We were playing a nice little game at night, when my Dad went flying along the sideline trying to stop the kick returner. He couldn't stop in time and his momentum carried him across the ice, so he had no choice but to run up the hillside. His skate caught in a hole, he felt his leg snap, and knew he had just broken the other leg in his initial game back from breaking the other one the year before. This time, it was a career-ending injury.

The ankle would not heal and he had to have numerous surgeries before the doctors finally fixed it so that he could at least walk on it. It was a devastating injury that turned out changing my father's life. Even to this day, he has a hard time walking on that leg, but he keeps going, and he never lets it get him down. I don't know anyone tougher than my dad.

My Dad related, "It always got a little rough down there on the pond, that's probably why I got hurt. I am still paying for it to this day, but it was a lot of fun and the memories from it will last forever."[3]

Football on ice never really resurfaced after my Dad's second broken leg. Without him, it would never be the same. He always made it fun, and I know the injury really hindered the rest of his life, but I was thankful for the times we all shared playing under the lights on that frozen pond.

MEET THE TEAM

Before I go into the playground and junior high years, I will give a run down of the seniors and underclassmen of the 1986 team. This will make it easier to follow along as the book progresses.

SENIORS

#12 Denny Martin (5-10, 150) Quarterback/Holder: A great athlete that was very fast. He was an accurate passer that could throw the deep ball. Denny had the skills to allow our offense to do many things that our opponents couldn't. I knew Denny since kindergarten.

#21 Andy Groll (5-10, 165) Blocking back/Rotator: Grew up wanting to be a lineman, wanted to play just one game in a pair of giant black gloves, get down in a four-point stance, and blast into a blocker. Enjoyed every second on the field, but liked playing defense a lot more than offense.

#22 Phil Girlie (5-7, 155) Blocking back/Rotator: Great hitter and sure tackler, we played beside each other on defense and split time on offense. We usually went head-to-head in practice. He may have had more passion for football than anyone. Phil was a great hitter and delivered some great hits throughout his career. He was just a great teammate and I enjoyed all of the time we spent together on the field.

#25 Steve Deitrick (5-8, 165) Fullback/Linebacker: Also referred to as Deek, quickest guy off of the ball, had great leg drive, all around great football player, had tremendous football skills, and was always in the action. One of the true leader's of the team. Steve could have played any position on the field and played it well. He was a great warrior and hitter. With his toughness and quickness, he was a force of destruction.

#56 Jaime Briseno (5-7, 165) Guard/Nose guard: Smart, agile, excellent trap blocker, would come in at nose guard on passing downs because he could always find a way to get pressure on the QB. Jaime just did his job and didn't say anything about it. We didn't realize how good he was until we watched the film.

#60 John Finn (5-11, 205) Center/Long Snapper: Phenomenal blocker that would get downfield and deliver blocks, never have I seen anyone that could snap the ball harder or quicker. Coach McCord referred to him as the quickest center he ever coached.

#61 Tim Boals (5-11, 180) Offensive Tackle: Loved to pull and trap people, his bear crawl blocks were classic, always sustained his blocks, and he was the player most likely to make you laugh. Tim was also a real fine pass blocker.

#63 Mike Wilson (5-9, 160) Guard/Linebacker: Mike was very fast and had great footwork. Also known as Harley Man, (for his love of Harley Davidson motorcycles), the ultimate team player that allowed us to get outside because of his speed at the guard position.

#64 Eric Burket (5-11, 175) Guard/Defensive End: Tenacious and hard to block. He was great at holding his ground and creating a pile, yet had the speed to get outside and make the tackle.

#71 Marv Andrews (5-9, 210) Nose guard: Strongest guy on the team, nicest guy off of the field, but had a mean streak on it. Referred to as Marvelous, was immovable in the middle and a great run stuffer.

#75 Aaron Roth (5-11, 175) Offensive Tackle/Defensive Tackle: High energy player, was always jumping around, had great technique, played much bigger than he was, and was a tremendous football player. He played low and angled well.

#76 Jeff Okuly (5-11, 185) Offensive Tackle/Defensive Tackle: Had great technique, always stayed low, tough as nails, quiet and all business, referred to as Oak. He always did his job while putting a beating on his opponents. He was a phenomenal run stuffer as well as a great pass rusher.

#77 George Schaffer (5-10, 210) Offensive tackle: Great team-mate that did anything asked of him, player you could count on for anything. George was willing to do anything to help the team.

#84 Tolly Hanna (5-10, 175) Tight End: A great hook blocker that allowed backs to get outside. Tolly ran good routes and had sure hands. His blocking paved the way for our sweeps.

#85 Johnny Armes (5-11, 155) Safety: A great cover man that made big plays and was a good teammate. He always practiced hard and did whatever he had to. Johnny played the first part of the year with a cast on his hand, so he was definitely a gamer.

#87 Rob Giesige (5-11, 160) Defensive End: An intense player that was smart and crafty. With his toughness he was the perfect defensive end. He was very well conditioned and probably in the best shape of anyone on the team. He was true to his school and never slacked off even in practice. Rob was fiercely competitive in everything he did. When he moved to Ayersville in the third grade, we became instant friends.

UNDERCLASSMEN

JUNIORS

#10 Todd Hanna (5-10, 155) Safety: Brother of Tolly, and he always seemed to be around the ball. Todd made some key plays during the year. He was good at run support and could deliver a good hit.

#18 Shelby Dawson (5-10, 165) Tight End: My first cousin, who really came on later in the year to score some touchdowns and allow us to run a lot of double tight end sets. Shelby caught everything thrown at him while also being a good blocker. He was excellent at running after the catch.

#20 Travis Lewis (5-7, 155) Tailback/Kick Returner: He filled in when Chris Schlachter was hurt at tailback. Travis was fast and had good moves. His play while Chris was out helped to carry the team. Even when Chris came back, he was still valuable at returning kicks and giving him a break carrying the ball

#26 Jason Guilford (5-4, 125) Blocking Back: He always gave his all. Jason was a real fine downfield blocker and made up for his lack of size with a gritty determination.

#33 Scott Kolb (5-7, 155) Fullback/Linebacker: He filled in for Deek at fullback and Harley Man at linebacker. Scott was hard nosed, played hard, and was a great special teams performer. He made some big plays throughout the season.

#44 Chris Schlachter (6-2, 205) Tailback/Kicker: He was a big, fast, punishing runner that could turn it on in the open field. Chris was known as Fat Boy, but it had nothing to do with his physique. He could run over people, but possessed breakaway speed. Chris was an all-around great athlete, and I spent a lot of time with him, since we played three sports together.

#83 Randy Richard (5-9, 145) Split End/Defensive End: He received a lot of playing time at the end of the year, giving Jerry Carnahan a break when he had to play defense. Randy was a good downfield blocker that also played some defensive end due to injuries. He was quick and did a great job.

#88 Jerry Carnahan (5-10, 140) Split End/Punter: He was a great athlete and never dropped a pass. I played three sports with Jerry so I was around him a lot as well. For his size, he had the strongest legs on the team. He was known as Jear Bear. The car rides in his brown Pinto were classic.

SOPHOMORE

#67 Don Andrews (5-7, 140) Special Teams: Marv's brother and a key performer on special teams. He was a good hard nosed player that would do anything asked of him.

FRESHMAN

#72 Matt Lloyd (5-7, 175) Defensive Tackle: He gave Aaron Roth and Jeff Okuly a breather on defense. Matt was a tough player even as a freshman. He made them and the rest of the linemen work hard in practice, enabling them to be ready for game night.

THE REST OF THE TEAM

Juniors
#28 Dave Mack
#45 Corey Ankney
#68 Doug Brown
#69 Tim Kuhlman
#78 Erick McCoy
#79 John Phillips

Sophomores
#11 Joe Florence
#15 Ron Leatherman
#31 Greg Cross
#32 Steve Briseno
#40 Dave Delano
#51 Chris Stiltner
#54 Chris Schaffer
#55 Mike Jones
#62 Denny Dearth
#70 Tim Wagner
#74 Rick Caryer
#81 Denny Kuhlman
#82 Scott Tyrrell

Freshmen
#14 Scott Seigman
#16 Aaron Giesige
#17 Jeff Askins
#19 Eric Waldron
#23 Sean DeWolfe
#34 Terry Schlosser
#50 Matt Reineke
#65 Lonnie Gerschutz
#66 Jeremy Stark
#86 Robert Temple

THE COACHES

Coach Craig McCord was our head coach. He coached the offensive line as well as the linebackers. He called all of the defensive plays as well. Coach McCord was the original coach when Ayersville started varsity football in 1976. He was known for his calm approach and stirring speeches. He commanded our attention and he got it. We would have done anything he asked.

Coach Bill Ondrus called the offensive plays along with coaching the defensive backs, the running backs and quarterbacks. He had been with Coach McCord since the 1980 season. Coach O was a fierce competitor that could be fun, yet stern. We all enjoyed being around him

Coach Don Hammersmith, also known as Coach Beef was the defensive line coach and also helped Coach McCord with the offensive line. He had played on the line previously for Coach McCord and was a senior on the 1980 team. The 1986 season would be his second year coaching the line. He was a great teacher of technique, and another fun guy to be around. He had the respect of his linemen and the rest of the team as well.

Coach Norman Beck coached the offensive and defensive ends, it was his first year coaching with Coach McCord, and none of us knew anything about Coach Beck at the time. He had a fiery side to him and we all respected him for it. He did an awesome job with his ends on both sides of the ball.

Coach Jeff Maag helped Coach Ondrus with the backs and quarterbacks on offense. Defensively he coached the defensive ends with Coach Beck. He was a former quarterback under Coach McCord, and was a senior in 1981. He was a fairly quiet guy that would come up with some inspiration at just the right time. He knew the offense well since he was a former signal-caller with the Pilots.

THE MANAGERS

Without question, The Pilot managers played a key role in the football program. This was a group of high school girls that were invaluable to our team.

They would wash our game jerseys and game pants, clean the locker room, be ready with water, tape, or any other piece of equipment when we needed it. They also took care of all of the practice equipment, and in general, did all of the things nobody else wanted to do.

We had a group of phenomenal ladies. Not only did they do all of the things behind the scenes to make everything run smoothly, they were our biggest and most loyal fans. They would actually get in the face of anyone opposing us. I hope that we always gave them the respect they deserved, because they were a big part of our success.

Some of them even took classes in the summer so that they could help tape ankles and do other trainer related duties. They were there to work, and they worked as hard as anybody on the team, if not harder.

> Kim (McCord) Engel confirmed. "Dad sent us managers to camp over the summer to learn how to tape ankles so that we could help the coaches after school on Friday night. It felt like we really knew how to do something (other than wash jerseys)."[4]

The managers consisted of seniors: Kim McCord, Kristen Bell and Amy Shinabery, junior, Ann Shinabery and sophomores, Missy McCord, Pam Roth and Deb Mansfield.

Kim and Missy were both Coach McCord's daughters and Amy and Ann Shinabery were also sisters. Pam Roth was Aaron Roth's sister. Needless to say, there were quite a few family connections in the Ayersville football program.

All of the hard work they performed was still no match for all of the support they gave us. They were without a doubt our biggest fans and would be right on the sidelines during the games cheering us on. We could always hear them yelling support from the sidelines, even when we were out on the field. When we came off the field, one or more would be right there with a water bottle, and would grab any item we needed. They didn't wear a tool belt, but I don't think there was an item we could request that wouldn't be in one of their pockets.

Every Thursday when we would come back in from practice, there would be some sort of artwork on the chalkboard depicting our opponent on Friday night.

Amy Shinabery was an excellent artist and would use her imagination and artistic skills to create something we all appreciated as we filed in after practice. I am sure all of the managers helped in this endeavor to inspire us before our big game. We all couldn't wait to see what they had come up with, and it was talked about even before practice was over on Thursday nights.

Another member of the team was Coach McCord's eight-year-old son Jonathan. He was on the field anytime we were. If he wasn't at Coach McCord's side, he was usually with one of the seniors. He was also one of our biggest fans, and he would do little duties wherever he could. When you look at the pictures from the season, Jonathan was usually somewhere in the foreground or background of the image.

PLAYGROUND YEARS/ JUNIOR HIGH

Every year on the first day of school, the principal would give the morning announcements over the public address system. It always ended the same way, "There will be NO tackle football on the playground and violator's will be dealt with swiftly and harshly."

We always knew that it was coming, but we always hoped that by some miracle, some vindication for every school boy, tackle football would be allowed and we could cream each other at will.

This should never take place since tackle football without pads can be very dangerous. There wasn't a year that went by without broken bones, cuts, broken noses or other serious injuries.

We would always start the year off slow, but sooner or later, we would be playing full tackle football. That's when an injury would happen, or we would get caught and that would be the end of it.

John Finn, who would later be an All-Ohio center on the 1986 team, was the best running back on the playground. He had slick moves, was hard to bring down, and I found him the hardest to tackle of any kid I played against. In those playground years, I would have wagered that John would some day be a Heisman Trophy winning running back, he was that good.

To realize how close the group of seniors on the 1986 team was, you have to realize that when we played on the playground, we were all playing together. I can remember games and plays from each and every one of the 16 seniors.

One year after we had been caught playing tackle football, we all came up with a tremendous idea that couldn't fail.

We couldn't play tackle football because we were being watched like hawks, but maybe we could play something else and still get some good hits on each other.

We traded in the football for a soccer ball, and thus formed the infamous tackle soccer.

It was anything goes soccer, we could tackle, grab and trip, anything but touch the ball with your hands. The object was still to kick the ball through the goal on each end, but it was somewhat harder, considering anytime we got near the ball, somebody was going to completely clobber us.

It worked like a charm at first, the teachers all thought we had finally given up on tackle football and were playing just a nice friendly game of soccer. All created by the fabulous illusion of a soccer ball instead of a football.

This went on for some time until a playground teacher wandered over one day and told us to quit roughhousing.

I think it was Phil Girlie that said, "We aren't doing anything wrong, there is no rule against us playing soccer."

That seemed to satisfy the teacher at the time, so we went on playing.

It was probably a week or so later when the same teacher came over and said, "You boys aren't fooling me, I know exactly what you're doing. You're playing tackle football with a soccer ball."

Off she went with our soccer ball and that was the end of tackle soccer.

The next day, the announcements were modified somewhat. After all of the morning business was concluded, the very last statement was, "There will be NO tackle anything on the playground, this includes, but is not limited to, football and SOCCER." Our crafty little concept was a blast while it lasted, but it was obviously foiled by Ayersville's wise playground instructors.

My most cherished memories of the playground come from the cold days of winter. When the sky opened up and dropped the soft glistening flakes we all call snow, it was time for the best playground football of the year.

The heavy winter coats we wore, served as the perfect padding for those games played on the soft fluffy snow covered playground. It was pure football and I loved every second of it.

I remember during one excessively snowy winter, we played some four-on-four football everyday. It was Phil Girlie, Marv Andrews, Rob Giesige and me, against John Finn, Steve Deitrick and I can't remember exactly who their other two team members were. I would guess it was Denny Martin, Tim Boals, Jamie Briseno or Mike Wilson.

Those were the days: Slipping, sliding and lumbering across the deep snow to tackle one another. I don't think we even kept score, because we had so much fun just playing the game.

After recess was over, we would all head back to the classroom with snow caked to our socks and pants. For the rest of the day, we sat in the classroom with puddles under our desks from the melting snow, while we longed for the next day when we could do it all over again.

JUNIOR HIGH

My football career at Ayersville began in the seventh-grade. I don't think any of us had an opportunity to play organized football until then. It just wasn't available anywhere. The eighth-graders took up all of the playing time, except for one seventh-grader that year. Eric Burket started both ways as the lone seventh-grader having an impact. Later on, this would raise a question mark on the unknown probability of our chances in our senior year. Once the 1985 season was over, we would be left without the class above us for the 1986 season. There were some great football players in the class ahead of us, guys I looked up to. I will go into more detail on those players later on.

The eighth-graders, plus Burket, lost two games to Wayne Trace that year. They lost one in the regular season and the other in the GMC championship game, for a respectable 4-2 record. It was a good season, and what most of us got to do was scrimmage against them. I was happy enough with that.

Getting to hit people with pads on was so cool. I loved every minute of it. My Dad would always ask how practice went on the way home from picking me up. I think I always told him the same thing, "I had a great practice, don't be surprised if you see me out there in the next game."

I knew that would never happen, I think he knew it as well. He never said anything or pressured me. He was very supportive at all times.

When our eighth-grade year was upon us, I couldn't wait for football, finally my big chance to play. I figured it was the seventh-graders time to stand on the sidelines. I never liked offense, so I set my sights on being a defensive starter. Tackling was what I liked more than anything and figured I'd let somebody else play offense.

The first game of the year was against Wayne Trace, the team that had beaten us the year before. I was the starting outside line-backer and I was overjoyous and couldn't wait for the game. On game day, I found out that I had a long way to go before I would ever be a football player. It didn't seem like I could do anything right and I felt lost out there. The result of the game was not at all how I imagined it. We lost the game in decisive fashion, 22-7.

Wayne Trace seemed to be able to pass the ball like we weren't even out there. Coach Grant and Coach Sprague thought it was my fault.

Apparently, I was supposed to cover the flat on pass plays. I was very raw at that point in my career and all I wanted to do was tackle the guy with the ball. When I charged after the quarterback and he kept dropping it over me for an easy completion, it probably wasn't the way the coaching staff wanted me to play defense. I was sent directly to the bench and would no longer be playing that position, or any other starting position for that matter.

Back to the bench I went, while some seventh-graders were starting. I couldn't believe it.

I dejectedly thought to myself, *maybe I am never going to be a football player; I am just not good enough.* I was again a practice player and even though I was unhappy about not getting to play in the games anymore, I still loved to play during practice. I don't know how it happened, but for some reason, I started playing quarterback against the first-team defense in practice. I had played my classmates all the time on the playground and hoped I could take it to them.

At quarterback in junior high, we basically just handed the ball off all the time. I couldn't stand it, there was never anybody to hit. Finally, Coach Grant, who ran the scout team, called for a quarterback sneak. I took it up the middle all the way through the defense for a score. We ran it a few more times, all with the same result.

We had two games left in the season when I was put in as one of the starting halfbacks. We ran the straight T in junior high, very basic; sweeps and dives were our plays. My football career was resurrected. Who would have known that playing quarterback would result in renewing my passion for the game?

Little did I know, the position I hated to play more than anything would continue to haunt me throughout my career at Ayersville.

We ended the year with a 1-4 record, it did not seem like we had any football players at all in our class. We all loved playing the game, but apparently, we just didn't have the skills required to be winners. With a 1-4 record, I don't think anyone had high hopes for our high school career after that fateful season.

My introduction to Coach Craig McCord and high school football happened at the end of our eighth-grade season. Even though he was a junior high teacher and we had known him for awhile, this was when we actually met the REAL Coach McCord. Mr. McCord had been our science teacher in junior high, but outside of football, he was definitely not the same person. Once he was involved in something football, his intensity soared. He wasn't this nice smiling teacher I had known in class. He was the commander of his personal wrecking crew, the Ayersville Pilot football team.

For the very last home varsity game, the eighth-graders always suited up and joined the high school varsity team. I think Coach McCord did this to give us all a feeling of what football would be like in high school. I am grateful that he did, because after our night with him, I was going to play high school football.

We of course dressed in the junior high lockers because there just wasn't enough room in the varsity locker room. We were laughing and carrying on like usual, getting ready to go screw around. Little did we know, it just wasn't allowed when you played on Friday nights under Coach McCord.

We finally got called up to the varsity locker room, which was on the east side of the school and was accessible up a flight of stairs on the interior of the building or a set of stairs on the outside of the school. The locker room was also located on the deck overlooking the school's swimming pool. The outside door led right out to the practice fields and other outside facilities of the school.

At the time, I never knew this locker room even existed and I had been going to Ayersville my entire life. Once inside, the locker room was immaculate, absolutely gorgeous. There were signs, a chalk board and equipment - awesome football equipment - pads, helmets, tape and all kinds of things I had never seen before.

The atmosphere was unforgettable and I can still feel it today. I was in a place where warriors got ready for battle, the past, the present and the future.

Dave Temple, the Diamond brothers, Jim Froelich, Bob Lamb, John Whiteford, Chuck Florence, Jeff Bauman, Jim Hunt, Bill Davenport, Tony Dockery, Mike Smith, Ken Marckel, Ron Leininger, Coach Beef, Coach Maag, all the greats from before had been there.

Next, I remember the sound, there wasn't any. *Why weren't they talking?* Nobody was saying anything to anyone. It finally dawned on me, the warriors were getting ready to do battle. They were really concentrating. It was way more serious than the goofing around we were used to. If we wanted to be winners, we had to act like winners and concentrate on the job that needed to be done. I wanted to be a part of this, some day I wanted to be sitting there with a scowl on my face preparing for the job I had to do.

When Coach McCord came into the room, he was not the science teacher anymore. He was like Superman, and as intense as a TV preacher. He had a scowl on his face and he went into his pre-game material with so much gusto that I thought the walls would crumble. It was intimidating, but I think we all wanted to have a chance to play for him. There was so much structure to the rest of the night. Lines were straight, motions were crisp; when the team spoke, they spoke in unison. It was not a bunch of individuals, it was a TEAM, they had a job to do and they all did it together.

The team went on to lose on that night to Edgerton by a score of 8-7, but the die had been cast. There were a bunch of eighth-graders that were hungry to play for Coach McCord.

At the end of our eighth-grade year, Coach McCord called a meeting for anyone that wanted to play football the next year. He told us to start working, that whatever we wanted, we could achieve it. He was very positive, and basically let us know, that if we worked for it, we could be winners. At the time, none of us knew what we would accomplish. The 1986 season was still four years away.

Anyone that was going to be playing football received a letter from Coach McCord right before summer outlining what he wanted us to work on and that the weight room would be open three days a week in the morning and in the evening.

I always played baseball in the summer, so I didn't really think that I needed to participate much, but I did show up every once in awhile. Coaches couldn't do any coaching until the state's designated day when football practice officially started, so we were basically on our own. We would lift weights at the different stations, and then go outside and do jump rope work and agility drills over two boards. It was a good workout, designed to make everyone stronger and quicker. It was summer baseball season for me, so at that time, I was more concerned with those practices and games than I was with football.

I really enjoyed baseball, but I wish I would have spent a lot more time at the sessions. It would have benefited me tremendously to have used the sessions to get stronger and quicker in my early high school years.

FRESHMAN YEAR

I will save most of the practice details and different aspects of Ayersville varsity football under Coach Craig McCord for when I get into that magical 1986 season, but I will touch base on all of the other pertinent information leading up to that year to give the reader a better understanding of things to come.

My freshman year and high school football career started off in a less than desirable way. One week before the opening day of football practice, I flipped my moped and passed out with the muffler searing the flesh all along my right leg.

I had been lying there for awhile before a passer-by found me and pulled the moped off of me. A moped is kind of a joke in the first place, because it is not considered to be a very cool mode of transportation. I have to tell you though, we all had them, and they saved our parents a bunch of money and time by not having to drive us back and forth to practice.

A moped is basically a bicycle with a motor, quite capable of doing up to 40 miles per hour. The one I had would do a good 35 miles per hour. The day I wrecked it, a road crew had been paving the road I lived on and there was a fairly steep slope on the edge of the road because they hadn't put the stone along it yet. I drove off the edge, lost control, flipping the moped tooling along at 35 MPH.

A guy in a pickup truck found me, and I told him to just take me home. I only lived a half mile up the road from where I wrecked. He wanted to take me to the hospital because my entire right leg had a deep burn where the muffler laid on it, my shirt was basically torn off, exposing many cuts to my torso, and I was bleeding from a gash on my chin. I insisted that he just take me home. I never knew this Good Samaritan or found out who it was later on, so if you're reading this and you once picked up a kid from a moped crash that wouldn't go to the hospital, I issue you a much over due Thank You.

Once inside our house, only my sister, Teresa, was home, thankfully. She basically told me to get in the bath tub because I was bleeding all over the house. She looked me over and replied, "You look like you got ran over by a truck."

> Teresa remembered not being very compassionate. "I took the day off from work so that I could clean the house and get ready for a Tupper-ware party. I was busy cleaning the house and getting food ready when you came walking into the house dripping blood all over. You looked like a mess, but I didn't have time to deal with you because I really needed to get things finished for the party. I was so mad that you were bleeding all over the clean floors. I told you to get in the bath tub and take care of yourself because I had too much work to do, and you were obviously not dying."[5]

Finally, my parents came home, and after some discussion, it was decided that nothing was life threatening and I wouldn't have to go to the emergency room.

Everything healed up pretty well by the first day of practice, except the burn on my leg. The burn went right over my knee and was so deep that I couldn't bend my leg at all. I could only walk by dragging the leg along without bending it. I would not be able to run, therefore, practice would be quite challenging. I wasn't going to miss it though, and limped along as fast as I could to all of the different drills, participating however I was able.

We were going to have a really good Ayersville team in 1983. Quite a few starters were coming back from the 1982 team that went 6-3-1. The team had a good group of seniors that were very motivated about winning. As freshmen, we were going to be relied on heavily as scout team participants and for other less desirable duties.

The returning lettermen were Seniors: #15 Todd Yeager (5-8, 155), #23 Charlie Ankney (5-7, 150), #26 Robert Girlie (5-8, 155),

#34 Mike Finn (5-10, 180), #55 Brian Wittler (6-2, 195), #60 Pat Vogel (5-9, 170), #61 Ed Chavez (5-11, 160), #62 Randy McCoy (6-1, 195), #76 Mark Vittorio (5-11, 240), #77 Mike Batt (6-0, 185) and #87 Chad Teague (6-1, 160).

Juniors: #11 Brad Schlachter (6-3, 185), #17 Charlie Askins (5-8, 135) and #33 Kevin Gerschutz (5-8, 145).

Sophomores: #10 Brian Allen (5-8, 150), #32 Bob Froelich (5-5, 160) and #46 Steve Thieroff (5-9, 160).

Once my leg healed, I was finally ready for full participation in practices, which happened right around the day we suited up in full pads.

The first game of 1983 was against McComb. Ayersville had never played McComb before, but supposedly they had a magnificent team in 1983. Jerry Mapes was McComb's all-everything halfback and he would have to be contained if we were to have any chance of winning.

The 1983 Ayersville team played them very tough on the road that year. It was a back and forth affair with the game finally ending in a 28-21 McComb win. We found out, that year and in the years to come, McComb had a very solid football program. That same year in 1983, McComb went on to become the eventual state champions in Division V by beating Newark Catholic 6-0 in the championship.

Looking back, I don't think anyone on the 1983 team realized just how good McComb was that year and how close they came to beating the eventual state champs.

Game number two on the schedule for that year was the Fairview Apaches. Coach McCord always got psyched up for the Apaches. They had a great program and there was a reason for his enthusiasm on Fairview week. Ayersville had never beaten them before. In all seven games since Ayersville started varsity football in the 1976 season, Fairview had won, and done so in dominating fashion. That finally changed in 1983, Ayersville won 20-13. The turning point in the game came from a freshman.

Denny Martin received some playing time at safety in the first half of the game. It was late in the second quarter when the Fairview star halfback turned the corner and had one man to beat for an easy trip into the end zone. The man standing between him and the goalline was none other than Denny Martin.

Now, Denny was a great athlete, but he had never been known for his defensive abilities and was considered a quarterback prodigy. That being said, Denny lowered his shoulder and performed one of the finest tackles I have ever seen. Not only did he dump the ball carrier, he managed to hit him hard enough to cause a fumble, which Ayersville recovered. The play turned the entire momentum into our favor and we went on to beat Fairview for the first time ever.

At halftime of the game, I asked Denny what he was thinking on the play. "When he was coming at me, I thought I was going to pass out," said Martin. "I don't know what happened, but then he went down and the ball came loose."

It was one of many fine plays that Denny would make in his career, but one of the rare standout defensive plays he made since he'd go on to become our offensive trigger man.

As freshmen, we did not only have scout team to look forward to, but also the junior varsity games. A few sophomores that didn't play in the varsity games would also play on the team.

Coach Ondrus was in charge of the junior varsity games at that time and he had prided himself in the fact that he had never lost one. We won our first two games and then the unexpected happened. Our freshman quarterback, Denny Martin, developed a staph infection that would hospitalize him, and end his season. I was once again called on to be the signal-caller of the offense. I hated playing quarterback and went back to playing strictly offense with Martin sidelined, so much for getting to hit somebody. Just dandy, the kibosh had been put on my days of lambasting the opposition.

"My freshman year started off with a bang and ended with a thud," recalled Denny Martin. "Our second game of the year was against Fairview. I was a freshman playing defensive back and as I came up to tackle Brian English from Fairview ... my helmet hit the football and he fumbled and we recovered. We went on to score after the turnover and beat Fairview for the first time in our history. I got the Tackle of the Game and later was awarded with the Tackle of the Year on that same hit. That was the bang. The thud was that during the next week's practice, I ended up in Parkview Hospital in Fort Wayne, Indiana and Defiance Hospital for the next six weeks being treated for a Staph Infection and Endocarditis of the heart."[6]

"Being stuck in the hospital for six weeks during football season was the worst … although on the weekends some of my team-mates would make the trip up to Fort Wayne to spend some time with me and that meant a lot! I missed the rest of my football season as a freshman and also my basketball season due to the illness that started with a small scrape on my back," continued Martin.[7]

I was not cut out to be a quarterback. I did not feel comfortable, literally right from the snap. Here is an instance showing exactly how inept I was at being a quarterback.

We ran a drill in practice where the varsity quarterback, his backup and the JV quarterback, all lined up under our respective centers. Then, on the varsity quarterback's cadence, we took the snap, dropped back, and delivered the ball to a receiver running a pre-determined pass route. It was supposed to all be done in unison with three precise passes being delivered to their respective receiver at the exact same moment.

There I was under center, when John Finn (the JV center) started squirming and laughing. Coach McCord always liked to give it to John, I think mostly because he was the youngest of three brothers playing for the team that year.

All at once, Coach McCord screamed, "John, why don't you share what's so funny about the little drill we're trying to run here." John said, "Coach, you really don't want to know".

Obviously, Coach McCord was not content with Finn's attempt to squirm his way out of the little ordeal.

"Yes, I do want to know, and if you don't tell me, you're going to be running fence busters for the rest of practice."

John finally relented, "It's Groll, Coach, he doesn't put his hands where they need to go when he is taking the snap and it tickles."

That's all it took to bring everyone around to laughter, for obvious reasons. Coach McCord was not one to have his practices disrupted, so he just turned his back and yelled, "Then you need to show him where to stick … (he caught himself quickly), put them then."

It was too late, there was an outbreak of laughter at that point. Whenever I took a snap after that, I don't know if I was imagining it or not, but I would always detect a hint of laughter from John.

My first junior varsity game at quarterback turned out to be another blessing in disguise. As much as I hated playing quarterback, I think it paved the way for the rest of my career in football. In my first game as the JV quarterback I was mainly asked to hand the ball off. I didn't run any option or throw many passes in the first half. It was a close game and in the second half, we had a third-and-long, and in came a pass play from the sideline. The play was pro right 36 pass.

It consisted of sticking the ball in the fullback's belly as he dove into the six hole (between the tackle and tight end), then pulling it out and dropping back a couple of steps before delivering the pass. The tight end, who lined up on the right, was the primary receiver and he was running straight down the field. At the time, I had no clue what routes any of the receivers were running.

I took the snap, stuck the ball in the fullback's belly, pulled it out, and without even looking up, just threw the ball downfield. I heard a bunch of cheering, and thought, *oh great, it had to be intercepted.* To my astonishment, the ball was caught by our wide-open tight end, Dan Bakle. It was a 30-some-yard touchdown pass. I seriously just threw the ball downfield trying to get rid of it.

Later on in the game, the same play was called. I did exactly the same thing. I just threw the ball without even looking. Once again the ball was caught by Bakle and he went in for another long score. After the second touchdown, Dan Bakle probably thought I was the best quarterback he had ever played with.

Little did he know, I had no idea where he was at when I threw the ball, or if anyone was in the general area. Coach Ondrus was fooled too, I never told him that I didn't look up, and I just threw the ball downfield to get rid of it. He had somehow thought he found a quarterback and I wasn't going to tell him anything different.

The rest of our junior varsity season went on the same way. I completed the pass many more times. As the year progressed, I began to understand where the receivers were on each play and was on my way to be coming a quarterback. The pro right 36 pass never seemed to work as well as it did in the first game I played. Maybe not looking at your receivers, and trying really hard to make sure you get the ball in the fullback's belly before you throw the pass does something to open up the defense. I do believe that as we became more comfortable with a play, the fakes became less and less emphatic.

We won the next three JV games and then faced a Liberty Center JV team for the first time. We arrived at their school and the Liberty Center guys were huge. They definitely didn't look like freshmen, with a few sophomores sprinkled in. We went on to become the very first team to lose under Coach Ondrus' tutelage. They were good, but I played awful. I fumbled a few snaps and just never got the offense going.

> Jeff Okuly talked about a play during this game. "I was the JV kicker and after we scored towards the end of the game, Coach Ondrus called for an on-side kick. I was supposed to kick it left, but you (the author) kept trying to get me to kick it to the right side where you were lined up. Just as I was running forward to kick the ball, you called out to me from my right side, 'Oak, they are expecting it on the left side, kick it over here.' I relented and kind of had my feet crossed up when I struck the ball. The result was a spinning kick that actually went backwards. Thanks to you, I think I got the blooper of the year award."[8]

The very last JV game was at home against Edgerton and we trailed with just a little under a minute to play in the game. I dropped back on third down and hit Brian Pessefall on a slant route for a 13-yard touchdown. I actually knew the route he was running, and saw that he was open before I threw the ball. Finally, I felt like an actual quarterback. The pass completion turned out to be the game winner when we held on for the victory. Our junior varsity team finished the year with a 6-1 record, not bad, but it had been Coach O's first loss, therefore, we felt like we had failed. Once again, it looked like our class was going to be a complete disappointment when our senior year rolled around.

The varsity continued their winning ways with wins over Edon (14-6), Antwerp (32-0), Hilltop (40-14), Hicksville (6-0), Holgate (22-14) Wayne Trace (27-8) and Tinora (14-0). This set up a final game showdown with Edgerton for the Green Meadows Conference championship.

As the year progressed, a few freshmen started to see some time on special teams at the varsity level with Rob Giesige, Jeff Okuly and Steve Deitrick seeing the field. If Denny Martin wouldn't have been sidelined with the infection, he may have even lettered our freshmen year.

> Rob Giesige related this, "I was put on the kickoff team towards the end of the year. I took senior Ed Chavez's spot and he was not happy with me. The first time I ran down the field, I got clobbered, and as I was coming off of the field, he was coming on. He yelled, 'Way to get drilled out there freshman!'"[9]

The rest of us only saw action in the games against Antwerp and Hilltop after those games were out of reach. In the game against Antwerp, I intercepted the first pass of my football career. No one cared and it didn't figure into the outcome of the game. It was a long, up-for-grabs throw towards the end of the game. At the time, I cherished the interception. After playing very sparingly when I was an eighth-grader, and the way my high school career was shaping up, I thought to myself, *one interception may be the high point of my career.*

Would I ever intercept another pass? Would I be a practice player for my entire career, even when I was a senior? Those were the questions going through my head.

On the line in the showdown against Edgerton was the Pilots' very first outright GMC championship in football. Plenty of hype also surrounded that game.

However, I was not there for any of it. Since I wasn't playing, I didn't think it would be a real big deal if I wasn't there for the game. Earlier in the year, my Mom and Dad planned a week-long pheasant hunting trip out west to South Dakota. My two brothers, Darrel and Lynn, were going, and I of course wanted to be a part of it, since I had never even seen a pheasant before. We left the weekend before the Edgerton game and did not return until the following Sunday.

My parents made all of the arrangements with the school for my absence, but it was up to me to tell Coach McCord that I would be missing the clash for the GMC crown. I didn't think he would care very much, since I had no chance of playing in the game anyway.

I wasn't nervous or even thinking it was a big deal when I told him, but I do remember his response, "You're going where, and doing what?" I replied, "We're going to South Dakota pheasant hunting."

Still trying to grasp what I was telling him, Coach McCord still seemed a bit puzzled, "Why do you have to go to South Dakota to hunt pheasants?"

"Because you can't find any pheasants around here anymore, and South Dakota has hundreds of them."

Still not completely satisfied, he followed up with another question, "Your whole family is going?"

"Yes, except for my sisters."

He couldn't understand this very well at first, in his defense, we weren't going on the normal family vacation and it may have sounded like I made the whole thing up. Our family really liked to hunt, and the pheasant hunting was only legal and good right around the end of October and beginning of November. School had to be missed, there was just no other choice. Since I wasn't really playing varsity football, the decision was made that we would go the last week of football season so that I could be back for the first week of freshmen basketball practice.

Once he finally understood the entire situation, he went from confused to disappointed, "You do realize that your part of this team, and that I expect all team members to be here for all practices and games?"

I don't think I had a reply for him, because he was really disappointed in me. As he walked away, even though I felt like I was letting him down and had made a huge mistake, I felt a new respect for Coach McCord. If he cared that much about some freshman that wouldn't sniff the playing field, even if 20 guys got hurt, how much did he care about the entire team? The team meant a lot to him, right down to the last player, and at the time I thought to myself, *I may very well be that last player.*

The pheasant hunting trip ended up being an incredible family experience. Not only did I see my first pheasant, I saw thousands of pheasants, sometimes hundreds at the same time. It was an experience of a lifetime and we brought back three coolers full of one of my all time favorite things to eat.

The 1983 season ended with the Pilots losing to the Edgerton Bulldogs, 18-0, to finish the season at 8-2, which resulted in a second-place finish in the Green Meadows Conference. It was a disappointing end to a very fine season. I do not know many details from the game since I was hundreds of miles away in South Dakota. We didn't watch the film, and because it was such a disappointing loss, nobody really talked about it.

> Steve Deitrick talked about what his freshman year meant to him. "In the game against Hicksville, when we were still getting role model influence on the sidelines, well at least for me in figuring out who I most wanted to play like … Robert Girlie, Chad Teague, Ed Chavez, Kevin Gerschutz, etc. Basically, it was anyone that could hit like a two-ton shithouse. The specific one in this case was Charlie Ankney. As he came staggering off the field, barely still on his feet with a big old smile on his face, and blood just gushing down all over his face from inside his helmet, saying something like, 'I drilled him Coach, did you see that, Coach? I just drilled him! How was that?"[10]

The senior leadership on the 1983 team paved the way for us as freshmen. I know many of us that played with them would remember the experience when we were on our journey three years later in 1986.

SOPHOMORE YEAR

With the graduation of the 11 seniors from the 1983 team, there were a lot of holes that needed to be plugged on the 1984 team. On the offensive side of the ball, senior Brad Schlachter (Chris's older brother) would be returning at quarterback along with fellow senior Charlie Askins at split end. They were the only two starters returning on offense. On the defensive side of the ball, junior, Bob Froelich returned at nose guard. Seniors Paul Fry and Brad Schlachter returned at the defensive end positions while junior Steve Thieroff was back at linebacker and Charlie Askins at safety. This Pilot team in 1984 also needed an entire new offensive line and backfield, as well as some key components on defense.

The seniors on the team were: #11 Brad Schlachter (6-4, 195), #17 Charlie Askins (5-8, 150), #33 Kevin Gerschutz (5-8, 165), #63 Brandon Knoll (5-8, 160), #77 Pat Finn (6-1, 196), #81 Shannon Erman (6-1, 175), #85 Paul Fry (5-11, 175), #86 Doug Nagel (6-3, 170) and #87 Ray Shockey (5-10, 160).

The junior lettermen were: #23 Brian Allen (5-9, 165), #24 Eric Guilford (5-5, 135), #32 Bob Froelich (5-6, 170) and #46 Steve Thieroff (5-10, 170).

There were no sophomore returning lettermen. I can't recall any other time this had happened and it looked as if our class would possibly be the ones to bring the whole house of cards tumbling down on the Ayersville tradition.

Steve Deitrick recalled this as well. "I think we were the first class ever to NOT have a freshman letter if I remember right from all the crap we took collectively as "the weak class". Hmmm, I guess we proved some folks wrong after all didn't we?"[11]

In talking with manager Kristen (Bell) Warren, Steve and I were wrong. "I think I received a letter before all of you guys did, because I got one my freshman year." She ended up being the lone four-year letterwinner of our class.[12]

When practice started up in 1984, I was again hindered by an injury. I was pitching in a baseball tournament the week before practice started, when my right elbow just locked up and I couldn't bend it. I never went to the doctor, so I didn't really know what was wrong with it other than it wouldn't bend past 90 degrees. After a few days, I could get it to bend again, but it was painful, and it made a grinding noise.

When practice started up, it was very sore, making it extremely difficult to do certain drills and calisthenics, most notably push-ups. We were in the middle of push-ups, when Coach Ondrus walked by and saw me laboring with each one. I had not told anybody about my arm because I didn't want to come into football camp each year being one of those guys looking for excuses to get out of work. Especially since the year before I had the burnt leg and couldn't do any running.

Coach Ondrus singled me out right away, and started going on and on about what a pathetic push-up technique I had.

"You have to bend both arms and get down there," he yelled.

Now mind you, my right arm didn't bend very well, so I was doing a lot of the twisting, one arm bent and one arm straight deals. He then placed his foot squarely on my back and proceeded to help me bend my right arm. It did hurt, but I made it through without him or any of the other coaches finding out about my arm injury.

Early on during the annual picture day, when the team, individual and specialty pictures were taken, I ran right smack into a real reality check. The picture for the returning lettermen was being taken, and I lamented on the fact that it could possibly take me until my senior year until I got a varsity football letter, if I got a letter at all. I thought to myself, *I may never be in the returning lettermen picture.*

This really bothered me, I didn't feel like I was fast enough or big enough, and I was determined to work hard to get to a level where I could contribute. I really didn't think there was any chance in the world that I would receive a varsity letter in my sophomore year, but hard work always paid off.

On the day we selected our jerseys for the year, I was determined to get rid of the #16 jersey that I wore my freshman year. I was really reaching, but I figured maybe if I didn't have a quarterback number, they couldn't play me at quarterback anymore. I always liked the #21, but junior Drew Gardner wore that number. However, with the depleted offensive line, Drew was moving to guard and would have to take #60.

Oh yeah, I was through wearing a traditional quarterback's number with #21 available. I had the number I wanted and my signal-calling days would finally be over because I didn't have the right number to play there. In the back of my mind, I always thought to myself, *I do not want to spend my entire football career as a BACKUP quarterback.*

There were more sophomores that changed jersey numbers that year, but the changes were due to totally different reasons. Denny Martin changed from #12 to #10, but I don't know why. Rob Giesige changed from #19 to #65 because Coach McCord was going to make a guard out of him. Finally, Jeff Okuly changed from #75 to #76, and that story is best told by Jeff himself.

> "I overslept on the day we were supposed to get our pads and jerseys. I drove as fast as I could to the school, but I arrived too late, and all of the sophomores had already got their pads and selected their number for the year. Aaron Roth didn't play his freshman year and he selected the #75. I was so mad at myself for oversleeping that I just took the #76 and accepted it as punishment for not waking up on time."[13]

Jeff Okuly is a real stand-up guy, and I did not know this until he related the story to me years later. For him to take responsibility for this incident speaks volumes about his character. He overslept, so he just accepted it for what it was.

Once again, we opened the season at home against McComb and they were the defending Division V state champs. They had a nice team and defeated us 21-6. I actually played in two plays during the game because Eric Guilford was hurt. Plus, there was no backup for Kevin Gerschutz, who was playing both ways at blocking back and rotator.

The next game was against Fairview at their place and they were out for revenge. We had beaten them for the first time in 1983, and they were ready for us. Before the game, while we were getting dressed, someone found a note that was left for us, or should I say Brad Schlachter in particular. Brad was big, fast and had a great arm. He was returning for his second year at quarterback as well as his fourth year at defensive end. He was well known, and in the pre-season write-up, the local newspaper anointed him the top quarterback in the area. It went as far as to say he wasn't only big and strong, but he could run the 40-yard dash in 4.75 seconds.

Written on the note directed at Brad was a simple poem.

Here lies Brad Schlachter
He runs the 40 in 4.75
After we get done with him tonight
He will no longer be alive

The challenge had been issued, and I know everyone was fired up and ready to go. It was a game that changed the rest of the year for me. It was also a game that I would like to forget.

The defensive secondary had been hit hard by injuries and just wasn't playing well at all. I don't know how it happened, but I found myself getting a lot of playing time in this game. Fairview had a high-powered running attack, so we were running a 5-3 defense most of the night. When we went to a 5-3 defense, the safeties would play the outsides as cornerbacks, while one rotator moved up into the third linebacker spot. The other rotator would drop back and play the middle of the field like a free safety. I was playing the middle free safety a lot in the second half. We were clinging to a 14-10 lead in the middle of the fourth quarter when I committed the most devastating error of the entire season. Coach Ondrus always preached that the cardinal rule of a defensive back was to never get beat deep. He would harp and harp all the time in practice about it.

On that crucial play, I was playing the middle safety position. The Fairview quarterback pitched the ball to their halfback on a sweep right, just like they had been doing the entire game. I was in position, flowing to the ball, when something just didn't seem quite right. The halfback pulled up to throw, and flashing behind me was Fairview's tight end. Suddenly, I was sick to my stomach. I tried to stop flowing toward the ball carrier and get deep to defend the halfback pass. In my sudden panic attack, I tripped over my own feet and fell down like a wounded sparrow.

Lying there on the ground, I saw the halfback release the pass, and as it sailed over me, I begged for the receiver to drop it and keep me from being completely humiliated. I heard a huge roar from the crowd. I prayed that it was from our side and not Fairview's. I turned my head just in time to watch the receiver cross the goalline on a 43-yard touchdown to give Fairview a 16-14 advantage.

I tried to hide right there in the middle of the field. Picture a cat trying to lay low, concealing his whole body, with the grass around him. I was doing my best impersonation of a cat right then. If the grass would have been longer, I swear I would have hid there forever, or maybe crawled out to the end zone and ran as fast as I could all the way back to Ayersville. It was not to be, Fairview had an excellent groundskeeper and the grass was mowed right down, nice and neat.

Nothing could spare me the jog of shame back to our sideline. Jog of shame it definitely was, our crowd was silent. I felt like every eye was on me, cursing me and wondering why that sophomore was in there to begin with, he was obviously horrible. He couldn't even stay on his feet. Coach Ondrus glared right through me, and I could tell he was completely and utterly angry.

I waited for the screaming, but it never came. I think it might have been better if he had screamed at me, but he didn't, he never said a word to me. Actually, I don't think he said a word to me for the rest of the season. I always respected and looked up to Coach Ondrus, I think everyone did. He was a true blessing to Ayersville football. He was smart, funny and a fierce competitor. Letting him down was punishment enough for me. We went on to lose the game 24-14 and started our season off at 0-2.

We had been decimated by injuries at the start of the 1984 season, especially after our game against the Fairview Apaches. Notably, starting linebacker junior Brian Allen was out for the year with a neck injury. Our next game was at home against the Edon Blue Bombers. After my screw up in the Fairview game, I didn't have high hopes for playing much the rest of the season. Once again, I did not possess enough talent to make a contribution on the field and I hurt the team because of it. Things were looking very bleak for #21's playing career. I thought to myself, *face it, you're going to be a scrub for life.*

One day in practice, as if fate stepped in, that all changed. The first-team offense was running plays against our simulated Edon defense. To get ready for our next opponent, the coaches made out a scouting report with the different formations and the playing style of our next opponent's defense. We would then assemble a scout team to give our first-team offense a look at what they would be facing on Friday night. After a few walkthroughs, we went live, and the first-team offense went full go against the scout team.

Coach Dave Welty always ran the scout team defense. He was the linebackers coach and called the defensive plays during the varsity games. He was intense and had been with Coach McCord since football started at Ayersville in 1974. He did not put up with any crap and had a no non-sense way of handling things.

The first-team offense was just dominating the scout team that day, when he grabbed my shoulder pads and pushed me towards the practice field and growled, "Get in there and play middle line-backer." I looked at him and mumbled something about not being a linebacker. All he said was, "I don't care what you are, get in there and play middle linebacker." I replied, "I don't know what I am supposed to do, I only know the formations of Edon's secondary." At that point, he became fed up and said, "How hard is it? Just tackle the guy with the ball."

I thought, *okay, whatever; I will just do as he said.* I ended up making a few tackles. I was having some real fun because most of the time I wasn't doing any assignment and just blitzing to get after the ball carrier. We ended up stopping the first-team offense pretty much dead in their tracks.

It was obvious that Coach McCord was getting rather steamed with the offense, because if they couldn't move the ball against our scout team, how could they move it against Edon? On the next play, I blitzed through the guard/center gap and tackled the quarterback before he could even hand the ball off. Coach McCord totally went off, "Coach Welty, that's not how Edon plays defense, we can't get anything accomplished here if we can't even get our plays off." Coach Welty responded, "Sorry Coach, I thought we were going full speed, I can't help it if my guys are busting into your backfield."

Coach McCord was mostly frustrated with the fact that we were 0-2 and not the situation at hand. He then proceeded to smack the five linemen, one at a time, in the face mask with his clipboard. This we had seen before and would see many more times in practice when Coach McCord was unhappy with his linemen.

Coach Welty was very pleased. Whenever a scout team coach could take a bunch of scrub players and get the best of the starters, he had to be proud that his job was well done and the team would be better prepared for Friday night. As we were breaking up to go into conditioning drills, Coach Welty put his hand on my helmet and said, "That's how a linebacker plays, tomorrow you will be with me in defensive groups."

I didn't think much about it and thought surely that would never happen. I had always envied linebackers because they were always in the action and were hitting people on every play. Linebacker was beyond my wildest dreams.

When practice came around the following day, as we were heading off for defensive groups, Coach McCord stopped me and said, "You will be with Coach Welty today, he needs another linebacker since Brian Allen is out for the year."

I was ecstatic, *me a linebacker?* I could hardly believe it. I was sure Coach Welty had made the request and Coach Ondrus was probably happier than could be since I screwed up so badly in the Fairview game. Getting me out of his secondary probably felt like he was losing a bad tooth.

When Coach Welty selected me to be one of his linebackers, I looked up to him like he was the greatest. The only thing that would have made me happier was if Coach McCord would have made me one of his linemen. I dreamed of being in the trenches, and to actually get a chance to play linebacker was closer than I thought I would ever get.

I became Coach Welty's shadow. Wherever he went, I went. On the scout team, I begged to play nose guard, hoping my advancement to the trenches could continue. I worked harder than I had ever worked before, because I really felt like Coach Welty was giving me the chance I had always wanted. I would have run through a wall to show him I had what it took to play linebacker.

Linebacker was something new and I loved the new drills we performed. I had all new assignments to learn and it kept me very interested. I wasn't expecting much playing time, if any, because junior Steve Thieroff and sophomores Steve Deitrick and Mike Wilson were ahead of me for playing time. In the 5-2 defense, only two linebackers were needed and when we went to a 5-3, one of the rotators would become the other linebacker.

Against Edon, I played in quite a few plays at linebacker and found myself a member of the special teams. I loved being on the kickoff team, as it was usually the first step in a player's career. When you found yourself playing on the kickoff team, it wouldn't be long before you secured a position on the defense. Coach McCord always groomed his younger players by allowing some sophomores and maybe a freshman or two on the kickoff team. We ended up winning the game against Edon, 8-7. Our offense had still not played well, but our defense had improved enough for us to get the win.

The next game on the schedule was against National Trail. Antwerp did not field a team in 1984, so we picked up National Trail in Antwerp's place. We were scheduled to play National Trail on a Saturday afternoon at their place. We had never played them before and none of us really knew what to expect. We left very early Saturday morning because it was a very long bus ride, and Coach McCord wanted us to have some time in between the bus ride and the game itself to relax and get ready to play.

We beat National Trail (26-6), and evened our record at 2-2. The offense came alive and rushed for 230 yards. The defense played spectacular and limited National Trail to only 10 yards rushing. Steve Deitrick played great at linebacker and had 13 tackles. I received more playing time at linebacker and finished with nine tackles and a couple of quarterback sacks.

The Hilltop Cadets came to our place for our next game. Steve Deitrick broke his arm in the National Trail game, so sophomore Mike Wilson moved into the starting spot alongside Thieroff at linebacker. I was probably going to be receiving even more playing time at linebacker, as the new injury to Deitrick took its toll.

The defense didn't play quite as well against Hilltop, but we still won the game, 56-22, and it looked as if our offense was coming around. The Schlachter brothers carried the load with freshman Chris rushing for 86 yards and senior Brad scoring twice while tossing a pair of touchdowns. Our season record stood at 3-2.

It was after this game when we were watching the game field that I received a nickname that stuck with me throughout school and even after. Coach McCord was rolling the tape and running it back and forth. Just before he went on to the next play, he would announce who got credit for the tackle. He would call it out and another coach would mark it down. It was always an exciting time and many players anticipated their name being called.

On different occasions, players would make comments, kind of helping Coach McCord decipher who actually made the first hit and who really brought the ball carrier down. Coach McCord always tolerated it some, but once it got out of control and there was arguing back and forth, he would call an immediate halt. It was time to give Coach McCord complete control over the decision.

During one film viewing session, Brandon Knoll could be seen taking on two blockers. As Brandon was about to make contact with the ball carrier, there was a flash of blue jersey flying in to put a hit on the ball carrier just before he got his hands on the runner.

Coach McCord ran it back and forth a couple of times, then announced, "Solo tackle to Groll and assist to Knoll."

At that point, Brandon stood up and proclaimed, "That little weasel. Coach, I was taking on two blockers and he just came sliding in there like a weasel to get that solo tackle, the weasel does it all the time." After that, I was simply known as "Weasel".

We were on the road to Hicksville for our next game. A single play in the game became a stepping stone for my career, and one of my favorite plays of my entire playing days.

Hicksville was back to punt and the call in our huddle was punt return right. Punt return right meant that the five down linemen were to hand shiver the man in front of them, make sure the ball was kicked, and then run straight down the line to about 15 yards from the sideline. Next, they'd turn and run downfield, stopping when they were downfield about 25 yards. They would then set up and form a wall five yards apart from each other.

The goal of the return man was to catch the ball and take off for the right sideline. If the return man could get there, the blockers would be waiting and ready to dish out some punishment.

Getting the return man to the wall was where I came in. The right side linebacker's job was to make sure the ball was punted, run straight down the line of scrimmage to a point 15 yards from the right sideline, then run downfield until I was parallel with the ball carrier. From there, I wouldn't stop like the rest of the linemen in the wall, but continue towards the return man. If anyone was chasing the return man, it was my job to block them, enabling the return man to get to the wall, or "peel them off" as it was called.

The peel off blocks would sometimes result in hellacious hits. Sometimes, the defender had his eye on the ball carrier and never saw the block coming. In practice, underclassmen got flattened by these blocks often. To me, this was the most devastating play in football. Through my years playing football for Ayersville, I saw the most bone-crushing hits in practice and in games from the peel off blocks.

During the punt return against Hicksville, it was my responsibility to deliver the peel off block. I watched the punter kick the ball away, sprinted right down the line of scrimmage until I was 15 yards from the sideline, turned up field and ran as fast as I could. As I turned up field, I saw Denny Martin waiting on the punt to drop. After Denny caught the ball and started heading for the sideline, I was parallel to him and started running directly toward him. I saw three Hicksville defenders in hot pursuit of Denny.

Would I get there in time? I ran as fast as I could. If I didn't make it, Denny would be tackled and I would receive some sour looks from the coaches. I was at full speed, Denny was at full speed, and the Hicksville defenders were at full speed. The closest one reached out and grabbed Denny's jersey and was preparing to bring him down just as I arrived.

I was at full speed and the defender never saw me coming. It was the most bone-crushing hit of my career. I just ran right through the defender, sending him sailing into one of the other guys chasing Denny. The guy I hit slammed into the other guy so hard that he went over backwards and tripped up the other guy chasing Denny. The wall was then waiting, and once Denny made it to the wall, he always went the whole way. It was a 68-yard touchdown, or so we thought. An official threw a late flag. I had been called for clipping.

Coach McCord went ballistic, "How can you call that a clip, the guy was running straight at him. Your just calling it a clip because two of those guys are lying out there hurt."

I am sorry that Denny didn't get the touchdown return, but that hit was the best one of my career. When we watched film the following Monday, Coach McCord kept running it back and forth grumbling about the bad call and in disbelief that three guys were taken out by the block. It was more of a domino thing than anything else, but it was nice to see those guys wiped out just when they thought they had Denny tackled.

We went on to win the Hicksville game, 33-12, to up our record to 4-2. Bob Froelich had 108 yards rushing and hit paydirt twice.

Our next game was at home against the undefeated Holgate Tigers. They had been rolling up some very impressive wins and were without a doubt the best team in the area. There was a pep rally on Friday, where a production company had come in and put together a slide show to some very upbeat music as different pictures flashed against the big screen in our auditorium.

When we gathered in the auditorium, we didn't have any idea of what was to come. The lights were turned off and the song "Eye of the Tiger" started playing, as different still shots were flashed on the screen of us at practice and during games. Everyone started screaming and it was an intense and moving pep rally. After the pep rally, we went to the locker room to get our equipment in order before we went home and ate dinner and prepared for the game. As I was leaving the locker room, Coach McCord stopped me and informed me, "You will be starting at linebacker tonight, don't be intimidated, just play like you know how."

I was jubilant, but nervous at the same time. Holgate had a group of fast and quick running backs that had been putting up some extraordinary numbers. My first start would be a real challenge and I hoped I could make the most of it.

We played them pretty tough in the first half; I tried to concentrate on doing my assignment and to not make any mistakes. In the second quarter, they ran a sweep left, and as I skated in pursuit down the line, I was completely annihilated by a crack-back block. I was knocked right on my butt. The play went for about 30 yards and I was dreading Monday's film session, as that play was just plain pathetic on my part. I just hoped it wouldn't be replayed too many times.

Holgate went on to defeat us, 41-12, dropping us to 4-3. I did not play all that bad and ended up making a lot of tackles in the game. Holgate was just a much superior team than us in 1984. The Tigers went on to win the GMC title and finished undefeated in the regular season. They also made a nice run in the Division V state playoffs until a few key injuries ended their year.

We traveled to Wayne Trace and battled the Raiders after the lopsided setback to Holgate in 1984. We defeated them fairly easily,

43-20, improving our record to 5-3. The offense rolled up 313 yards rushing, with many backs contributing, while the defense recovered five fumbles, sacked the quarterback five times and had one interception. I had one of my best games to that date with nine tackles and two quarterback sacks.

Our last away game of the year was against the Tinora Rams. Coach McCord never called them by name the entire time I was at Ayersville. He would only refer to them as, "That team across the river."

Tinora was always a big game and it didn't matter what the records were. There were always pads cracking when we took on the Rams.

I had become fairly comfortable at the linebacker position. Coach Dave Welty did a great job in practice of teaching us to hit hard and fill holes. He had a repertoire of drills in practice where it was like a meat grinder, because all we did was crash into each other taking on lead blockers and ball carriers. I loved every second of it. I was finally playing smash-mouth football with contact on every play.

Since I was starting, Coach Welty was my complete hero. I was an actual starting linebacker for him, and I felt like I was his personal warrior. When he would coach me on certain things, I was totally transfixed and I would do whatever he said.

Starting alongside Steve Thieroff was a tremendous benefit to my career. He knew what everyone was doing on every play. He was a true football player and could deliver hard hits. He flew to the ball and always kept himself in position to make the play. Ayersville had a history of producing some very fine and outstanding linebackers, I think Steve would be right at the top of the list. He started every game as a sophomore on a very good 1983 team. It was plainly attributed to the talent Steve Thieroff possessed. As talented as he was, it was his mind for the game that set him apart from others. I think he could have had a tremendous career coaching football. I learned more from him than anyone else I ever played with.

He gave me every bit of knowledge he had, "Keep your shoulders square with the line of scrimmage at all times. Use your hands to keep blockers off of your legs. If a back comes through your hole, put him on his back so he can't get out into a pass pattern. Do your assignment and then fly to the ball. If a lead blocker is coming through the hole, you better fill that hole and create a pile. If you're getting blown off the ball, drop down and don't lose any more ground."

In an earlier game in 1984, I kept falling for the fake on a cross trap. A cross trap is where the quarterback fakes a handoff to a back going one way, and then hands it to another back going in the opposite direction. Every time they ran it to my side, it was for a nice gain. When they ran it to Steve's side, he made the tackle.

I finally got disgusted and said to him, "Steve, how in the heck do you keep sniffing out that cross trap, they fake me out every time?" He looked at me and replied, "Aren't you reading the guards? The guards will always lead you right to the ball carrier."

I had to stop and think about this, he was right, guards were usually lead blockers. If they pulled, usually the ball carrier would be right behind them. If they came straight at you, you better meet them, because the play was coming right up the middle. This analogy from Steve Thieroff would stay in my mind for the rest of my playing days.

During the first half of the Tinora game, everything was going great for us as a team. The defense was playing great. I had made an interception early on and it seemed like I was always in the right place to make a tackle.

I was in front of the defensive huddle, alongside Thieroff, waiting on him to get the play from the sideline and make the call, when nose guard Bob Froelich looked at me and said, "You better get out of here, there is blood all over you."

I looked at him, and then looked down, and sure enough, blood was dripping all over my jersey. At the time, I didn't know where it was coming from. The play before the huddle, I had made a tackle on the ball carrier where I felt something slam into my face mask, but I didn't think anything had happened to make me bleed.

I ran to the sideline, where Coach McCord examined my chin. My chin was where the blood was coming from apparently. Coach notified me that I had a pretty big gash on my chin and I would need some stitches.

I said to him, "After the game?" We were still in the first half at the time. He just looked at me like I was crazy and shook his head, "No, not after the game, right now, it's a bad cut."

Somebody found my Dad, and soon he was driving me to the emergency room. I just went there in my uniform, because I really thought after a few quick stitches, I could get right back out onto the field. Once we arrived at the ER, it took a little bit of time before the ER doctor came through the curtain to put some stitches in. I told him to hurry up because I had to get back to the game. He just looked at me incredulously and replied, "I have to do this right or it will leave a nasty scar, and what will your wife think about that one day when you get married?"

He put some numbing stuff in my chin with a needle and said he would be back in a little bit. I asked, "Why?" He said, "To give it some time to get numb." I said, "No, stitch it up now, I really want to get back to the game." He said, "Alright then, fine," and got started stitching it up.

After 13 stitches later, and him complaining the whole entire time that I was rushing him, and not allowing him to do his job properly, my Dad and I were out the door. I do have a nasty scar there, but you know what, my wife says that she kind of likes it. So what did that doctor know?

This was where my Dad was just the coolest. We got out of there, started running to the car, hopped in, and he squealed the tires as he pulled out of the parking lot. He had our yellow Oldsmobile screaming across the Maumee River Bridge and heading for the Tinora High School doing over 100 miles an hour. How many fathers would do this? Risk a speeding ticket, just to try and get their son back to a football game. Mine did, and that tells you what kind of father he was. At the time, I had to take a vow of silence so that my Mom wouldn't find out. Sorry Dad, I guess Mom is going to find out about it now.

We got back and everyone was walking off of the field. The game was over and we had won, 34-0. Even though we had won, I was dejected that I missed a whole half of football because of a stupid gash on my chin that wasn't even life threatening. I really think we could have slapped a couple pieces of athletic tape across it and I would have been fine. I made up my mind to never go to a coach if I was bleeding or injured, that way I could stay on the field. The win brought our record to 6-3 and we had one game left against Edgerton at home.

It would be the final game for the seniors, but maybe I wouldn't be allowed to play with my stitched up chin. Coach McCord cut out a piece of knee pad in the shape of a football, and then cut a hole in the center of it. He referred to it as a donut and told me that it would fit under my chin strap to keep the pressure off of my stitched up chin. I would be able to play in the last game of the year after all.

Due to personal reasons, Coach Welty was not going to be at the Edgerton game that year. He pulled Steve Thieroff and me aside, and told us that we would be running the defense and making all of the defensive calls. I was sad that he couldn't be there because he had believed in me and gave me a chance, but at the same time I was thinking, *hot freakin tamale, the game is going to be a total blitz-fest because I will bug Thieroff to call a blitz on every play.*

I was in Thieroff's ear all night, "Let's run pro right or left." It was my favorite play. When the offense came out of the huddle, we would make a right or left call depending on the strength of the opponent's formation. If it was a left call, the nose guard would angle right, and I, as the right side linebacker, would blitz through the opposite guard hole. If it was a right call, the nose guard would angle left and the left side linebacker would blitz through the opposite guard hole.

On the play, it always seemed like we went through the line of scrimmage untouched and had a straight shot at a ball carrier or a passing quarterback. The Edgerton game was no different; we were in their backfield a lot. After awhile, Thieroff started ignoring me and made calls appropriate to down and distance, but I am sure while he was sleeping that night, the words, "Let's run pro right or left," echoed in his ear.

The Edgerton game was the seniors' last game, and they played harder than I had ever seen them play before. Brad Schlachter ran for 125 yards and a touchdown and threw for another touchdown. His defensive effort was even more impressive: nine tackles, two caused fumbles, one fumble recovery, one QB sack and an interception from his defensive end position. Seniors Charlie Askins and Kevin Gerschutz had 14 tackles each. Edgerton was driving late in the game with less than two minutes to go, when Brad Schlachter intercepted a screen pass and gave us the victory, 21-14. We finished the year with a 7-3 record.

Unlike the previous year, my family did not plan our annual pheasant hunting trip to South Dakota for the last week of football in 1984. We left the morning after the Edgerton game. The year before, I had felt like I let the coaches and team down by missing the final week. Even if my parents would have planned the trip for the final week, I wouldn't have gone; I was having too much fun playing football. That said a lot about my passion for football because the next year's annual pheasant hunting trip to South Dakota was anticipated as soon as we arrived home from the previous one.

It was a fun and interesting year for me. Playing linebacker had been a dream come true. I started and received a lot of playing time as a sophomore, it was not like junior high where I could never seem to be on the field taking on blockers and tackling ball carriers. I didn't realize it at the time, but it was my last game at the linebacker position in our standard 5-2 defense.

Playing linebacker my sophomore year was probably the most memorable event of my entire football career. I absolutely loved every second of it. The year of 1984 completely enhanced my desire to be on the football field. My experiences that year left me hungrier than I had ever been before to strap on the pads and helmet.

JUNIOR YEAR

Everyone was excited for the 1985 season to start. We had a lot of guys coming back, and our outlook was good to contend for our first ever outright GMC championship. We even had some aspirations of making the playoffs for the first time.

But before the football season began, our summer baseball team enjoyed a great ACME campaign. Brian Allen, Denny Martin, Rob Giesige, Aaron Roth, Mike Wilson and I, had to put football on hold until we finished the ACME State Tournament. We had advanced all the way through the sectional and district tournaments before we traveled to Piqua, Ohio for the double-elimination State Tournament. We won our first game, lost our second game, won the third game and then we were eliminated when we lost the fourth game. The long baseball season was over and the highly-anticipated football season was upon us.

The seniors on the team were: #23 Brian Allen (B.A.) (5-10, 170), #24 Eric Guilford (5-5, 140), #32 Bob Froelich (5-6, 175), #34 John Lewis (5-11, 160), #46 Steve Thieroff (5-9, 180), #54 Steve Santo (5-11, 195), #60 Drew Gardner (5-7, 145), #71 Sam Burns (5-9, 245) #72 Mike Schlosser (5-9, 180), #82 Brian Pessefall (6-0, 170) and #84 Dan Bakle (6-0, 190).

Returning underclassmen lettermen were juniors: #12 Denny Martin (5-10, 145), #21 Andy Groll (5-9, 155), #25 Steve Deitrick (5-6, 160), #63 Mike Wilson (5-7, 160), #68 Rob Giesige (5-10, 150) and #76 Jeff Okuly (5-10, 180), along with sophomore: #44 Chris Schlachter (5-11, 185).

When practice started in 1985, I was informed early on that I would no longer be practicing at linebacker; I would be back at my original rotator position. Steve Thieroff was back for his fourth year at linebacker, Brian Allen was back from his injury, Steve Deitrick was back from his as well and Mike Wilson was there too. The defensive secondary, however, had lost three starters off of the 1984 team. I wasn't even going to ask, or voice my desire to remain a linebacker. It just didn't make any sense from a team standpoint.

We were stacked at linebacker, and needed to revamp three-quarters of our secondary. It wasn't as disappointing as I thought it was going to be. Coach Ondrus would be coaching me again, I missed being around him during practice, and his football personality was matched by none. He was fun, yet intense, witty, and always smiling unless somebody angered him.

He was just one of those guys that everyone wanted to be around, and over the years, I acquired many memories of the times we shared. Even though he was a fun guy, we knew better than to get under his skin because he wasn't scared of anything and he was tougher than all of us.

On the first day of defensive groups, I thought it would be funny if I ran off with the linebackers to their group. Girlie, Guilford and Gardner started yelling at me, "Hey Groll, get back here, you're with us this year."

The linebackers were trying to chase me off because there was always a long-standing friendly rivalry over who the hardest hitters were, defensive backs or linebackers. They were chasing me and yelling, "Get out of here, you light-hitting defensive back, you can't take the hits we dish out."

Finally, Coach Ondrus yelled out, "You guys just keep him over there, Groll has a little problem of tripping over white lines when he is trying to cover somebody."

It was the very first time he had ever mentioned my falling down, and allowing the go-ahead touchdown in the Fairview game from the year before. Coach McCord, who would be coaching the linebackers in 1985, finally broke it up with, "A.G. (he always called me by my initials) get your butt over there, and Coach Ondrus, see if you can teach him how to back peddle without falling down."

Phil Girlie would go on to name our secondary that year "The Killer G's", Girlie and Guilford at the safeties, and Gardner and Groll at the rotators. Whenever the linebackers would start their smack talk, Phil would say, "Do you hear that buzzing, baby? That's "The Killer G's" coming for you."

We would once again start the season off against McComb at their place. Would 1985 be the year we finally beat McComb? We sure wanted it; all we could think about was beating McComb and finally starting our season off with a win instead of a loss.

It was a hard-hitting battle, our defense played fairly well, but our offense couldn't get much going and we fell for the third year in a row to McComb, 13-7. What a let down, starting the season off with a loss made it an uphill challenge the rest of the season. We needed more work; our 1985 team had all of the tools to be successful. We would surely be practicing longer and harder in the weeks to come.

> Rob Giesige talked about a key moment in the game. "We were down by a touchdown and someone needed to make a play. McComb was punting, and we had a punt return right called. I told Brian Allen that I was going to try and block the punt. I asked Brian if he could take my guy. Brian said, 'I got your guy, I got my guy, and I got any other guy that wants a piece.' I almost blocked the punt to give us a chance for the win, but came up short. Brian Allen was always good for a laugh."[14]

On week two we would welcome in the Fairview Apaches. Personally I needed to play well in the game to avenge my mistake in the 1984 match-up. When Friday night rolled around, it was the hottest game I ever played in. It was just unbelievably hot and humid.

Fairview scored a touchdown first and looked to take a commanding lead with a second. They had a first-and-10 on our nine-yard line, when I intercepted a pass in the end zone, halting their drive. Finally, I felt like I had avenged my mistake from the previous year. Eric Guilford then scored for us, making the score tantamount at 7-7.

Fairview kicked a field goal and led 10-7 before Brian Allen ran for a touchdown late in the fourth quarter and with the extra point, put us ahead, 14-10. Fairview came right back and marched down the field. It was so hot during that game that a few of us were sucking air big time and I was one of them. Sam Burns, the biggest guy on our team, must not have felt the heat, as he made three consecutive extraordinary plays, culminating in him sacking the Fairview quarterback on fourth down when they had the ball first-and-goal inside our 10-yard line. We escaped victorious, 14-10.

> Steve Deitrick recalled a memorable play from the game. "During the Fairview game, I caught an Apache back coming across the middle on a slant. I laid him OUT; bring the cart because he's crying that he thinks his wrist is busted. I'm just standing over him screaming, get that crap out of here, you aren't catching that ball on me jerk-wad! The ref wasn't real pleased with me, to say the least, but hey, no flag, so I'm good! Ahhh, I can still vividly picture that moment in my head"[15]

After the game, I remember having to be checked over by the emergency medical squad. They took three of us inside the ambulance and monitored our heart rate and other vital signs for heat exhaustion. Bob Froelich, Steve Thieroff and I all sat in there breathing hard and trying to catch our breath. Maybe I needed to work a little harder on conditioning. Obviously, I was not in good enough shape.

During our Monday film session, it was brought to my attention as well. It was late in the game on Fairview's final drive. They were just running the ball right down our throats. On one particular play, they picked up 15 yards off tackle. Coach Ondrus made the remark, "Where is Groll at, rotators have to stuff those off tackle plays." Coach McCord ran it back, played it again, and there I was standing straight up, hand wrestling with the tight end as he was taking me out of the play. Coach McCord remarked, "Oh gee fer socks, he is sucking wind and playing with the tight end." Conditioning that week was going to be brutal. I knew I was going to be pushed extra hard after that.

The highlight of the film session was of course the 245-pound Sam Burns making tackles in the backfield on the final three plays. Coach McCord used this as a little motivation, "Look at Sam out there at 245 pounds making plays, what kind of excuse do you other guys have? 'Oh, it's so hot! We are so tired!' That's a bunch of crap, get in shape!"

Another highlight of the film session was of Eric Guilford. Fairview had busted two kickoffs and had one man to beat, our kickoff safety, Eric Guilford. Coach McCord always kept one man back on our kickoffs, just in case the other team broke one to prevent a touchdown. Eric Guilford was that guy and both times he made fine open-field tackles.

On the second one, we could actually see Eric waving his hand and motioning for the ball carrier to come right at him. For some reason, the ball carrier did, and Eric performed a perfect form tackle with his head up, right in the numbers, as he wrapped his arms around the back of the ball carriers thighs, and lifted, dumping the return man squarely on his back. All Coach McCord kept saying was, "Now that's a perfect tackle, just look at that form. He wanted that guy to come right at him. He just waved him in, now that's a great play." He ran it back, over and over, saying the same thing.

Week three was against the Edon Blue Bombers at their field. The rout was on right out of the chutes. Denny Martin took off on a 64-yard touchdown gallop on the first play of the game. On the night, eight different players scored for the Pilots. Rob Giesige had eight tackles and two quarterback sacks. I had eight stops and my second interception of the season. The Pilots stood at 2-1 with an impressive 52-0 thumping of Edon.

Week four and we were back at home against the Antwerp Archers. They were trying to resurrect their program after not having a team the year before. It was another easy victory, as the Pilots rolled up 390 yards on the ground in a lopsided 61-24 win. On our fourth Friday night of the season, nine different players scored for Ayersville. The starters only played until the half and the JV team took over the rest of the game. I had nine tackles and two more picks. The defense continued their stalking of the opposing quarterback with five more sacks.

> Rob Giesige was having some fun from his defensive end position and said. "One of the Antwerp halfbacks kept coming over to block me and he was throwing a forearm into my helmet. I thought, *whatever, go ahead and hit me in the face mask.* This continued throughout the first half and I was having some fun with it. When that halfback came out for the second half, he had his forearm wrapped up so much he looked like Popeye. I guess he was getting the worst of the battle."[16]

On Monday, right before the film session started, Coach McCord addressed us as a team. None of us knew what was going on when we filed into the locker room. Before the film started, he said, "Caught on this tape is something that will not be tolerated on this team, or any other Ayersville football team."

Now, we were all worried, what could be on the tape, and who was the perpetrator? I hadn't seen the coaches like this before, especially after a win. All of the players were completely quiet as the film began to roll. It stayed that way all through the film. We all had looks of concern on our face and were just waiting and praying we hadn't done anything wrong. I tried to think back and there was nothing I could think of that happened during the game. Apparently, I totally missed the monumental event.

Finally, Coach McCord said, "Under no circumstances will an Ayersville player act this way. We do not take cheap shots, play dirty, or act disrespectful to anyone. We need to be a class act, hold ourselves to higher standards and play the game the way it was meant to be played."

He then started the projector; I didn't see anything other than our defense chase down a sweep for no gain. The tackle was clean and nobody piled on.

He ran it again and said, "Brian Allen what do you have to say for yourself?" We all tried to find #23 as the play unfolded. There he was, trailing the play from his weak-side linebacker position. An Archer was lying on the ground and as Brian passed by, he lifted his leg and kicked him right in the helmet. The player fortunately wasn't hurt, and with the helmet on, wasn't fazed by the kick.

It was no consolation to Coach McCord, he was fuming. Brian finally responded, "I was just trying to jump over him, Coach."

"No you weren't, see me after practice," Coach McCord replied. He ran it back again, smacked the table hard and said in a low voice, "This will not be tolerated." I think everyone of us got the point loud and clear.

Coach McCord always stressed clean-hitting football, just the way it was supposed to be played. You play hard, you hit hard, but you don't play dirty, cheat or take short cuts. Coach McCord was a class act; he was shaping our lives forever, not just in football.

He had Brian Allen out there running, doing push-ups and bear crawls long after we had showered and went home. As a few of us were walking to our cars, there were no signs that it would let up. He was still out there running. I am sure that once he was done, since everyone else had left, Coach McCord had quite the chat with B.A.

I asked Brian the next day how long he was out there. He replied, "I don't know, but it was really dark when he was done with me."

I really liked Brian Allen and considered him one of my friends. He could be mean if he didn't like you, and he was prone to causing trouble and getting into it. But if you really got to know Brian, there wasn't anything he wouldn't do for you. I experienced one of those instances my sophomore year.

I had gone back to his house one hot summer day after baseball practice. We were both dying of thirst. He opened the refrigerator, pulled out a two-liter of soda, and unscrewed the cap. The bottle was about empty and I figured he would just gulp it down. He didn't, he shoved the bottle into my chest and said, "Here you drink it, there isn't enough for both of us, and I will just drink some water."

That was the B.A. that I knew, and he will always be my friend. To his testament, Brian never did anything like what he did against Antwerp again. I think part of him changed that day. He became a great teammate and leader to go along with all of the athletic skills he possessed. He had always been tough and afraid of nothing, that day he understood the difference of being tough and acting tough. He had something to be afraid of as well, the wrath of Coach McCord if he ever did something like that again.

Week five we were back on the road again to take on the Hilltop Cadets and they put us in an early hole by grabbing a 12-0 lead. Our defense got a strict lecture, and we didn't allow them to score the rest of the game. Our offense went on to score 32 unanswered points. Steve Thieroff scored three times and Steve Deitrick scored twice. I had nine stops, Bob Froelich had seven tackles, a sack and a fumble recovery. Drew Gardner chipped in with a fumble recovery and an interception.

Week six brought the Hicksville Aces to town. Once again, there was an event that occurred that would get us all pumped up for the game. There had been a shoebox left in our locker room containing a bunch of marshmallows with the seniors' names written on them. A note was left in the box that said, "You guys hit like a bunch of... marshmallows."

Supposedly, they were from the Hicksville Aces. Were they really from our opponents, or from one of the Coaches, a parent, or possibly a concerned fan? We never found out or cared. We would go on to show them some hitting on Friday night. The offense rolled up 337 yards rushing. Brian Allen was back strong and ran for 129 yards after playing very minimally in the Hilltop game because of the kicking incident. Steve Deitrick had 13 tackles in the 27-14 Ayersville win. There was some major hitting in the game and our record improved to 5-1.

Tolly Hanna recalled an incident from the game. "I'm not sure exactly when this happened but Jeff Okuly had a nasty dislocated finger (ringer finger at a 90 degree angle) after a kickoff. He ran off the field calling for Coach. Coach immediately sent him to Mr. Baldwin (our Athletic Director. at the time). Mr. Baldwin just grabbed Jeff's finger, popped it right back in place, taped it up and Jeff was back out on the field. I saw the whole thing and about yakked.[17]

Week seven was against the team ranked 14th in Division V, the Holgate Tigers. In 1984 they had beat up on us pretty good, and they had quite a few players back. It was going to be a hard-hitting game, that's for sure.

Our defense dominated the game. Early on, I was having all kinds of trouble keeping track of the ball. I felt lost out there. I couldn't tell if it was a pass play or running play. Their quarterback must have been doing a great job hiding the ball because I was getting no read at all on where the ball was going. We were in the huddle and I asked, "Is anyone else having trouble following the ball?" Of course Steve Thieroff chimed in, "Read the guards, they will tell you what kind of play is being run and where it's going." Point taken, I didn't have any trouble after that.

Offensively, we just couldn't punch the ball into the end zone. We kept getting down close, only to see our drives stall. I think it happened three times. Coach Ondrus was getting a little bit upset because we couldn't get the ball in the end zone and he was voicing his displeasure.

"Doesn't anybody want to score? When you get down here this close, you have to smell that end zone."

I had played hardly any offense all that year, basically because I just plain didn't like playing offense. I only wanted to be a defensive player. I for sure hadn't carried the ball that year. I was getting kind of sick of not being able to score as well and replied back to him, "I can smell it, Coach."

He looked at me, rolled his eyes, and then sent somebody else in with the play. The play was run and we were stopped for no gain on second down at the Holgate seven. Coach Ondrus was livid. He grabbed somebody else and shoved them onto the field with the play, and on their way to the huddle, he screamed, "Get it into the end zone."

We ran a sweep that got snuffed out after a one-yard gain. That brought up third down on their six. I was standing right on his hip, and breathing on his neck. There was no way he could have avoided me. I don't know why I said it, or where it came from, but I looked at Coach Ondrus and said, "Give me the ball, I will not be denied."

He looked at me, hesitated, grabbed my arm, and said, "I-right blast right reverse, you better score." I ran to the huddle with the play and took the place of blocking back. The formation I-right meant the blocking back would line up on the right side, outside the tackle, and a couple of yards off of the line of scrimmage. The quarterback would fake a handoff to the tailback running through the two hole and then hand the ball to me as I passed behind him. The play was to be run outside, behind a pulling and leading guard.

The line blocked great, but there was still one guy between me and the goalline. He hit me on my right side and didn't wrap me up. I stumbled, put my hand down to keep my balance, and continued into the end zone. Finally, we had scored! As I ran off the field, I glanced at Coach Ondrus; he was shaking his head mumbling something about, "Not being denied."

Brian Allen went on to score another touchdown, and we came out of the game with a 13-0 shutout victory. Bob Froelich played a great game from his nose guard position with seven tackles, one blocked punt and a trio of sacks.

Week eight brought the Wayne Trace Raiders to Ayersville. There had been a lot of rain and the field was pretty muddy. The game had actually been cancelled on Friday night because of the storm. We were set to play on Saturday night instead.

Our punt return team scored a touchdown on a Denny Martin 54-yard return. Our punt rush team also got into the act and was all over the Raider punter, causing him to lose the ball early in the game. I scooped it up and took it 17 yards for another score.

Steve Thieroff had one of the best hitting games I had ever seen. He was the peel off blocker on our punt return team that night. The first time, he delivered a crushing block to get Denny around the corner on his 54-yard dash to glory. The guy Steve hit needed to be carried off the field. He did this two more times before the game was over. Each time the guy had to be carried off the field. Steve made some nice clean hard hits as the Wayne Trace guys just kept chasing Denny without paying any attention.

The third time, the Wayne Trace coach went nuts on their sideline, screaming at the officials to do something since his guys were getting creamed by Thieroff. Coach McCord looked at Coach Ondrus and said, "Maybe we better not set any more punt returns up tonight. Those guys just don't keep their heads up when they are running down the field and they are getting blasted."

> "I remember Thieroff's punt return peel off blocks. He knocked out so many players, that they ran out of ambulances. Their coach was out there screaming about 'unnecessary roughness' and how he should be thrown out of the game for 'hitting too hard.' For the record, they were all legit hits and no penalties. We laughed our butts off at the game, after the game and on film day," related Steve Deitrick.[18]

We went on to win 26-0 as our defense pitched its second straight bagel. Our record stood at 7-1. Thieroff had nine tackles and two fumble recoveries while Steve Deitrick had seven tackles and a sack to lead our defense.

Week nine brought "That team across the river" to our bank of the Maumee River. Tinora had a highly-touted defense in 1985, so it was going to be a battle.

It was a good game, but the Pilots prevailed. Brian Allen rushed for 127 yards, Bob Froelich ran for our only touchdown and Chris Schlachter kicked the first field goal of his career to give us the 10-0 victory. It was a tough-hitting game, and once again, our defense hung a goose egg on the opponent's side of the scoreboard. Steve Thieroff had 10 tackles, one sack and an interception while Eric Burket added nine tackles and two sacks.

Week 10 took us northwest to Edgerton to take on the Bulldogs. We were 8-1, but still didn't have enough computer points to make the playoffs. Would we get enough to make the playoffs if we beat Edgerton? I hoped so, and thought we stood a good chance if we went 9-1.

My parents had it all set up so that we could leave right after the Edgerton game to go on our annual pilgrimage to South Dakota in search of ringneck pheasants. I was not going if we made the playoffs. I wanted to make the playoffs bad, and arrangements had been made, that if we made the playoffs, I could stay home.

Winning the game would also give us our first ever GMC title. Spirits were high, and all through school that week, everyone was focused on the big game. It was spirit week, so everyday there was something exciting happening, culminating with a pep rally on Friday to celebrate the seniors last regular season game. We still hoped to make the playoffs to extend the season even longer. Hopefully, we would be playing for a few more weeks yet, and the excitement would continue.

Steve Thieroff and Steve Deitrick scored in the first half and we had the lead at halftime, 13-7. In the fourth quarter, Edgerton put together an extensive drive and scored the go-ahead TD to take a 14-13 advantage.

The Bulldogs only enjoyed the lead for a short time, fortunately.

Coach McCord had put in a new kickoff return a few weeks prior to the Edgerton game. It was called kickoff return middle. Each man on the kickoff return team was assigned to block a player on the opposing team. The assigned player to block would be determined by counting from the left side to the right side. The two opponents running down the center of the field would be double teamed, while the rest of the guys blocked one-on-one, concentrating on the center of the field and allowing the outside guys to run free and hopefully never be a factor in the play since it was going right up the middle.

Steve Deitrick and I were to double team the man fifth from the left. The kickoff was good and high. Steve and I ran side-by-side and leveled the number five man. Everyone else must have done their assignment, because when we both looked up from lying on top of the guy we blocked, John Lewis was cashing in on the fine blocking and was darting into the end zone to complete an 81-yard TD return. Everyone ran and piled on; we ended up receiving a penalty for excessive celebration and I made a note to try and never let that happen again. The game was never over until the final whistle.

We had the lead back, 19-14. We held on and won the GMC title for the first time ever. I wasn't really excited about that, I wanted to make the playoffs. I wanted the season to continue, we went 9-1, and surely we could go to the playoffs. This had been one of my best games ever, I finished with 18 tackles and Steve Thieroff ended his career with 16 tackles.

After we had showered, we always went out by the buses and got something to eat and drink and talked about the game. I was more concerned with finding out if we were going to be in the playoffs since my family would be heading off to South Dakota if we hadn't.

Coach McCord was probably tired of me following him around and asking him if we would be in. Going into the game, we knew some major upsets had to happen, but I still hadn't lost hope.

Finally, he told me to go on the trip to South Dakota, we weren't going to make it, but he couldn't be absolutely sure until Sunday night. Unless things hadn't been figured correctly, we were most definitely out, but the official results wouldn't be made until Sunday. I dejectedly left and we were on our way to South Dakota. I told him that we would call on Sunday night and make sure we were in fact not going to be in the playoffs.

We would be all the way in South Dakota by then, but I didn't care if I had to hitch hike back, I would be back for practice and the playoffs. On Sunday, I found out that we indeed did not make the playoffs. Football was over for the year, and I would no longer have the chance to play alongside the seniors that would be graduating.

> My Dad felt those seniors had a lot to do with our success in 1986. "I thought that class set the tone for you guys the following year. You have to give credit where credit was due. That was a great year, and everyone wanted to do a little better the next year. They kind of got the ball rolling in the right direction."[19]

Steve Thieroff, Brian Allen, Bob Froelich, Drew Gardner and Eric Guilford were all leaders, and guys I enjoyed being around everyday on the football field. They couldn't be replaced and it just wouldn't be the same the next year without them.

Being on the open plains of South Dakota, where it is so peaceful and you feel so free, was the best place possible to forget about football being over for the season. Hunting pheasants with my parents, brothers, and trudging through corn fields, milo patches and shelter belts was the next best thing to being on the football field.

PART II:
Senior Year

CONDITIONING

Coach McCord would always gather the soon-to-be senior class together at the end of their junior year. He would let them know that they would be the leaders of the team next year. We would need to put in the work. He always stressed the importance of senior leadership. This had been evident from the first three years we played for him. Seniors were held in higher regard, Coach McCord did not put up with any crap at all from a senior.

He expected them to know the program and be seasoned enough to follow through with the team concept without being told. In other words, seniors were held to a much higher standard than anyone else. He informed us that he indeed expected us to uphold the Ayersville football tradition. We were to in return, uphold that tradition to the younger guys.

Our senior year would be upon us and it would be our last chance to play Ayersville football. He then issued a challenge, "What kind of senior class would we be? Would we be one of the classes that screwed around and got our butts kicked on Friday nights?" He went on to tell us, "In the past, I had some great senior classes and some not so great senior classes." He ended the meeting with a simple challenge, "What do you seniors want to be remembered for when you're gone?"

I think most of our feelings on being a senior meant that the team was ours. We would have access to all of the finest things, from pads, tape, helmets, locker space, water, snacks, complete control of the music in the locker room, all the way down to being the first in line for everything. If football was fun before, the senior year would be the best of them all.

The coaches even treated the seniors differently. It was as if we belonged to an elite squad of commandos. As a senior, we would be responsible for the entire unit. We would be the leaders. What kind of senior class would we be, what would we be remembered for? Would we be a disappointment, or would we become a group of overachievers?

Just before school let out for the summer, we would be having our annual strength, quickness, agility and speed tests.

In 1986, it was held on a day we didn't have school. We reported to all of the different stations to be evaluated. Things such as bench press, squat, 20-yard agility run, 40-yard dash and 160-yard run were on the agenda. Later on in the summer, Coach McCord would send out a letter with the results. The letter challenged us to work hard and prepare to win. The following is an excerpt from the actual letter I received that summer.

> Right now is the time and place that your desire to be a winner is most important. Practically all players will try hard to win on game night, but by then it is sometimes too late to be a winner. BEAT THEM NOW WHILE WE HAVE TIME.

Coach McCord was exactly right. You never want to go into a game thinking, we did not prepare for this at all. Time was running out, it wouldn't be long before our senior year of football would be upon us.

While school was out for the summer, not only would I be participating in the summer ACME baseball season, I would be working on basketball and football as well. It was going to be a really busy summer.

The Fairview Summer League was a basketball league that contained players from all over the area. We would all drive to Fairview, and from there, play in pick-up games on the two courts they had. The different participants were thrown together and mixed up so that around 10 teams consisted of a conglomeration of players from the different schools. It was a fun time and not only did we get to practice our skills, we got to know players from the opposing schools as well. Denny Martin, Jerry Carnahan and I were all participating, and we rode back and forth together.

> Denny Martin remembered the car rides to and from Fairview more than the basketball. "Remember when we would ride with Carnahan in his Pinto? Jerry would get flying along at 55 miles an hour and then pull up on his emergency brake. We would go skidding all over the road and about crash."[20]

Since Denny brought it up, I have to talk a little bit about Jerry Carnahan's brown Pinto. First of all, it had a sunroof that would completely come out, so we could actually stand up and have our entire upper body above the car. I am sure the reader can use their imagination to figure out all of the things we used that freedom for.

His Pinto was also a stick shift, so the emergency brake was located right on the center console. Just as Denny said, Carnahan loved to get flying along and pull up on that thing. Tires would screech and Jerry would fight the steering wheel like crazy to keep the car under control.

During one instance, we were coming back from Fairview, when Denny was the one that actually pulled the emergency brake up. Jerry was unaware that he was doing it, and we were traveling at about 60 miles an hour when Denny jerked it up. Jerry fought like crazy to keep his Pinto under control, and we ended up coming to a sideways stop right in the middle of State Route 281. To make things worse, a semi-truck was bearing down on us from the other direction. We all started to panic when Jerry found the emergency brake stuck. Carnahan, Martin and I grabbed that thing simultaneously and jerked on it to get it free. Once free, Jerry dumped the clutch, and we sped out of there as fast as we could.

On a totally different occasion, five of us were riding with Jerry to an away summer ACME baseball game. We were on a stone road, when he decided to pull the brake up while we were doing 55. On the gravel, the tires didn't catch, and we totally spun out of control and ended up in a ditch on the Pinto's side. We had a baseball game to get to and if we didn't show up we would be in some serious trouble. We all piled out of the Pinto and the five of us hauled the infamous Carnahan Pinto out of the ditch. Fortunately, we made it to the game on time.

The rides in that Pinto were classic, but now back to the Fairview Summer League.

In between games, anyone who wasn't playing, sat in the bleachers, caught their breath and talked back and forth with each other.

On one occasion, I was sitting there resting and not really involved in any conversation, when the topic of football came up. Dave Maugel, a big, strong kid from Edgerton was in the group talking about how hard the guys from Edgerton were working. I was sitting down a couple of rows and within earshot, so I just listened in on the conversation without saying anything. He went on to say how he couldn't believe how strong and fast the backs on the Edgerton team were going to be for the 1986 season.

Apparently, they were putting in some major work in the off-season to get stronger and faster. The Edgerton team was going to be the program's best ever, and they were loaded at every position. They would have a three-headed monster of a backfield that would be strong and fast and another guy in the backfield that would possibly be the fastest player in the area. They also would have a seasoned line that was big, strong and quick.

Everyone talking in the group seemed to agree, Edgerton would be the best football team in the area. We had beaten them the year before with a long kickoff return in the fourth quarter, but most of their guys were back and we lost some key performers. In my mind, I granted that they may actually be the frontrunners to win the Green Meadows Conference and head to the playoffs. I also knew, we had some guys that were very hungry for some playoff football, and we wouldn't go down without putting up a strict resistance.

Would we be able to beat Edgerton in 1986? We wouldn't be able to find out until the final week of the season. We had nine games to play before then, and if we didn't win them, we probably wouldn't make the playoffs. We found that out in 1985. So my thoughts were on McComb and the first week of the season.

Nobody was even mentioning the Ayersville team as one of the better teams for the upcoming season. I was hoping we could prove them all wrong. Just listening to all of the talk, I couldn't wait for week 10 on the football schedule, when we would face the Edgerton Bulldogs.

In the summer before my senior year, most of my training came from the old-fashioned way. There was always something that needed done around the farm at our house, from splitting and hauling wood, to bailing hay and pulling weeds in the field. Chris Schlachter was also known to find an odd job, here and there. He would get a group of us together so that we could make some much needed spending money. We bailed hay at a dairy farm, painted barns and homes. Whatever he came up with, I was usually a willing participant.

The one job he came up with that I wish I never would have signed on for was detasseling corn. There was a farmer that raised seed corn, and in order for it to grow right or be premium seed, the tassel had to be cut off during the hottest days of summer.

It was smoldering in those corn fields. There was no air flow because we were in the middle of the tall stalks of corn. We walked up and down, row after row of corn, cutting or breaking off the tassel. Not only was it hot, but each time we would reach up and cut the tassel, the chaff and pollen would fall down our sweaty neck and stick, becoming a perfect form of natures itching powder. After about five minutes, we were not only hot and sweaty, but itched all over. Our arms would get tired and sore from constantly reaching over our head. I absolutely hated the job, but enduring it would make the upcoming two-a-days seem like nothing.

The annual Fourth of July celebration in Defiance, Ohio, would have an event that would, without a doubt, be the hardest training of the summer for me. My sister, Teresa, and her husband, Mark, along with my other sister, Tammy, and her fiancé, Doug, were entering the homemade raft race. I decided that if they could do it, and be all pumped up about it, maybe I should get some guys together and enter a raft as well.

We could surely beat them. Jeff Okuly, Jerry Carnahan and Steve Waldron would be my team members for the race. Jeff had access and was pretty handy with a torch and welder, while Jerry Carnahan had six, 55 gallon steel barrels in his barn. It was then our idea to cut the top half off of four barrels and weld them together to form sort of a canoe with four individual seats.

We then welded a 10-foot steel bar across the middle of the barrel canoe, and then welded the other two steel barrels to each side to keep the thing afloat. All we needed to complete our race-winning, super-fast stealth-canoe were paddles. We turned to our summer baseball coach and industrial arts teacher, Jim Leininger, a master woodcrafter. When we told him that we were entered in the raft race, had our steel barrel canoe all ready to go and needed some nice wooden paddles, he was more than happy to assist in our endeavor.

Now, Coach Leininger could sometimes be a jokester, and I think he knew what he was doing all along, but he was so enthusiastic about helping us that we just thought he knew what he was doing. He proceeded to find some scrap wood and cut out four identical paddles for us. We were standing there thinking, *wow, this man totally knows what he is doing*. He was making some very hardcore and tough-looking paddles. He used a very solid and heavy wood, it may have been oak, I don't remember.

The paddles were very wide, thick, and they had nice baseball bat sized handles. They looked like war-clubs and possibly weighed 15 pounds each. We didn't think they could have looked any better. They looked like they had came from the gladiator days, and we felt like warriors with them in our hands.

We thanked him immensely and as we left, he wished us the best of luck in the race. I am sure he laughed for hours after we left.

On the Fourth of July, the race would take place on the Auglaize/Maumee River and would consist of about a four-mile stretch of the river. We were very confident and ready to showcase our rafting skills when we arrived just before the start in Jeff's dad's pick-up truck with our raft behind us on a trailer. It was a perfect setting. People were staring and shaking their heads. They must have known the victors had arrived!

My sisters' crew was cracking up laughing at us when we unloaded the stealth raft. When we pulled our war-club paddles from out of the back of the truck, the laughing stopped. I think a lot of jaws dropped wide open when they saw the extreme size and bulk of the objects that would propel us down the river.

Later on I realized, as everyone else watched, I don't think the silence and blank faces were attributed to fear. I think it may have been compassion.

My family rivals' raft was a little more sophisticated and consisted of some bicycles frames on a raft driving a paddle wheel on the back. Theirs might have been a little nicer, but we were young and in great shape. How could anybody beat us?

Other rafts arrived, and to our surprise, looked like real watercraft. There was one much like ours, only with plastic barrels and a long piece of plastic pipe on one side to keep theirs afloat. They even fashioned some sort of point on their raft that made it look like it would just knife right through the water and be impossible to control. We had the surface area of our two side barrels to keep us straight as an arrow. (I didn't know it at the time, but it was more like as straight as a cargo-ship.) However, they had thin plastic kayak paddles, and they couldn't be any match for our war-club paddles. Those things we so wimpy, lightweight and sleek that we figured we would paddle circles around them. How would they ever be able to move water like our hefty and bulky paddles?

Once all the rafts were lined up in the water, the starter signaled ready, set, and then a gun blasted to signal the beginning of the race. The race was on and we started paddling furiously. All of the other rafts were out in front, but surely we could over take them if we paddled harder.

The raft using the wimpy plastic kayak paddles was just flying and pulled away from us like we were sitting still. We put our heads down and paddled even harder, surely we could catch up then. Out of breath and exhausted, we finally looked up. We were all alone and the other rafts were drifting out of sight. We labored all down the river, cursing the heavy steel barrels, especially the two on each side of us that held us back.

To make matters worse, Coach Leininger's war-club paddles were not made for breakneck canoeing. They were incredibly heavy and bulky. Those paddles probably sounded like a stick of dynamite going off to the fish every time we splashed them into the water. Halfway to the finish line, we started sinking, and once again, we tried to paddle like crazy to get to shore. It was to no avail, we had taken on water and were even heavier.

> While maybe not real hilarious to us at the time, Jeff Okuly looked back on our ordeal on the water that day with a chuckle, "Do you remember when we went under the Hopkins St. Bridge? (Jim) Leininger was leaning over that bridge laughing at us. He knew full well what he had done. Even though we had no rafting skills, that was one of the funnest things I did all summer long."[21]

Finally, a rescue boat pulled up and threw us a line so they could pull us to shore. If the situation wasn't embarrassing enough, the rescue boat had to pull so hard, I thought they would surely sink with us. If nothing else, I am sure we took a few years off of the rescue boats motor that day.

Lastly, completely exhausted, out of breath, humiliated and dejected, we made it to shore and finished the race dead last. That day on the river, we worked harder than in any other conditioning session of my life.

Somewhere, at the bottom of the Maumee River, lies four pieces of solid oak wood, shaped like paddles, resting peacefully. Those war-club paddles were so heavy they didn't even float away when we threw them into the muddy water. They just sank like a ton of bricks.

The summer of 1986 was my last year of summer baseball. We had a good year, but fell one game short of making it to the State ACME Tournament. With baseball being over, I started getting ready for football season. There were a few weeks left before practice started, so I started to attend weightlifting and conditioning more regularly since I had nothing else going on at the time.

Every year I felt like football officially started when the football team would take a trip to Wilmington, Ohio to watch the Cincinnati Bengals practice for one day. It was always a lot of fun and everyone was back together. Our official practices would then be starting in a few days. Watching the Bengals practice was always interesting. It was an experience to get to watch those famous players gritting it out in practice. I remember guys like Tim Krumrie, Dave Remington, Max Montoya, Anthony Munoz and Chris Collinsworth, to name a few. I remembered mostly linemen because I always thought they were the toughest and best players. After watching them practice, we would eat lunch and swim in the university pool before heading home.

Since it was our senior year, it was our last trip to Wilmington to see the Bengals. I realized the trip was one in a long line of last things I would be doing as an Ayersville football player.

The trip to the Bengals' training camp in 1986 was much like the ones before it. We screwed around, watched some football, ate and swam in the pool. The only difference was a meeting with one of the Bengal coaches where he addressed only the seniors. He told us to enjoy our last high school year, there would be nothing like it. Being a senior was indeed going to be something special. It was evident we were the focal point of the team.

How good would the team in 1986 be, would we finally beat McComb, could we finally get to the playoffs?

We had Denny Martin back for his second year under center. Steve Deitrick had proven that he could take over the fullback spot. Chris Schlachter had the potential to be the best tailback we had in a long time. The line would be quick and had many guys coming back for a more expanded role. John Finn moved back to Ayersville for his senior year. We were glad to have him after his year away and he would become our center. Mike Wilson and Jaime Briseno would play at the two guard positions. Tim Boals would be one tackle, with George Schaffer backing him up, while Jeff Okuly and Aaron Roth would switch on and off at the other tackle spot. Tolly Hanna, Rob Giesige and Shelby Dawson were set to play at tight end. Jerry Carnahan would be our new split end while Phil Girlie and I would split time at blocking back.

A blocking back is not a familiar term in football. I think Coach McCord came up with this name when we put three guys in the backfield. That's where the blocking back would line up to become the lead blocker on power plays. I would say a blocking back was very similar to a normal flanker. A blocking back could line up all over the field.

Coach McCord had stressed in our team meeting the spring before that we would try to keep our strongest defense possible on the field at all times. We would switch guys around on offense to give them a break so the defense could always be fresh. Steve Deitrick was the only one going both ways without splitting time with somebody else. Scott Kolb would emerge to give him a break on and off through the season, but Steve Deitrick was going to be on the field more than anybody.

Our base defense was the 5-2. Marv Andrews would anchor the line at nose guard with Jaime Briseno playing on certain downs. Okuly and Roth were back at the tackles. Eric Burket and Giesige both returned at the bookend spots. Even though we graduated our starting linebackers, both Deitrick and Wilson had experience there and became starters. I was back at rotator, Phil Girlie moved up from his safety spot to the other rotator. Johnny Armes and Todd Hanna rounded out the defense at the safety spots. On special teams, Chris Schlachter would be the kicker, Jerry Carnahan the punter, Denny Martin would return punts and Travis Lewis would return the kickoffs.

In our secondary, the safeties played on the outside and were more like a cornerback. I don't know why the term rotator was used, but they played more like a free safety and strong safety. Both rotators would line up five to seven yards deep just outside the offensive tackle's shoulder. Depending on the larger side of the field and the formation, one rotator would be responsible for the flat, while the other rotator would drop to the deep middle on pass plays, much like a free safety. It is a confusing concept and you may want to refer to the defensive diagrams at the end of the book to understand our defensive formation.

In the basic zone coverage of our secondary, we would make a call depending on the larger side of the field first, and then the formation second. If the call was to the right, we would shout out "Roger." If the call was to the left, we would yell "Louie." When this became repetitive, we would shout out any name that began with an "R" for a right call, or an "L" for a left call. It was just a basic and rudimentary call, but it served its purpose. After playing with Phil Girlie for so long, we ended up rarely shouting out the call so as to not alert the offense. We would basically look at each other and know which way we would rotate. A quick look back at our safeties, Armes and Hanna, was all that was needed to know they knew as well.

Depending on different situations, we would sometimes run a 5-3. Basically, the left rotator would move up and play outside linebacker with one linebacker playing middle linebacker and the other moving to the other outside linebacker position. The right side rotator would slide to the middle of the field and play middle safety. We would occasionally run a 6-2 goalline defense. For this, an extra nose guard would line up beside the other nose guard over the center. The two linebackers would play normal and there would be three defensive backs.

After a long summer of waiting for football to begin, practice started, or should I say conditioning got started. We worked our butts off to get into shape before we strapped on the pads and got ready to hit. Conditioning practices started early in the afternoon. We would line up, the 16 seniors in alphabetical order across the front, facing all of the underclassmen. The rest of the team lined up from juniors down to freshmen and the lines were straight and crisp. It always took the freshmen a while to understand this wasn't junior high football anymore and they better find their place in line and remember where it was for the next day. Straggling around and sloppiness would not be tolerated and everyone liked to make sure the freshmen were learning this quickly. They usually caught on quickly, but if they didn't, an upperclassman was there to make sure they knocked that crap off or it would be a really long season for them.

We did push-ups, sit-ups, leg lifts and a little thing called "guts". Guts were a drill where we would run in place, and when the whistle blew, we dropped our chest directly to the ground and yelled "Guts!", then bounced back up to our feet and continued running in place.

It was one of the most hated drills, sometimes it seemed like we did "guts" for a half hour or longer. I can remember in the years before my senior year thinking, *I will never make it through practice if we don't stop doing "guts".*

However, during my senior year, the early-season conditioning didn't seem to be as hard for me. Maybe I was finally in good enough shape heading into it. Every year, kids puked from the early-season conditioning. It was no different in 1986. In between different drills, we always made sure the ground was clear of puke before taking our spot. We would run and we would run, 40s, 60s and even 100s. Sometimes we would run the dreaded fence busters, where we would touch the fence on the north side of the school property and then run down and touch the fence on the south side of the property. I would guess it was approximately 300 or 400 yards between the fences. There were days when we followed up 40-40's with a fence buster.

The words I never wanted to hear at the end of practice were when Coach McCord would say, "Let's finish up with a cross country and don't round the corners."

Rob Giesige and Jerry Carnahan lived for those words, they both loved long-distance running, and it was a friendly competition between them to see who could come in first. I think Rob always did, but then again I wasn't there to see it. I did not like long-distance running, or for that matter, any running that didn't involve chasing somebody with a ball or running from somebody while I carried a ball.

> Rob Giesige was the cross country champion of our class and shared his experience. "I remember running a cross-country at the end of practice our freshman year. I was going to pass senior Chad Teague for the win at the end, when I heard Chad say, "Don't pass me you piece of shit freshman."[22]

A cross country consisted of running the fence line all around the school property. We started at the northwest side and ran along the fence to the northeast side. This was also the northeast corner of the football field. We would then head to the southeast corner of the property past the football field's visiting bleachers. Then we ran along the left field line of the varsity baseball field until we made it to the left field fence and southeast corner of the property. We then followed the fence along the outfield until we ended up in right field. There, the fence ended, and we would wrap around to the other side and continue along it until we made it to the left field fence of the middle school ball field, which was adjacent to the varsity field on the west side of the varsity field. From there, we would then continue along the outfield fence until once again we were in right field and the fence ended.

Once there, we were at the elementary ball field in the southwest corner of the property and we wrapped around the fence and ran the outfield fence of that one as well. From there, it was a race along the west side of the property back to the area right out in front of the football locker room.

I get winded just thinking about it. The whole time we ran it, coaches would strategically place themselves along the bends in the fence and scream at us that winners never cut corners. Did we want to be winners or would we cut the corners of the fence line? It was always tempting to cut the corners, we were tired and if we could just save ourselves that little bit of extra distance, we could finish faster.

I think this says a lot about life in general. Take the easy way out and you may accomplish something faster and easier, but if you didn't cut the corners, in the end, you would be rewarded with something much more valuable.

Coach McCord taught us some real life lessons, all that we learned could be applied to life in general. I don't really know how long those cross countries were, but after a hard practice, it seemed like it was five miles. Actually, it was probably closer to two miles.

During the days of conditioning practice, Coach McCord would use the time following conditioning to lay words of inspiration on us. We would be standing upright and breathing deeply since we were not allowed to bend at the waist to get air. If anyone was bent over, it did not take words from the coaches to get them upright. There was always a teammate close by that would tell them to get their head up. If that didn't do it, there would be more teammates saying the same thing. If someone was having a particular tough time of it, practically the whole team would issue words of encouragement. There was a lot of cheering and general hoopla while we were conditioning. Everyone would try to get pumped up to make the pain go away.

There would also be times of complaining and whining. If that happened, the coaches were on it immediately, they would say we weren't tough enough and maybe we should just go home and cry about it. The words challenged our manhood, and the seniors would get the hint and tell everyone to pick it up and quit whining since it was our team.

Coach McCord would walk through the lines while we did conditioning and say, "Winners do things losers don't like to do." The words were so powerful to me then and now.

I think a lot can be taken from those words. It's a fact that success is usually achieved by putting in hard work and doing the things nobody else wants to do. If it was easy, then everybody would be doing it. What separates the winners is the fact they do the things nobody else wants to do.

He would go on to say, "What do you think Fairview is doing? McComb has beat us three straight times, do you think they aren't over at their place working hard? Are they working harder than us, is that why they keep beating us? I am sure Edgerton is over there working their butts off so they can go 10-0, win the GMC and go to the playoffs. Do they want it more than we do?" Coach McCord did not berate us, he almost always used challenging words to get us to realize, if we were going to be winners, we were the ones responsible for it.

The coaches would take turns. Coach Ondrus would usually use some type of humor to get his point across; Coach Beef would use his passion and serious side to inspire us; Coach Beck would use some sort of high-octane pitch to whip us into a fury.

That brings me to Coach Norman Beck. I said before that none of us knew anything about Coach Beck. It was his first year coaching us and he wasn't a teacher at the school. All we knew was that he was from Archbold, Ohio, which is about 20 miles north of Ayersville in Fulton County. This was enough to put us all on guard. Here was a guy that had shown allegiance to another school, how could he possibly be as dedicated to Ayersville as we were? There was always some grumbling about the new guy early on. Call it crazy, but we felt he was some kind of spy sent to infiltrate the team and cause us to have a miserable season.

He came out one day wearing an Ayersville hat with a big block A on the front. There was some mumbling about the A standing for Archbold, and why did we have some guy from Archbold coaching our Ayersville team?

We would split up by class and go through conditioning drills with each of the coaches after calisthenics in the early days of conditioning practice.

When we split up, Coach Beck yelled, "I want the seniors." We ran to his group and he just started ripping into us. We were doing monkey rolls and he had us going at it with so much intensity we were all gasping for air. Monkey rolls are where three guys line up and the end guy rolls over the next guy and so on. We were constantly getting to our feet to dive over the next guy that just rolled over the other guy. It could be a grueling drill when we had three guys working hard at it.

After we were all utterly exhausted and couldn't say anything if we tried, he started screaming at us, "This A on my hat stands for Ayersville. I am 100 percent dedicated to this program, and I will work you guys like crazy to make sure you succeed. I am tired of the bitching and complaining. I believe in you seniors and you need to believe in me. I think this can be a great team and I want to be a part of it."

Apparently, he had overheard some of the comments and the way he handled it was perfect. This said a lot about his character, he handled the situation himself, and he came right after us without involving anyone else. Maybe we should all be like Coach Beck, instead of doing our whining behind someone's back.

He gained my respect that day and I think he gained the respect of each and every one of the seniors. Coach Beck was then one of us, we then trusted him and we were ready to go to work for him. Nothing about him being from another school was ever said again. As far as we were concerned, that day he became an Ayersville Pilot.

Conditioning practices lingered on until the day two-a-day practices started. Before they started, we got our equipment. It was a monumental day for all of us and the excitement was high. Each class had a set time when they were to arrive at the locker room and get their equipment.

On the deck overlooking the pool would be stacks of practice pants, thigh pads, hip pads and rib pads. Inside the locker room, in the equipment cage, there would be helmets, shoulder pads, game jerseys and game pants. I already had my cleats, a pair of black low top Nike's with screw in cleats, and they were the best pair of shoes I have ever worn.

As seniors, we finally got the first pick of everything. On the deck, I selected a gold pair of practice pants, the thigh pads, hip pads, knee pads and butt pad. Then moved to a stack of rib pads and grabbed a decent pair of those. There were new blue shiny mesh practice jerseys. The seniors wore blue and everyone else wore gold. I grabbed one of those and went inside the locker room.

I always liked to joke with Jerry Carnahan about his gold under-classman jersey. When he, along with the other underclassmen, was waiting for us seniors to finish drinking from the "rain-train", I would ask him, "Do you know why you have to wait for us to finish?" I wouldn't give him a chance to reply and then I would say, "It's because," and then I reached out and grabbed his jersey and finished with, "That's gold Jerry."

Inside the locker room, there would be the two most coveted items for me, the helmet and shoulder pads. I selected a nice Bike helmet that inflated with air, and attached to it was an old metal face mask with four cross bars. I preferred the face mask that came down lower on your face because of the gash I got on my chin my sophomore year. I didn't want that to happen again. A lot of guys selected the new style of face mask. They were made from a light-weight plastic that was supposed to be as strong as the steel ones. I liked the old style better, even though they weren't as lightweight and fancy. I then picked up a nice pair of shoulder pads, ones that fit just right. From there, I selected a pair of gold game pants and I was done. I would still be wearing the #21 jersey.

I didn't select any arm pads at all. I liked to be able to feel the ball right against my skin when I carried it. I always felt like it was easier to hang onto that way. As much as I thought all of the arm pads and gloves looked cool when I was younger, I just really didn't need them and didn't select any of them. I stopped and looked at the black gloves for a moment and thought to myself, *as much as I dreamed of one day wearing a pair of black gloves, the position I play just doesn't warrant them.* My mind drifted even further to me fumbling handoffs and dropping interceptions because I had to fulfill my lifelong dream and wear a big pair of black gloves.

I would take solace in the fact that Jeff Okuly's locker was right next to mine. He would surely have a pair of the black gloves and every chance I got, I would be putting those bad boys on and acting like a tough linemen.

I did look at my #21 jerseys. There was a blue one with gold numbers for our home games and a white one with blue numbers for our away games. I was somewhat disappointed when I saw they were brand new. My jerseys from the previous two years were gone. I am sure my mother would be pleased though. She had put more sewing thread into those jerseys than there was original material. They had been ripped, torn and sometimes came out of a game with big holes in them. I remember after one game, she was so disgusted with the state of my blue jersey she just kept going back and forth across my jersey with the sewing machine, shaking her head the whole time until the holes had been filled in with thread. They were in horrible shape, but I was still disappointed to get new jerseys.

Picking out our equipment was a monumental task for one senior in particular. Aaron Roth may have not only played bigger than he was, but he looked bigger than he was from all the pads he wore. We would always look at his locker with all his pads lying around and say to each other, "Roth has a pad for just about everything, including pads for some of the other pads."

He had all of the standard issued equipment, plus a shoulder harness, a horse collar, elbow pads, arm pads, hand pads and black gloves. Plus, he selected a whole array of duplicates and pads I didn't even know what they were used for. I always thought he could start a used equipment store right out of his locker.

As we walked out the door, we were handed an un-molded mouth piece with a strap. Once I got home, I couldn't wait to form my mouthpiece. I got some water boiling on the stove and then I would dip the mouthpiece into the boiling water for 15 seconds, then take it out and stick it in my mouth. I would then bite down on it a little bit to suck the air out of it, which gave me a perfectly fitted mouthpiece. When I got back to the locker room for the next practice, I would affix the strap to the face mask, tape it down good with some athletic tape and my equipment was set to go.

I have to make some references to Coach McCord at this point, because anyone that played for him has those memories etched in their mind and the story would not be complete without them.

His absolute favorite saying when he was disgusted with something was, "Gee fer socks." I have no clue what it actually meant, and I don't think anybody else does either. I have no idea where he came up with it, but he said it all the time during practice.

> Coach McCord clarified, "I picked up gee fer socks and cheese and crackers from an old high school coach of mine. He had been in the Navy and he used those expressions all of the time."[23]

His trademark scolding would always be done with him in a players face and end with a rap on the face mask or helmet with the clipboard he always carried around. CRACK, that thing would just echo across the practice field.

Coach McCord would never degrade us or swear at us, he would sure get our attention with that clipboard, though. It never did any damage, but it was an effective way to get his point across.

In most instances, the two were combined for a much better effect. Steve Santo, a senior offensive lineman in 1985, was the recipient of the two on numerous occasions.

It went something like this, "Oh, gee fer socks, Santo, how hard is it to stay low and get your block when you're double-teaming a guy? That's just pathetic." CRACK, went the clipboard across his face mask, "Now run it again."

Kim (McCord) Engel talked about the infamous clipboard. "Dad would never let us get him a new one. He had that one all duct taped together and it was completely falling apart, probably from the beatings it took."[24]

TWO-A-DAYS

On the first day of two-a-day practices, Coach McCord gathered us around after the morning practice on Monday and told us it was time to elect the Team Champ. He went on to explain what the Team Champ meant. We should vote for the player who would uphold the school and the team in a positive way. If you could pick only one player to go out on the football field, the field of battle, or anywhere else, and go against a player of an opposing team. If they won, we won, if they lost, we lost. Who would you want playing for our team? That's the person you should vote for. In the past, we had some good ones and we have had some bad ones. It was your choice.

We would then go into the locker room and vote for the player of our choice and then head home for lunch. I thought about it, and I didn't think I could pick a bad one out of the other 15 seniors on the team. I thought any of them would make a fine Team Champ.

I kind of faced a dilemma on who to choose. I thought if I had to pick, it was between two guys. Jeff Okuly, he was big, quick, tough, strong and had a never-say-die spirit. I thought if I had to have one guy out there, he was the one. Then there was Rob Giesige, he was a fierce competitor in everything he did. If a battle was taking place, I knew he would die before he gave up. He was also very good at anything he did, so I am sure he would have made a good Team Champ. Jeff was more of a quiet, serious leader and Rob was more vocal and fiery. I know I went back and forth in my mind over who to choose, but I can't remember which name I actually wrote on my slip of paper. Steve Deitrick is who I thought would be our Team Champ. He was a great player and dished out some good hits. He

91

was going to be going both ways and everyone respected the hard nosed style with which he played the game.

When we returned for the afternoon practice, the Team Champ was announced. Coach McCord said, "The Team Champ for this team, the Pilot football team of 1986 is ... Andy Groll."

I was shocked and really didn't know how to feel. I didn't expect to ever become the Team Champ, I was horrible in junior high, and only hoped to get a varsity football letter before I became a senior. It hadn't been that long ago when I wondered if I was ever going to even be starter on the team. As a freshman, I only hoped to see some playing time as a senior and being named Team Champ was beyond my wildest dreams. I wasn't one of the more vocal leaders on the team. I just wanted to play football. As team champ, I got a blue star to wear on the side of my helmet, and I would call out all of the different stretching exercises during games and practices.

I decided that I would not change my attitude about anything else, as far as I was concerned, every one of the seniors was a Team Champ. I would not act differently. I would not become a loud-mouth vocal leader. It was my style to play hard, give it everything I had and to never quit. I would not change how I played the game, and it wasn't going to give me any reason to treat anyone differently. We all knew what we wanted to accomplish, there were 16 dedicated seniors on the team, and I believed we would all lead the team together. Being Team Champ did not make me any different from anybody else, it was an incredible honor, and I hoped I would be remembered as one of the good ones instead of the not so good ones, but in our own way, we had 16 Team Champ's on the team.

I remembered thinking at the time, *I better not be hiding on offense anymore, what kind of Team Champ would that make me?* I really didn't like offense, but I would do whatever it took, and besides, it was my last year and I wanted to be a part of everything.

Two-a-day practices started at 8 a.m. We would do our normal stretching and then head off for defensive groups. In our defensive groups we went over our coverages, responsibilities and did some drills. Coach Ondrus always started it off the same way. "Rotators are responsible for the run first and the pass second. Safeties are responsible for the pass first and the run second." He would make us repeat it back to him over and over. Then his cardinal rule for a defensive back, "Never ever get beat deep. If you do, you might as well go stand on the other sideline."

He would then go over alignment. When he asked me to tell everyone where the rotators lined up, I said, "On the outside shoulder of the offensive tackle and two to three yards deep." Coach Ondrus snapped at me, "Groll, you know the rotators line up five to seven yards deep. Just because you never line up right doesn't mean you can cause everyone else to line up wrong as well." Coach Ondrus was absolutely fastidious about details.

It had been a long-standing point of topic when we watched our previous game film for him to point out, "Look at where you're lined up on that play. Okuly (the defensive tackle in front of me) can't even get down into his four-point stance because you're crowding him and the linebackers are playing behind you. You're a defensive back, stay five to seven yards off of the line of scrimmage." I would always reply back, "Coach, those guys have the play stopped before I can get to the ball carrier if I play that deep."

"I don't care, do your assignment," he would shoot back at me." I would usually line up correctly early in the game, but sooner or later I would creep forward, and get in trouble on film day.

Another thing we went over extensively in defensive back groups was our read step. When the ball was snapped, we were supposed to start back pedaling until the play took shape and we knew if it was a passing play or running play. If we couldn't tell, or the play unfolded slowly, we were to remain backpedaling to get depth so as to not let anyone behind us. I struggled with the read step mightily. When I was a linebacker, we would make our move, usually forward, and then read the play. I really liked those assignments because I was headed towards the ball. Moving away from it just felt foreign to me.

This instance explains my problem with the read step perfectly. One day in my junior year on film day, Coach McCord came up with a rating system for the coaches to give us on each play. We would get a number with zero being the lowest to four being the highest on each play. Our position coach would give us a slip of paper with a number for each play before we started watching the film: A 0 meant we did absolutely nothing right and had a negative impact on the play, a 1 meant we didn't do our assignment but it didn't have an impact on the play, a 2 meant we did our assignment but it didn't effect the play, a 3 meant we did our assignment and it had an impact on the play, while a 4 was where we did everything perfectly and made a great play.

The film started to roll and I looked at my sheet. I had a whole bunch of 1s on there. There were a couple of plays where I tackled the ball carrier in the backfield. They should have been at least 3s I thought. Then all at once I had a 4 on the sheet. I couldn't wait for the play to roll across the screen. I did absolutely nothing as the ball carrier was tackled at the line of scrimmage.

I looked at Coach Ondrus and said, "Coach O, I think you have this sheet all mixed up, I didn't do anything on that play and got a 4 and the one before it I made a tackle in the backfield and you gave me a 1." He looked at me and said, "Nope, that sheets right. If you watch, on that play, YOU ACTUALLY TAKE A READ STEP, and I figured that will be as close to a perfect play as you have a chance of ever making since you NEVER seem to be able to take a read step and start the play off doing your assignment." I replied back, "Come on Coach, that quarterback isn't hiding the ball at all. I can tell what play they are running as soon as the ball is snapped."

"Just shut up, and start taking your read step," ended the conversation.

I knew Coach Ondrus was right, once we played better teams, a read step would be very important to the success of the defensive backfield. Coach Ondrus was a coach we could joke around with as long as we didn't take it too far. I never wanted to get there, and I respected him immensely as a coach and believed in everything he told me.

After defensive groups, we would do some team up, where the whole team would get together and go over our defenses and run pursuit drills. A pursuit drill was where a defensive play would be called and we would then all make our initial moves. Then Coach

McCord would send an underclassman off with the ball. We were to take the proper path to the ball carrier and tap them since we weren't allowed to have any contact yet.

Of course we were all itching to hit people and occasionally somebody would get a little rough with the person carrying the ball, and they would get knocked down. If the runner got knocked down, or somebody pushed them, Coach McCord would get irate and scream, "I need the ball carrier on his feet, how am I supposed to see what route all of you are taking if the ball carrier is on the ground. The next person that knocks him down is going to be running fence busters." After that, there was a lot of gentle taps.

We would then go into all of the special teams. Coach McCord stressed special teams play, and we would work on every one of them each day in practice until he was satisfied with their performance.

The morning practice would end with the dreaded conditioning, the extra weight and tightness of the equipment only added to the harshness of the workout. We would run sprints, do distance running, or other activities that would get us into playing condition. Sometimes we would split up by class and other times we would stay together as a team to perform conditioning. Morning practice would end around 11:00 am. We would then shower and go home to rest and eat some lunch. Most of the time, we were just thirsty and we drank more than we ate.

The afternoon practice would start at 1:00 pm. During the hot and dry days of August, we were required to weigh in before and after each practice, in order to monitor our weight loss in case a medical condition arose. The coaches would monitor it, and some people would forget or just be too lazy to do it. They would be reminded to weigh in and out. Then one day after practice, the guillotine would fall and Coach McCord would ask, "Coach Ondrus, who forgot to weigh in or out." Coach Ondrus would read off the names and they would have to stay after for some extra conditioning. Usually, they would remember and take the time to weigh in and out after that.

We would then go back out in shorts, shoulder pads and helmets for the passing segment of our practice at 1:00 pm. We of course would go through our stretching routine again before we started running our passing drills, and then we finished up with the entire offense running pass plays. Once Coach McCord was satisfied, we would go back inside, take off our helmets and shoulder pads, grab whatever we could get our hands on to drink and go to the school cafeteria to go over the plays we would be putting in during the afternoon practice. The time in the cafeteria was a welcome break and everyone enjoyed the time together where we weren't being worked like crazy, and we could sit down and relax.

When the classroom segment was finished, we would get in full pads and head out to our designated area for offensive groups. The offensive back group usually went to the outfield grass on the elementary baseball diamond by the tennis courts. We would then re-stretch while we were in our groups before running drills and practicing the plays we just went over.

Then the team would come together and the offense would run play after play until Coach McCord was satisfied with our performance. During the sessions, even though we couldn't have contact yet, we were expected to be going at full speed. The linemen had to stay low, fire out and get downfield, while the backs were off and running at full speed until the whistle blew to end the play.

Occasionally, somebody would dog it, and then the whistle wouldn't blow. At that point, everybody better get moving like it was going to be a 200-yard touchdown run or Coach McCord would chime in with, "Dave Temple used to run every play until he was in the end zone. You played with him Coach Hammersmith, how good was he?" We always hated to hear Coach Hammersmith's response. "He was a good one Coach, maybe the best." would come the reply.

Coach McCord always got his point across and whoever had the ball on the next play, kept running even after the whistle blew. Of course we would have to wait for the ball to get back before we could run the next play. This always resulted in everyone hustling and the whistle would come faster and more emphatic the harder we went at it. We wanted to be the best team EVER. We did not like any reference to a team or player that worked harder than we did, even if it was in the past.

We were done running plays when Coach McCord was content and there wasn't much of a time frame with those drills ... we quit when he was satisfied.

Then it was more conditioning and running. Finally, we were done and after a quick pep talk from Coach McCord, we hit the showers, by then it was starting to get dark.

After we went home and had our dinner, I don't know about anybody else on the team, but I was whipped. I remember sleeping very well on the nights of those long two-a-day practices. When morning came around, we woke up to do it all over again.

Coach McCord always referred to that part of the year as "The dog days of August" and that they were. On the particularly hot days, we would be getting ready for our stretching routine, when Coach Ondrus would emerge from the locker room steps and swing some sort of tube on a rope around and around in the air. This always got our attention. He was supposedly testing the air for the humidity. I don't know if it was just a tall tale or what, but supposedly if the humidity was too high, we couldn't practice. We always watched thinking today might be the day practice could be cancelled. When he was done, he would look at the tube, examine it a little bit, shake his head some, and get a funny look on his face. We would be watching him the whole time, "Was this it?" He was going to say it's too humid, practice was cancelled, and maybe we could go swimming.

He would then lean out over the steps and yell out to us, "It says it's a perfect day to practice football." Then he'd get the unmistakable Coach Ondrus grin on his face. I don't think the magic tube even worked, it was just his idea of having fun with us. I am sure he came up with it all on his own because he sure seemed to be fond of this maneuver.

During our practice sessions, we would always try to move to different areas on the school property to avoid killing all the grass, but in August, it didn't seem to matter. The ground was always hard, the grass was brown and dead and there was a layer of dry dirt and dust just under the lifeless grass. When we were down on the ground, we could feel the heat like it was coming right out of the hot magma from the center of the earth. We would usually get one water break in the morning and one water break in the afternoon.

Coach Ondrus had developed a plastic pipe with holes in it supported by legs on each end, which he called "The Rain Train". A garden hose would be attached to it, and when it was turned on, it would spray forth 10 beautiful streams of delicious water. We would all crowd around it, seniors first of course, and drink just enough to quench our thirst. If we drank too much, there was always the chance of that sick to the stomach feeling and then conditioning would be brutal.

We all looked forward to the first day of contact, it would be the day when we could finally hit somebody, and start putting some big time smack downs on people. Maybe some of the underclassmen didn't look forward to it, but I am sure most of them did. Our first taste of contact would come in the form of the seven-man sled. I really enjoyed practicing with the seven-man sled. I can remember looking at it parked in the grass when I was in grade school thinking it would be so nice to one day be there with six of my classmates, driving that thing backwards while everyone else cheered.

> Coach McCord reminded me of this about the seven-man sled. "Do you remember the first day of hitting, when we had to get out the sled? It was parked in the corner by the fence. A summer's worth of weeds would be growing through and around it. I would have you guys drive that thing all the way to the practice area, you guys would be whipped by the time we made it there, because it was a long way."[25]

Once we had driven the sled to the practice area, we would start out in a long line and one by one, run up, thrust our hands out in front of our bodies, hitting the sled with a shove, or what we called a hand shiver. We would continue down the line until we gave each of the pads a hand shiver. When the first guy moved to the second pad, the next guy in line would hit the first pad and so forth down the line until there was a steady rhythm of all of the pads being hit - all at the same time. This would continue until everyone had gone through the line a few times. When there was a group of guys that could really hit, the sled would really jump backwards when the timing was perfect and all seven players were hitting it at exactly the same time. The timing was everything, and the upper classmen on the team were really good at it, because the sled would be bouncing way back on the hits we were giving it.

Next, seven of us would get down in a four-point stance about one foot away from each of the pads on the sled, and on the whistle, explode with our legs and spring forward. We would hit the pad in front of us with our hands and the front of our helmets, while falling right on our stomachs. When we were freshmen, the hits usually did nothing more than bounce the sled up and down a little, as seniors, our hits would make the sled fly back about seven yards. It made for some great competition to see what group could bounce the sled back the farthest. We had two full groups of seniors along with one group of the remaining two seniors and the first five juniors, who could lay some pretty good licks on the sled. I had never seen the sled move like it did in 1986, we bounced the sled all over the practice field. We hoped it was a sign of good things to come when the season started.

Coach Beef acknowledged that the coaches saw something special in us early on. "During coaches meetings, we talked about how all of the guys on the team just did their jobs. They didn't ask why, they just did it. We would remark that we really had something here, these guys will do whatever we ask them to do."[26]

Coach Ondrus added this, "Whatever we did, we couldn't break you guys. Even during two-a-days when it was hot, you just asked for more."[27]

The next sled-drill was Coach Beef's favorite. He really liked to get on the back of the sled and ride it. We would get down in a three-point stance and on the whistle, hit the sled with a shoulder and keep driving it back until the whistle blew. The whistle would not come for minutes and therefore this was the most brutal of the sled drills. If one side of the sled was driving harder, the sled would not go in a straight line, and Coach Beef would start yelling at the end that was falling behind to pick it up or he would put all of his weight on their end.

The guy in the middle didn't have much control over the sled's course, but the three guys on each end could really change its course by who was pushing harder. Coach McCord would give the end pushing harder accolades by slapping them on the back and telling them great job, while telling the end falling behind that they needed to pick it up or the whistle would never be blown and smack them on the helmet with his clipboard.

We would finish up with a form tackle on the sled. Seven guys hitting, lifting up and driving with their feet into the sled. The key to this was to lift high enough so that the sled was tilting back far enough to keep it from moving or spinning. Once there, we could chop our feet until the whistle blew, then let go, allowing the sled to come crashing down. The sound of the sled crashing down always whipped everyone into frenzy and the next group would be ready and another hard hit was put on the sled.

We would go all through that days practice like normal, still no hitting, except for a couple of drills in offensive groups. One drill we would run involved the two-man sled. For that memorable drill, we would take a handoff, run into either side of the two-man sled, lift with our shoulder to deliver the blow and spin off to head down the field. If we did it just right and hit the sled hard enough, we could actually knock it onto its side, causing Coach Ondrus to have to flip it back over. We thoroughly enjoyed knocking the sled over, it was a great challenge and meant we delivered a tremendous blow. We had five guys that could do it that year, Deitrick, Girlie, Schlachter, Kolb and I, so Coach O spent quite a bit of time flipping it back up.

> It was one of Steve Deitrick's favorites. "The beat the guard drills every linebacker practice session was some hard hitting. It was funny how it was no longer dreaded the older we got. By the time senior year hit, it was just plain fun and something to look forward to, albeit not as fun as the defensive back butt-tackling drills or the "right of passage" in the offensive back drills when one finally was able to tip the two man sled on spin drills."[28]

The other drill that involved a little bit of hitting was "The Chute". "The Chute" consisted of a bunch of two-by-fours nailed together to form a tunnel about 10 yards long with old tires bolted to the inside. In order to make the tires bend and allow passage between them, we would have to be at full speed when we went into the chute to keep our momentum and get all the way through. To make it even harder, the top two-by-four was only about five feet tall to make sure we stayed low as we ran through it. If we stayed low and kept our legs driving, we would make it right out the other end. Occasionally, somebody would fall, causing everybody around to yell and scream, "GET UP!", until they made their way out the other end.

The season of 1986 was the first year there were no pranksters standing at the chute when someone ran through. Bending back a tire and letting it snap forward to doink someone on the helmet as they ran through was one of the favorite shenanigans pulled in previous years at "The Chute". Charlie Ankney, Brad Schlachter and Brian Allen all received great elation from their foolery at "The Chute" in the years previous to 1986, but that stuff didn't happen my senior year.

Throughout the whole practice, we waited and anticipated. If it was like the years past, we knew it was coming. After we were done running the offensive plays of the day, Coach McCord would get us all together and say, "Hey coach Ondrus, is today the first day of contact?"

"Yeah Coach, it is," reacted Coach O. "Are you sure, maybe we shouldn't hit today."

Then Coach McCord would shout out, "HOW ABOUT A LITTLE SCORE DRILL?" At that point, the upperclassmen all knew what to do. We would drag over some tires and set them up about 10 yards apart and 15 yards long. The drill would be run in just the small space and the seniors would go first. Three blockers would be selected and they would get down in a three-point stance, three defensive guys would be selected and they would get down in a four-point stance in front of the blockers. A quarterback would then get behind the middle blocker and two backs would stand behind the quarterback, one on each side. On the snap count, the quarterback would hand the ball off to one of the backs diving straight ahead.

Everyone would be crowded around screaming and yelling, it was the most noise we had made all year. The offense had three plays to get the 10 yards and score. The drill would be run over and over until everyone had a chance. I think everyone was hoarse when we got done with the score drill. The day of score drill was the one day out of the year that I was able to get down in a four-point stance and act like a lineman. It was a meat-grinder drill with bodies heaped in a pile and I absolutely loved it.

For me, the score drill holds the most unforgettable moments of my practice days. It was a right of passage, the day we became hitters. The score drill was the most anticipated practice activity. Coach McCord only ran it on the first day of hitting, it was as if the score drill were sacred. It was done only once a year, but if you would mention "score drill" to anyone that had played for Coach McCord, I am sure the response would be the same, "Oh man, score drill, that was the best part of practice."

> I asked Coach McCord why we only ran it once a year and how it came to be. "The score drill I picked up at a football clinic somewhere. We only ran it once because it was just a tradition to do it on the first day of hitting."[29]

Probably the most memorable event in defensive back groups once hitting started for the year was the butt-tackling drill. Coach Ondrus designed it himself. We would form two lines facing each other about 15 yards apart. One line was the ball carrier and the other was the tackler. Upon Coach Ondrus's whistle, the ball carrier would run forward and the tackler would run forward to meet them. Upon impact, the tackler would only wrap up the ball carrier, then let go. The ball carrier would then run backwards about five steps, the tackler would do the same, and the process would duplicate another time. The process would repeat, and on the third time, it was time for the defender to bring the ball carrier to the turf.

The process was to hit, bounce backwards, hit again, bounce backwards, and then go full out for the tackle. The ball carrier was not allowed to put any moves on the defender, enabling the drill to be all about pop, crack and destroy. The drill enabled the defender to put two good hits on a ball carrier before finally destroying them with a full tackle. The ball carrier could also deliver a blow, if the defender was too passive. The drill was well known throughout the entire team, and when we ran it in our defensive back group, lots of players paid more attention to our group than their own.

I performed the drill almost exclusively against Phil Girlie for all four years. We liked to hit and we delivered some great pops throughout those four years. On the days we didn't deliver good blows, Coach Ondrus would yell, "Knock off that buddy crap and hit each other, you sissies." After four years of hitting Phil, I didn't come across many people that could hit like him.

After beating on each other for weeks, we finally got a chance to hit someone in a different colored jersey during our first scrimmage in 1986 against North Baltimore.

We scrimmaged against North Baltimore on a Saturday and handled them fairly easily.

All I can remember from the scrimmage was the fact that our line was going to be really good that year. I had a couple of touchdown runs where I wasn't even touched in the scrimmage. It was all offensive line, anybody could have scored on those plays and there were no defenders near me.

When the scrimmage was over, Jeff Okuly, Jerry Carnahan and I headed off to Bowling Green, Ohio for the annual National Tractor Pulling Championships. Jeff's dad had a camper there and we stayed over night and watching the pulls on Sunday as well. It was a great time and I have many fond memories from it. I don't think Jeff has ever missed the pull; he has a camper now and he and Rob Giesige still go each and every year.

We returned in time for practice on Monday and got ready for our next scrimmage against Delphos St. John's. On the Saturday before school started, we scrimmaged against Delphos St. John's and it was nice to once again smack pads with somebody on another team. The result was much the same and we handled them fairly easily. Our defense played like we were hungry to hit somebody and the results were evident. It looked like our defense was as good as the unit in 1985, if not better. Offensively, our line just dominated the line of scrimmage. John Finn was going to be a great center, with Briseno and Wilson flanking him, Boals on his right side and Okuly/Roth on his left.

> "We knew we had the backs at the beginning of the season," recalled McCord. "The big key has been the offensive line gelling. We really saw how quick it was coming together after our second scrimmage. (After that) we knew we were going to have a good offensive line."[30]

Following our two scrimmages, we started school and began preparing for our opener in 1986 against McComb. Would 1986 be the year we finally beat McComb? I sure was ready to start the year off with a win. We had lost our openers to McComb for three straight years. Beating McComb was on everyone's mind. I know Phil Girlie, John Finn and Steve Deitrick were definitely ready for a victory. They wore white head bands with "Beat McComb" written on them with a Sharpie Marker the entire week. We found out the year before, that unless we went 10-0, we would never make the playoffs. It started with our first game; we would have to be perfect all year long to make it to the postseason.

With the regular season getting ready to start, there were a lot of newspaper articles written about what teams were going to be good and who were the players to watch. Our Ayersville team wasn't considered to be the team to beat in the GMC. We had lost some great players from the 1985 team and therefore it was assumed that the program would be down a bit in 1986. McComb was going to be good again, while Edgerton and Fairview were picked to battle for the GMC championship. I think it was predicted that we would go 7-3.

Once the school year started, we no longer were able to have two-a-day practices. We had to get in the locker room right after school ended and onto the practice field as quickly as possible. We didn't have as much time, but the practices went much the same way, defense first, special teams, then offense, followed by conditioning. We were out there until dark, and once daylight savings time was in effect, we were out there under the lights.

Our school lockers were always decorated with cool signs and it was attributed to the cheerleaders. Our cheerleaders probably did a lot of things that I never knew they were responsible for. They were all fairly quiet and shy, and did all of the stuff without ever taking credit for it. I never really got a chance to see them during a game for the obvious reasons, but every once in awhile, they would be on game film and I could tell they did a magnificent job keeping our crowd into the game. They even did some pretty neat formations and stunts.

The varsity cheerleaders were: Tina Trevino, Yvette Santo, Jina Stevens, Lori Geren, Shelli Joseph, Holly Porczak, Rita Sauer and Carla Pignataro.

The JV cheerleaders were: Marcia Sprow, Lori Minsel, Samantha Scott and Kris Sauer.

AUGUST 29, 1986

--- --- --- --- --- --- --- --- --- --- --- --- --- --- --- --- --- --- --- ---

MCCOMB PANTHERS
HOME
WEEK 1

On game days, we all went to the locker room after school. There were always signs, our lockers would be decorated, and there would be a game-day treat waiting on us at our lockers, all done by our parents the night before. The treats would range from an apple, a candy bar, to homemade cookies. For some reason, they were always the greatest thing in the world to us. Everyone anticipated the treat for the week.

After eating our treat, the assigned guys would get their ankles taped while the other guys went home. I always had to get my ankles taped, so I would have to stay. When I was finished, I always went home. If it was a home game, we always had more time than an away game. I would eat dinner, which would really consist of no set thing. My Mom knew my favorite things, and it was always one of them on game night. My Mom hated game nights because I was always in a horrible mood. I don't know why, but I was already in game mode and wasn't very nice at all. She would later tell me that she did not like the period before a game because I was always very mean and not myself. She would go on to say I would try and pick a fight, just to get fired up for the game.

"I could never figure it out for years why you would be so mean on game nights," stated my Mom. "Usually you were a very nice child and were so easy to get along with, but on game nights, you were always trying to pick a fight. It was just all of these nit-picky little things you complained about. You always tried to make me mad. Finally, I figured it out that you were just using me to get all psyched up for the game. I just hated the time period before a game."[31]

After I ate dinner, my only real ritual was to get a pair of scissors and cut up the tape on my ankles a little bit, so that it wasn't so tight. Sometimes I would nearly cut it off. I would then crank the song, "On the Dark Side" by John Cafferty and the Beaver Brown Band. I listened to the song over and over before a game. I just loved the beat and it always pumped me up.

Once we returned to the locker room, the game-day atmosphere was in full force. Coach McCord would have his record player set up and it would be playing all of the tunes of The Ohio State Marching Band. The music meant football to all of us; I preferred it to any of the normal rock songs playing before and after practice. Everyone was quiet and all business. If it was an away game, we would stuff our gear into the big mesh bags all of us carried, and load them into the Turbo Van. The Turbo Van was an old brown beat up van that the managers had fixed cardboard signs to the side panels, which stated just that, Turbo Van.

Steve Deitrick said, "Being a Michigan fan, it's ironic how the OSU band LP record playing during taping sessions and pre-game, along with the team prayer, and holding hands - because that's how the Buckeyes did it - are actually very fond memories."[32]

Once we were ready to leave, there was a bus for the seniors and juniors, and one for the sophomores and freshmen. The bus rides would be extremely quiet, nothing was ever said, but we knew we better be using the time to get prepared to play or Coach McCord would surely not be happy. It was never a problem, everyone was always focused on the game. As Coach McCord would constantly remind us, "We are in control of our own destiny."

Ever since we started playing organized sports in the seventh-grade, I rode the bus seated next to Rob Giesige. During football games, basketball games, it didn't matter. We always sat next to each other on the ride to the game. It was a little tradition that carried all the way through to our senior year.

The lid lifter to our 1986 season was at home against McComb, so we would be getting dressed in our own locker room. There was one article of clothing I wore for each and every game. It was a light blue half-shirt that had a picture of a surfboarder on the front. I don't know where I got it, and other than wearing it for every game, it had no significance to me. I just liked the way it fit and needed something under my shoulder pads so that the straps wouldn't dig into my arm pits. The shirt was my prized possession; I know it drove my Mom crazy on game nights if the shirt couldn't be located. I don't know what happened to it, but it came up missing after the season. I have images of my Mom standing over a bon-fire, cursing the shirt and its ability to come up missing just before a game, and then watching it burst into flames.

I wasn't the only one that had a piece of attire that was special for a game. Steve Deitrick related, "My rituals, I had to wear my cut off paint spattered "holy" sweat pants for pre and post-game wear … no substitutes. It was always two rounds of tape around the thigh pads … my signature. Pre-game field walks had to be "Hells Bells" by AC/DC and "Rock-n-Roll Party in the Street" by Axe in a loop on the walkman at volume 10 over and over and over … all about the focus! Game face meant war time, no talking about anything, just intensity for the task at hand."[33]

Manager Amy (Shinabery) Snyder also had an article she couldn't do without. "Booger, the green towel was for good luck. I was never without it during the season. Most of the senior guys would rub their faces with it at least once during a game."[34]

Once we were dressed and everyone was ready, we would head to the field as a team. We always went together and I cannot recall an instance where an opponent was on the field before us. We would run onto the field in our class lines. Once we were in our respective places for our stretching, everyone would start clapping slowly, and then increase the tempo until the clapping was at a fever pitch. We would then stop, yell and cheer, then start the process all over again. Once we were satisfied, we would then go into our Pilot Jacks. The Pilot Jacks were always done right before stretching, and before a game, everyone would be extra loud. A Pilot Jack was your basic jumping jack where we would yell out a letter when our hands were at the top until we spelled out PILOTS. Then we would yell out a letter at the top and bottom the second time around to increase the tempo.

It would go as follows: Up, P!, down and up, I!, down and up, L!, down and up, O!, down and up, T!, down and up, S!, down and up, P!, down, I!, up, L!, down, O!, up, T!, down, S!

Pilot Jacks were always followed by cheering and yelling, depending on the game, the cheering and yelling would go on for quite some time. As Team Champ, I would then yell out, "Fingers and wrists," and the stretching would begin. Sometimes I would let the screaming and yelling go on longer than other times. I felt it just depended on the game.

While we did all of our stretching exercises, Coach McCord would start with the seniors, and make his way down each line until he shook the hand of every player. I always thought highly of his maneuver, because it was a chance for everyone to be acknowledged personally by our great coach.

Once the stretching was done, we would line up and do jogging and running exercises in our class lines. We would then go to defensive groups and do drills. Then the punters and kickers would kick while the return men caught. The other guys would work on release blocking in the end zone. We would then come together and punt three times out of the end zone. From there it was to offensive groups, where we always did the handoff drill in lines facing each other. Next, the quarterbacks threw some passes. I always liked to air it out and have Denny Martin complete a long bomb to me before I could quit.

Then we would team up and run through our offensive plays until it was time to go back to the locker room.

Once back in the locker room, Coach McCord would deliver one of his inspirational speeches. He was a very good motivational speaker and used many of the terms we heard each day in practice. "You're in control of your own destiny. This is what we were working for in August. There are many seniors that played before you that would give anything to come back and have the opportunity you have tonight," continued Coach McCord. "Control the ball and keep their offense off of the field. Sustain your blocks. What will this senior class be remembered for? Leave it all out on the field."

Coach McCord would pick two seniors to be captains for each game. Everyone would get a chance. I liked this and felt everyone that put in all of the work during two-a-days deserved the chance to meet the captains of the other team at midfield, shake hands, and see the coin toss. For the first game against McComb, Denny Martin and I were chosen captains. When it was time, Coach McCord would grab the captains, tell them to either take the ball or defer to the second half, and what goal we wanted to defend. It was always a strategic move, would we want to jump right out and score on a team, or would we want to shut them down with our defense first? Which way was the wind blowing? Would we want to be heading into a certain direction in the fourth quarter so the wind would be helping us? The coaches always made the decision and relayed it on to the captains before sending them out.

The guys in the locker room would get some water, adjust their equipment and take care of their last minute restroom urges. Coach McCord would then go over all of the special teams, and who the back up was for each spot. We would then sit anxiously awaiting the captains' return. The captains would burst into the locker room and scream either, "We have the ball, or we are on defense first. We would all then start cheering.

On the opening night of 1986, it was defense. Coach would wait for the noise to subside then yell out, "Starting at middle guard, Marv Andrews." He would grab Marv and push him to the middle of the big circle that formed. Everyone would be screaming and yelling and Marv would be jumping up and down in the circle getting all revved up to play. Coach would then find the next guy he was looking for, grab him, and call out, "Starting at left tackle, Jeff Okuly," and he would push him into the circle with Marv. They would be bouncing around with their arms locked around each others shoulder, forming a circle in a circle.

Coach McCord would then move right down the line doing the same thing with each defensive starter. At right tackle, Aaron Roth, at left end, Eric Burket, at right end, Rob Giesige, at left linebacker, Mike Wilson, at right linebacker, Steve Deitrick, at left rotator, Andy Groll, at right rotator, Phil Girlie, at left safety, Johnny Armes, at right safety, Todd Hanna. The whole time everyone in the circle would be bouncing around getting revved up to play.

Once the whole defensive team was out there, the yelling would slowly subside. It was then time for silence. Coach McCord would say, "Seniors", and the seniors would fall into place with their knees on the floor and their heads to the carpet. Then "Juniors", they would fall into place behind the seniors, "Sophomores", they would fall in behind the juniors, "Freshmen", they would fall in behind the sophomores, and finally "Coaches", who gathered around us all.

Coach McCord would then go into the prayer. I can quote it word for word even to this day.

This is the beginning of a new day

God has given us this day to use as we will

We can waste it or use it for good

What we do today is important

Because we are exchanging a

Day out of our lives for it

When tomorrow comes, this day

Will be gone forever, leaving

In its place something that

We have traded

We want it to be gained not lost,

Good not evil, success not failure

Amen

We would then stand and make our way down the locker room steps. We would form four lines by class, seniors in the front, hold hands, and walk to the field. By then, the fans would be there and they would cheer as we marched across the grass to the football field. The young boys behind the stadium would stop playing long enough to stare in awe and amazement at us. Someday that would be them, and they couldn't wait for their chance to play high school football.

If they only knew, I sometimes would look at them in amazement and envy them. They had their whole high school careers ahead of them, and mine was coming to an end. I thought about my younger days, and how I would watch the players before me walk out onto the field, of the longing, and ache to strap on the pads to do battle. I knew what it felt like to want to be in the Ayersville Pilot uniform. I was wearing that uniform and standing in the front line. It all came down to our final season, finally we were seniors!

After making the walk from the locker room to the edge of the football field, we would gather in the southwest corner of the field. The band, cheerleaders and fans would form a tunnel, and at the end would be a big blue Ayersville Pilot banner hanging from two poles that were held up, one on each side. We would then run down the tunnel and jump up and touch the banner. Some guys would sprint out of there like a race horse in the Kentucky Derby and try to get to the banner first. I was one of the guys that hung back and got there in the middle of the pack. In just a few minutes it would be time to sprint down the field, either chasing somebody or running from somebody, and that's when I wanted to be poised and ready.

Starting the year off with McComb was a huge test to see if we had what it took to be good team in 1986. We had never beaten McComb, and they had a really strong football tradition under Coach Bill Banning, including the state title in 1983. They had ruined our chance for a perfect season and playoff run the year before, which left a really bad taste in our mouths.

There was some talk that a few of our players had been to their scrimmage the week before. I didn't know if there was any truth to it or not, but figured it could just be something made up to keep things interesting. The story was that they had met some students from McComb, including a few girls and became friends with them. I wasn't sure if it was true, but I know a few of us couldn't understand how any of our players could be friends with, or even talk to somebody from the school that ruined our season the year before

McComb had a fierce defense in 1985 and allowed only 36 points all year. We figured it would be another daunting task to score on them in 1986. Their quarterback, Scott Davis, was back and he could run as well as pass. They had a nice fullback in Brian Buck, so defensively, we would be challenged as well.

We kicked off to start the game, and since I had been selected by Coach McCord as the safety on the kickoff team, I was the leader in the huddle. We always ended the huddle for the kickoff in the same way. "Sprint down the field, stay in your lanes, breakdown and kill." Sometimes I would have Rob Giesige say it, because he truly loved flying down the field on the kickoff team. I had been one of those guys for two years, but now I had the task of preventing a touchdown if the return man broke through. It was a tedious task, but an important one, so I accepted it, and would be ready if the time ever came.

After the kickoff, both teams traded possessions, and then on our second drive, things started to come together. We took over on our own 25-yard line. We started to march down the field, with Denny Martin leading the way with 64 yards through the air. Tolly Hanna and Rob Giesige made some nice catch and runs to ignite our offense. We had the ball on the McComb five-yard line when it looked like Chris Schlachter would burst into the end zone after taking the handoff. He was hit just before he crossed the goalline and the ball popped loose right into the arms of McComb's Rob Killian. We had put together a really nice drive and failed to come away with any points.

From there, it was a defensive stalemate until late in the second quarter when we once again fumbled the ball over to McComb on their 37.

McComb started to move the ball fairly easily with four straight running plays and had the ball down on our 37-yard line after a couple of first downs. Our defense was trying to tighten against the run when Scott Davis surprised us by dropping back to pass and hitting Brian Buck over the middle for a 37-yard touchdown with 2:22 left in the first half. The kick failed, leaving McComb out in front, 6-0.

Our offense didn't give up and we threatened to get some points on the board just before the half. With 17 seconds to go, we had the ball at midfield when we ran one of our long desperation pass plays, twins left Ohio. The split end and blocking back would both line up wide on the left. Jerry Carnahan, the split end, would run an angle route to the center of the field to take his defender with him to open up the sideline. I was the blocking back, and would be running a down, out and up pattern to hopefully shake my defender and be open for a long pass.

I ran the down, and the defender was right with me, then I ran the out, and he broke out as well. Then I turned up the field and had two or three steps on the man covering me. I turned and the ball was in the air, it was thrown a little deep, so I turned to my outside shoulder and stuck out my arms. The ball landed softly into my awaiting hands and I thought I was off for a sure touchdown. I no more than started racing for the end zone when I was tripped up. Jerry Carnahan had not angled to the center of the field and his man was right in front of me.

It was Jerry's first start, and he must have been confused on the pattern he was supposed to run. I took full responsibility for it because I should have made sure he knew what to do as soon as we broke the huddle. The half ended with McComb out in front 6-0 and I don't think we ran a twins Ohio again for the rest of the season.

The half was brutal. We had lost two fumbles, one when we were about to score and another allowed them to score. We had numerous mental mistakes and we were beating ourselves. Coach McCord and the rest of the coaches really gave it to us at halftime. Something had to ignite our team or we would once again be starting the year off with a loss to the Panthers. I welcomed the screaming and yelling, and there sure was a lot of it. It was our senior year and we needed to dig deep and start playing some football. Once again, it looked like McComb's defense would be hard to score against. We needed to find a way to get the ball in the end zone.

> "WE TALKED (at halftime) about beating ourselves," said McCord. "I thought it was déjà vu. For awhile in the first half we beat ourselves."[35]

We made our way out of the locker room determined to play harder and smarter. Just before we made our way through the gate leading to the field, I saw the guy I looked for at the half of each home game. He was always slapping backs, shaking hands and yelling encouragement. I had known him from the years before and just referred to him as the brown coveralls guy, because no matter what the temperature was, he would wear a pair of big brown Carhardt coveralls. He always caught my eye, and when I was close enough, he would call me by name, slap me on the back, and say, "Let's get some good hits out there." I always asked who the guy was, but nobody ever seemed to know. I would tell them he had to be our biggest fan, "You know the guy I am talking about, the guy in the brown coveralls that always pumps us up before we get back out there for the half."

"Who are you talking about?" they'd ask. Nobody ever seemed to know who I was talking about. Now, I don't believe in a bunch of crazy crap, and don't talk to myself or anything, but maybe he was a ghost or I imagined the image because I really don't know how anybody could not notice the guy in brown coveralls.

We had the ball to start the third quarter and our offensive line came out strong. Tim Boals, Jaime Briseno, John Finn, Mike Wilson and the Okuly/Roth platoon were driving guys off of the line of scrimmage. We had a fourth-and-one call at our own 39-yard line, and Coach McCord decided he had the confidence in us to go for it. We got the first down, and on the next play, Steve Deitrick broke through the line on a perfectly blocked 32 trap and took it to the house for the touchdown. After the 59-yard touchdown gallop by Deitrick, John Finn pulled off his arm pads and emphatically slammed them on the ground to get ready for his long snap. He was making a statement, he had blown his man off of the line, and our offense was ready to roll. The kick by Schlachter was good, putting us out in front, 7-6.

The lead would only last a few seconds. With only 41 ticks off the clock after the ensuing kickoff, Scott Davis raced down the right sideline for a 68-yard touchdown. The two-point conversion failed, but McComb was back out in front, 12-7.

The touchdown run by Davis should never have happened. We had him stopped a few times but he got loose. When he was right along the sideline, Mike Wilson was giving chase, and had the angle on him, when Mike just stopped running. He must have thought he was out of bounds because Harley Man would never give up. I saw Mike slow down, so I slowed down as well and Davis raced into the end zone well ahead of us. I really think Mike would have run him down since he had the angle, and I had seen him do it many times, but it didn't matter. The whole defense had another mental lapse that we paid for on Davis' long jaunt into the end zone.

Our offense was forced to punt on our possession after the touchdown, and then our defense came up big. Deitrick and Giesige made a nice tackle in the backfield, causing a fumble. Aaron Roth fell on the loose pigskin and we had possession in great position to reclaim the lead at the McComb 32.

As Roth was running off of the field, he changed his sack dance into his fumble recovery dance. He ran off, jumped into the air and swung his arms all around in front of him like he was trying to kill a hundred flies. The Roth sack dance was a classic.

Three plays later, Travis Lewis took a quick pitch and dashed around the left edge for a 25-yard touchdown to put us back out in front. Chris Schlachter banged through the PAT for a 14-12 Ayersville edge.

Our defense played strong and didn't allow McComb to move the ball at all after Lewis put us out in front, ending the third quarter. Coach McCord would then have us all hold four fingers aloft as both teams switched sides for the final stanza. He incorporated this as, "The fourth quarter must always belong to us."

Once we received the ball back, we began a nice drive and faced a fourth-and-nine on the McComb 30. Steve Deitrick and Denny Martin took over from there. Martin hit Deitrick for 15 yards and a first down on a waggle right play before Deitrick carried three times for eight yards. Denny then hooked up with him for a seven-yard touchdown on a fourth-and-two call. The play again was a waggle right. The point after by Schlachter was again good and we had some breathing room with a 21-12 lead with only 7:34 left on the clock.

McComb came back and started to move the ball down field when our defense stepped up yet again. Davis tried a pass down the middle of the field, and I was there to intercept it, turning the ball back over to our offense. We ran some time off of the clock, punted, and then stopped the McComb offense on four downs.

With the ball safely back in our hands, we ran out the clock, finally beating the dreaded McComb Panthers, 21-12.

> "In the trenches is where football games are decided," explained McComb's Bill Banning, whose team managed only 13 plays in the second half and gained just seven yards after Davis' score. "We just couldn't do it. We couldn't sustain a drive all night long. You can't win football games that way."[36]

Would 1986 be the year we finally beat McComb? Yes it was! Deitrick rushed for 93 yards, and game captain, Denny Martin, was 10-for-14 for 142 yards passing and made some crucial fourth-down plays. I was the other game captain and led the defense with nine tackles and an interception while Aaron Roth had eight tackles and the huge fumble recovery that helped turn the tide into our favor.

The atmosphere in the locker room after the game was awesome. Parents and fans were all filtering in and out offering their congratulations. Apparently, everyone knew what a huge victory it was for us. The start of 1-0 sure sounded good after three straight years of McComb ushering in our season with losses.

Denny Martin was having a small get together at his house after the game, so a few of us went over there after we showered. We were sitting around talking about the game, when there was a knock at the door. When the door was opened, six strangers emerged, four girls and two boys. I didn't know them and thought they must be somebody Denny knew. They were finally introduced as the McComb students from the scrimmage the week before. I guess the story was true about a few players becoming friends with some McComb students at the scrimmage. Now that we had finally beaten them, I shook hands with all of them after they were introduced. Beating a school sure made a difference in how friendly we were to our opponents, and how the entire school was perceived.

STATISTICS

	McComb	Ayersville
First Downs	4	12
Rushing Yards	118	213
Passing Yards	53	142
Total Offense	171	355
Passes Attempted	8	14
Passes Completed	2	10
Had Intercepted	1	0
Fumbles	1	4
Fumbles Lost	1	2
Yards Penalized	20	15

McComb	0	6	6	0-	-12
Ayersville	0	0	14	7-	-21

MHS- Buck 37-yard pass from Davis (PAT kick failed)
AHS- Deitrick 59-yard run (PAT Schlachter kick)
MHS- Davis 68-yard run (PAT run failed)
AHS- Lewis 25-yard run (PAT Schlachter kick)
AHS- Deitrick 7-yard pass from Martin (PAT Schlachter kick)

SEPTEMBER 5, 1986

FAIRVIEW APACHES
AWAY
WEEK 2

Week two took us on the road to play Defiance County rival Fairview at "The Reservation". On the Monday before the game, there was another annual hunting occurrence that would conflict with my football schedule. Ever since I was in grade school, my parents would allow me to miss school for the first day of squirrel season. My note the next day was never a lie, it always stated that I was squirrel hunting and was signed by my parents. Some of my past teachers handled it well, others threw a fit and thought I was crazy, and my parents were wrong to allow me to miss school for such a thing.

In high school, our principal Ed McCord (no relation to Coach McCord) was familiar with our annual trip to South Dakota and me missing the first day for squirrel season. I didn't miss school for any other reason, didn't cause any trouble in school or the classroom, so we got along well. He never gave me any trouble whatsoever when I told him on the day before that I would be missing school to go squirrel hunting.

The only problem was, if we missed school, we couldn't practice. I remedied this by only missing a half a day of school, that way I would be eligible to practice. I know Coach McCord would not have been happy if I missed any practice, let alone one before the Fairview game.

Chris Schlachter, who was really nursing a bad ankle injury at the time and didn't get many carries in the McComb game, was my hunting partner on Monday morning. I doubt Coach McCord would have been very thrilled knowing I was going to be dragging him through the woods that morning.

We would be hunting in the woods right next to my house and Chris arrived before daybreak. We grabbed our gear and went off into the woods at first light. The area had a lot of ravines and is quite the rolling extravaganza of timber. When I hunted squirrels, I liked to cover as much ground as possible and we made our way up hills, through creek bottoms and over some dense undergrowth. I could tell his ankle was hurting, but Chris came along every step of the way. We had a great time, but when we were finally finished and made our way back to school, I am sure his ankle was in worse shape than when we started.

If Coach McCord would have known I had his prized tailback out all morning walking through the woods, he would have been more disgruntled with me than Chris. I was a senior, Chris was a junior, therefore, I should have been the one to know better and take the proper precautions. We made it back to school and reported in for our hard week of preparation for the Fairview game.

On Monday, we watched the film of the McComb game and then it was time for one of the most anticipated events of the season. The event took place on each Monday for the entire football season. The event brought out the five-year-old in all of us, IT WAS STICKER TIME! Coach McCord would hand out different stickers for all sorts of things: Touchdowns, QB sacks, interceptions, fumble recoveries, block and tackle of the game. Some stickers were even team oriented for shutouts or if the line didn't allow any QB sacks. We all loved the stickers and adorned our helmets with the precious things. My favorite sticker, and I think it was probably everyone's, was the skull-and-crossbones.

Practice was hard, and Coach McCord worked us like crazy because of his long standing rivalry with the Fairview Apaches. It had taken him until 1983 to beat them and he was really looking forward to evening the score against them. Fairview, along with Edgerton, was picked to be the cream of the crop in the Green Meadows Conference for the year. We needed a win so that as Coach McCord would say all week, "We could control our own destiny."

> "When we went to our defensive groups, the linemen group had something to look forward to each week" Coach Beef explained. "We had joke day once a week in our defensive line group. Everyone had a chance to participate. Guys like Finn and Boals participated more than the others, but we all shared some laughs. Sometimes, we would have to cut it short because Coach McCord would be watching us. He would always come over after defensive groups and say how hard the linebackers were working and he hoped we were working just as hard."[37]

It had been eight years since the Pilot program had started the year off at 2-0. It was long over due and the hard week of preparation was a testament that Coach McCord was ready to change that.

Fairview had also won their season opener. They had high hopes for the season, and wanted to start the conference schedule off with a win. They would definitely be ready for us since we beat them the year before in a real mêlée. They always had a competitive team, and a group of hard hitters, so the games we played against them were always tough and a hard-hitting affair.

It would be my first trip back to their field since 1984 when I tripped and fell down, allowing them to score the go-ahead touchdown in a 24-14 Fairview triumph. I wanted a win to avenge that dreaded defeat more than anyone.

The game did not start off well for us as Chris Schlachter fumbled on the second play from scrimmage and Fairview recovered. Chris was hurting and wasn't able to play up to his capabilities, so he was basically out for the rest of the game. Without Chris, a fellow junior, Travis Lewis, stepped in at tailback. He had run the ball well in the McComb game while Chris nursed his ankle, so he was a capable backup.

Six plays later, Fairview scored. Going into the game, we knew they had a good quarterback in Rod Bayliss and a fast and elusive runner in Todd Tadsen. We had focused all week in practice on controlling them. On the six-play drive, there was a key fourth down pass play that netted Fairview 19 yards and kept their drive alive when we had a chance to get the ball back. Tadsen went on to score on an eight-yard pass from Bayliss. The extra point failed, putting us down 6-0. The game started out like a repeat of our first week against McComb. Our secondary needed to step it up because both teams scored on us first via the pass.

On the ensuing kickoff, things started to turn around. Scott Kolb fielded the short kick on the 22 and blazed down the left sideline for 58 yards before he was tripped up. After Scott's great return, we had the ball deep in Fairview territory at their 20-yard line.

> "There were a couple of keys," McCord remarked. "The big thing that got us moving was the kickoff. I think the whole thing turned around."[38]

However, we could not get the offense rolling and faced a fourth-and-five at the 15. Coach McCord decided to go for it, and called one of his favorite plays, an I-left waggle left. On our waggle play, Coach McCord always stressed that it was run first, pass second for the quarterback. The play was a fake blast right, then the quarterback would get depth and roll out left. Both guards would pull and lead him around the end. The split end and blocking back would run deep routes to clear out the area, while the tight end would drag across the field as the primary receiver. Steve Deitrick, the fullback, would continue through the line, faking the blast play and get out into the flat as another receiver. Steve was excellent at finding the open area, and pretty much changed the way the play was ran, because he was almost always the primary receiver on the play. Denny Martin ran the waggle better than any quarterback in Ayersville history. He was fast enough to get outside, had an accurate arm and was a good decision maker on if he should run it or throw it. To go along with Denny's speed, Mike Wilson was a very fast guard and he had no trouble getting outside to lead block for Denny. We enjoyed a lot of success with the play because of the personnel we had.

Fourth-and-five to go, the call was a waggle left, Denny rolled out left and kept the ball. The play was going to be successful, he got the first down and slashed forward for more, a couple of nifty moves, great blocks, and he burst into the end zone. Schlachter came on for the point after and nailed it to put us up 7-6. We were right back in the game after our slow start.

> "Our defensive ends got killed," admitted (Fairview head coach) S.G. Brugler. "Denny Martin does a super job. They were quick and we weren't. They were a little quicker than I thought."[39]

Our defensive line came alive after we took the 7-6 lead and caused a Tadsen fumble that we recovered. We were back in business and looking to add to our advantage. It was short lived, however, as we returned the favor and fumbled the ball right back to the hosts.

Our defense held and we looked to get our offense rolling. It wasn't in the cards on that night. Once again, we turned the ball over as Martin threw an interception, at least we didn't fumble again. Our offense was just turning the ball over like crazy and Coach McCord would surely address the problem at halftime.

The defense once again came up big, especially Roth and Okuly, as they caused and recovered another Fairview fumble. We had the ball on the Fairview 45-yard line. With touchdown reservations we moved the ball well with a few runs, and some key passes sprinkled in to the Fairview 12. Martin dropped back and found Shelby Dawson open in the end zone for six. Schlachter once again came on to put the ball through the pipes and we led 14-6 with 4:24 left before the half.

Defensively, we continued to play well as we held and forced a Fairview punt. With two minutes left before the half, we continued to shoot ourselves in the foot with yet another fumble.

The fumble could have been the turning point of the game. The Apache side of the field was in a frenzy, loud enough that we couldn't hear the snap count. The Fairview faithful wanted a score to even things up before the intermission. We were digging in something fierce to keep it from happening. Not only did we stop them in four straight plays, we actually backed them up another seven yards. A statement was made and our defense wasn't going to give in.

After our defensive stand, we zapped the clock and headed into the half with a 14-6 cushion.

We ran to the area beside where our buses were parked for halftime. When it was hot out, Coach McCord didn't like to take us into the visiting locker room at the half. Plus, it was a long distance from the field at Fairview to the visiting locker room.

We gathered together, concealed by the two buses, to go over the first half. Coach McCord always had the buses parked in an obscure location and they were set up to block the view from the field. I always considered it our bus fort. I don't know if it was because he didn't want anyone from the other team spying on us, or if he didn't want any of us becoming distracted by the halftime show and fans milling around the field. I imagine it was a little bit of both.

With all of the fumbles and sloppy play, he was not in a good mood, even though we had the lead at the break. He ripped into us about all the work we did to keep the ball off of the ground in practice. We were killing ourselves, and if we didn't stop turning the ball over, sooner or later, we would get our lunch handed to us.

The second half began with our defense forcing a punt. Then with 3:26 left in the third quarter, Martin hit Steve Deitrick with a 14-yard touchdown pass. The extra point was good and we had a buffer zone with the benefit of a 21-6 advantage.

We exchanged possessions, and were set to punt, when the unthinkable happened. We muffed the punt snap and the ball got away from Jerry Carnahan. The Apaches recovered the ball near our end zone at the 10. Our defense couldn't hold and Fairview scored on a two-yard run by Tadsen. Fairview lined up to go for a two-point conversion, allowing them to make it a one possession game. They dropped back for a pass and the ball missed its target. It fell to the ground harmlessly which allowed us to maintain a two-possession lead, 21-12.

We once again couldn't move the ball on offense and were forced to punt from deep in our own territory. Fairview came after the punt, but Carnahan got it away and it rolled dead at the Fairview 48. The Apaches were on the march and faced a fourth-and-one at our 29. Our defense had been doing it all night and needed another big stop on the fourth-down play. We crashed the line of scrimmage with all 11 defenders, hoping to get a tackle in the backfield. Eric Burket crashed down on an inside move from his left end position and destroyed the ball carrier before he made it to the line of scrimmage. Our defense had turned the Fairview offense away again.

We took over possession at our own 30 and had the opportunity to run out the clock by moving the chains a few times. We kept the ball on the ground and stayed conservative with a nine-point edge. We couldn't pick up a first down, though, and had to punt. We executed a nice punt, stopped them again on downs and then ran out the clock for a 21-12 triumph.

After the teams shook hands, I could see Coach Beck on game film with his arms around his two defensive ends. He lifted Rob Giesige in the air and had an arm around Eric Burket. They had played a fabulous game and deserved a lot of credit for stopping Fairview's speed. Coach Beef then ran to his tackles and Jeff Okuly lifted Coach Beef into the air. Coach Beef slapped Okuly with his congratulations with one hand while he pulled Roth over and did the same with him. The two tackles had been chosen by Coach McCord before the game as our captains for the game. He couldn't have made a better choice because they both played magnificently.

Jeff Okuly had eight tackles and recovered two fumbles, while Aaron Roth had six stops, a fumble recovery and a sack.

Meanwhile, Denny Martin had a nice game on offense; in fact he was basically our whole offense and had a hand in all three of our trips into the end zone. He was 10-of-18 passing for 118 yards and two touchdowns to go along with a rushing touchdown.

As a team, we had not performed well at all; there were way too many mistakes and we had turned the ball over four times. Coach hated penalties and we had been penalized 60 yards to Fairview's five.

After our away games, we would always grab a quick shower, get dressed in our street clothes and congregate somewhere outside of the school where our buses had pulled up to take us home. Tables would be set up with sandwiches, chips and cookies. There would be coolers full of ice cold pop sitting nearby as well. After a win, those were the best of times; I can remember them better than some of the games. It was a chance to not only get something to eat and drink, but to share the game with the other players on the team, along with the coaches, parents and other fans that hung around.

The sandwiches served were the best ones I have ever eaten in my life. You're probably thinking there was something fancy about them, but you couldn't be more wrong. The sandwiches ranged from a plain piece of bologna on a couple slices of bread, to ham with pickle, lettuce, tomato, ketchup, mustard, cheese and mayo on a nice soft bun.

It never mattered to me, I wasn't picky at all, and every one of the sandwiches tasted great. Even if I would never in a million years put together some of the combinations we were served, I ate them all and enjoyed every one of them. You couldn't beat great food, good friends and a victory on Friday night.

STATISTICS

	Ayersville	Fairview
First Downs	7	7
Rushing Yards	84	60
Passing Yards	119	43
Total Offense	203	103
Passes Attempted	18	14
Passes Completed	10	4
Had Intercepted	1	0
Fumbles	4	5
Fumbles Lost	4	4
Yards Penalized	60	5

Ayersville	0	7	7	7-	-21
Fairview	6	0	0	6-	-12

FHS- Tadsen 8-yard pass from Bayliss (PAT kick failed)

AHS- Martin 15-yard run (PAT Schlachter kick)

AHS- Dawson 12-yard pass from Martin (PAT Schlachter kick)

AHS- Deitrick 14-yard pass from Martin (PAT Schlachter kick)

FHS- Tadsen 2-yard run (PAT pass failed)

LAUGHTER AND MEMORIES

This narrative explains Coach Ondrus' way of always making us want to play hard for him. He had a knack for being a players' coach and we knew that he truly cared about making football fun.

This case in point was in my sophomore season after the defensive secondary had played poorly in a scrimmage. We were headed to defensive groups when Coach McCord made the comment, "Hey Coach O, you had better really get after those guys since they stunk it up out there Saturday."

We were all thinking, *great, we are going to hear some hollering and be run to death.* To our surprise, as we gathered around in our corner of the practice area, Coach O lowered his voice and said, "Okay, I am going to rant and rave while you guys lay on the ground for push-ups and sit-ups. Just lay there unless I say, "Welty", (The last name of another coach at the time).

So we all got down in a push-up stance, and Coach O started yelling, "Down, down, down," and nobody moved. Then he started blasting us, "You guys are pathetic, just horrible, you can't tackle anybody." Then, "Welty," we all did a push-up. He went right back into it, "Down, down, down." This went on for quite some time where we did about 10 total push-ups to about 100 "downs". He was just tearing into us the whole time as loudly as he could.

Then the process repeated with us on our backs for sit-ups. Of course this drew a lot of attention towards the defensive back group from coaches and players alike. Whenever Coach O saw a lot of people staring, he let loose with a "Welty," thus creating the allusion that we were being worked to death over there. It must have worked perfectly because when groups were over and we teamed up, Coach

McCord was smirking along with everyone else. Rob Giesige came over to me and laughed like he always did, "You guys sure got your butts kicked over there." I just smiled, Coach O always made things interesting.

Another tribute to Coach O was when he introduced us to the infamous Buck Buck. At the end of certain practices for extra conditioning, we would split up by class and all go with a different coach. I think we were seniors at the time when we went off with Coach O for some extra conditioning.

He said, "Okay boys, today we are going to do a little thing called Buck Buck." At the time, I had never heard of it, I am not sure if anyone else had either since nobody said anything and everyone had a look of strenuous exercise fear on their face.

He went on to explain it to us. "Buck Buck is where you split up into teams of four. The first teammate leans over and puts his shoulder against a tree or post, pretty much like a three-point stance. The next three guys use the guy in front of them and brace themselves much the same way, forming a neat line of bodies."

Here is where it gets fun. "Someone from the other team then lines up about five yards behind the guys braced against the pole. He calls out, 'Buck Buck number one coming,' then runs up and belly flops on their backs. The guy that jumped on the other teams' backs holds on to create a pig pile on their backs. This continues with Buck Buck number two, three, four, and so on, until the whole pile collapses. The winner is the team that can hold up the most bodies."

I don't remember the teams, but I do remember it coming down to the team on the pole needing to hold one more body to be the winner. I was on top of the pile when one of the bigger kids on the team (I think it was Marv Andrews) comes running up yelling, "Buck Buck number six coming." When he leaped on the pile, we all tumbled into a heap. I don't think anybody cared who won because we all had so much fun playing this new game instead of running our butts off.

Coach O was our hero and every other class was envious of this fun and cool game we were playing. We played this many more times in our spare time. It was something all of us would remember for the rest of our lives.

Jerry Carnahan later on played me a cassette tape from a Bill Cosby stand-up act featuring Fat Albert that explained the origin of Buck Buck. If you have never heard it, you are missing out because it's very funny. Fat Albert was certainly the baddest back breaker of all time.

This brings me to another game we played in our spare time, definitely not during practice. Usually we played it during lunch or some other odd time. It was called Spread Eagle. I don't know who invented it or where it came from, but it was shown to me by none other than B.A. (Brian Allen). We could play with two guys or 10 guys, it didn't matter, and all we needed was a wall and a tennis ball.

Whoever was playing would line up about 10 to 15 yards from a wall and spread out in a line right beside each other. Whoever had the tennis ball would throw it at the wall so that it would bounce back on one, or a few hops at someone else in the line. This person needed to catch the ball without letting it hit the ground. If they did catch it cleanly, the process duplicated with them throwing it to someone else in the line. Now, if they dropped it or misplayed it, they would have to hurry up and run and touch the wall before someone else retrieved it and whipped it at them. The key was to hit them with the ball before they got to the wall. If they did make it to the wall, they couldn't be thrown at.

Of course there were some instances where someone had just touched the wall and then, whammo, they got nailed with the ball. This was a violation, resulting in Spread Eagle. Just as you might imagine, the violator that hit the person after they touched the wall, would then assume the position Spread Eagle; arms above the head, and legs spread apart with their face against the wall. Everyone else that was playing then got a free shot throwing the tennis ball as hard as they could at the person Spread Eagle.

The worst part about being Spread Eagle was not being able to see the ball coming at you and anticipating the thump as it bruised your flesh. When a lot of people were playing, you could expect to take at least six tennis balls square in the back. The only other rule was that if you hit someone in the head, it was also a Spread Eagle violation.

There was no winner to the game and really no object to it other than to beat up on each other. Not everyone wanted to play, for the obvious reasons, but a few of us loved it and played every chance we got.

I remember one time when B.A. was assuming the position of Spread Eagle, mostly because he liked hitting people in the head. I had the throw of all throws, and nailed him just below the butt and right between the legs. He must have not had tight underwear on because it caught him right in the balls (not an easy thing to happen because he was facing away from me), dropping him like he had just been shot. It wasn't where I was aiming, the object wasn't to harm anyone and we were all friends. He rolled around trying not to puke while we all laughed like crazy. B.A. never wanted any sympathy, he was one tough kid. I am sure I took many head shots later on, B.A. always got even.

It was a brutal game and I am sure the teachers, coaches and parents wouldn't have approved, but we didn't use golf balls or baseballs, and when you were Spread Eagle, you had your back turned and couldn't get hit in the face or anything. It was just good clean fun!

This occurrence happened during our freshman year. It was the week of the Hicksville game. The local newspaper, *The Crescent News*, would always pick the top performer from the week before and name them, *The Crescent News* Player of the Week. *The Crescent News* Player of the Week was J.J. Gloor and he played for the Hicksville Aces, our opponent that week. Coach McCord came out before practice, called us together, and took out a clipping containing the article and a picture of *The Crescent News* Player of the Week. He read it out loud and said, "Oh my, isn't he good, what will we do against a guy this good?"

He then took the article, crumpled it up, put it in his mouth, and started chewing. After he had it chewed up real good, he said, "I'll tell you what you do with a guy like this, you chew them up and spit them out." With that, he spat the newspaper pieces on the ground and walked away. There was an emphatic roar among all of us players. Coach McCord always wanted us ready for Friday nights. I am sure that wad of newspaper left an awful taste in his mouth, but he saw it as part of his job to have his team ready for the game on Friday.

On Friday right after school, we would always report to the locker room to get our ankles taped for the game. The backs that would be playing in the game were required to be there as well as a few select linemen. Coach McCord would always tell us to shave our ankles to make it easier for the tape to be taken off. A senior on the 1985 team, who I will not mention by name, hopped up on the table to have his ankles taped by Coach Ondrus. Once Coach O started taping his first ankle, he must have noticed something weird, because he called for everyone to come over and check it out. We all gathered around and Coach Ondrus started laughing and pointed to his leg, "Look at that, he shaved his whole leg! I think he must be trying out for the cheerleading squad."

We all then started laughing, and threw our little comments in there about how soft and nice his legs were. He defended himself, "I started shaving my ankle and it looked funny. I wanted it to all look the same, so I just shaved the whole thing."

Brian Allen then responded like he just couldn't believe someone would do this, "You dumbass, that's what girls do, boys don't shave their whole legs."

This player got quite a bit of teasing, but he took it well. It never seemed to bother him, but I don't think he ever shaved his leg again, not even his ankle.

I was also the recipient of a lot of teasing from Coach Ondrus when I got my ankles taped. It was for a different reason, but it still resulted in him calling people over. If someone new was in the locker room, he would make sure they saw it as well. He always said I had the worst feet of anyone he ever taped. He would always tell anyone within earshot, "Look at these feet, they are the worst. There is no arch, and the ankles are all screwed up. How can you run with feet that look like this?" I always responded, "It could be worse, they could smell like they look. If they did, I would make sure you were the one taping them every week."

After hearing this back in my sophomore year, Coach McCord told me I should go see a specialist. My parents took me to this foot doctor he recommended, where he made me these special hard plastic inserts to wear in my shoes. The doctor went as far as to wrap my feet with this liquid plaster that would then harden to give him an exact replica of my feet. From there, he could design the hard plastic inserts that would shape my feet in the perfect way. I wore the inserts, and you know what, the inserts didn't shape my feet at all. Instead, my feet shaped the inserts into the perfect form of my foot. That's right, I flattened those things right out. My feet had prevailed; there would be no changing them with expensive plastic.

Another comical event happened when it had been raining quite a bit and there were some nice mud puddles in the ditch by the practice field. After practice, Aaron Roth was out there diving and sliding in the big puddles. He was running, laying flat out and diving in those puddles, creating some great splashes. We were all kind of watching him and cheering him on. He was going all wild and crazy, putting on quite a show. Coach McCord came out of the locker room, looked out over the railing from the stairs leading up to the locker room, to see what was going on. About that time, Aaron ran, laid out and dove into the puddle, creating a huge splash. He got up and went into his famous sack dance, then saw Coach McCord. He stopped and walked away, dripping water like he was an emerging sunken ship. I looked at Jeff Okuly, he shook his head and said, "I don't know what he's thinking, he's acting like he is five years old." I said, "I am glad his locker is next to yours, it will take at least a month for all of the pads he wears to dry out." Aaron had a lot of fun that day and we all enjoyed watching him put on his display, all except for Okuly. Jeff was mumbling to himself the whole time in the locker room, as the wet pads were taken off and hung to dry, puddles developed right next to Jeff's locker

In our playing days, the technology wasn't the greatest. Coach McCord would always wear a headset so that he could communicate with the guys up in the press box. They would then relay different information down to him. Such as the opponents defensive and offensive alignments, plays that would work, and even if there was a certain player not performing well and needed to be pulled out and informed of such.

The headset he wore had a long cord running from the press box down to him that he would drag along behind him. It wasn't the age of wireless headsets yet, and I am sure the players on the sidelines today are thankful they don't have to deal with the dreaded cord.

When I was a junior, I didn't play a whole lot of offense and was able to see just how much the cord affected the sidelines. Coach McCord would always have to be right in line with the line of scrimmage, so as the ball moved down the field, he too roamed along with it. If there was a particular long gain, he would take off and pull the cord along behind. If you were on the sidelines, you better be paying attention or when the cord caught around your feet, it would stop him in his tracks. If the angle was right, it probably did put a nice bit of strain on his neck. He would then yell, "GET OFF THE CORD!" and then proceed to yank on it like he was pulling up an anchor from a boat. Everyone standing around that had their legs clear from the dreaded cord would also yell, "GET OFF THE CORD!" and nod at Coach McCord as if to make sure he knew it wasn't them that had committed this dubious transgression.

For some reason, I think it was to check on an injured player, Coach McCord had gone behind some players and circled around them and had created the perfect trap for an unsuspecting victim. The freshman, who shall remain nameless, was goofing around and not paying any attention to the game. Our offense made a nice gain and Coach McCord was off to pursue. The freshman was caught in a snare as the cord wrapped and tightened around his foot.

The jolt practically ripped the headphones right off of Coach McCord's head. He proceeded to yell, "GET OFF THE CORD!" and yanked on the cord like he was starting a lawn mower. The freshman went down and was dragged along like a trapped animal, the whole time trying to free his foot from the tangled cord. Everyone else that was free from the cord was shouting, "GET OFF THE CORD, GET OFF THE CORD!" making sure they could be heard, so as not to be blamed for this episode later on. Just when the cord was about to be untangled and free, one of our passes was intercepted and being returned back the other way.

Coach McCord was in no mood to deal with the cord problem anymore since the other team had just taken possession of the ball. He took the headphones off, grabbed the cord and trudged off down the sideline like he was in the world tug-of-war championship. The freshman fell back down and was dragged back to his original starting point and finally untangled himself from the dreaded cord.

I had to get on the field for defense since the ball had been intercepted, so I missed the aftermath, but I always wondered if Coach McCord found out who the perpetrator was. Once I got on the field for the defensive huddle, Brian Allen asked me, "Who was that dumbass caught in the cord?" I told him, and he said, "I would hate to be him, we could hear all of the yelling clear out on the field and it was distracting. I think that's why Denny threw the interception."

On some Saturday mornings following our Friday night games, Chris Schlachter and I would do some squirrel hunting. The Saturday morning after the Fairview game my senior year, he was going to introduce me to his way of hunting. We would travel to the Tiffin River and float down it in a small boat to save us a whole lot of walking. We arrived at the river just as the sun was coming up. It was a nice calm and peaceful morning, perfect for squirrel hunting. We dumped the boat in the river, tossed in a couple of paddles, and put our guns and ammunition on our respective seats. His seat was the back one and mine was the front one. I thought we were ready to go, but when I turned to look for him, he was headed back to the truck for something else. Finally, he got back to the river while lugging a fairly large cooler and a hefty grocery bag.

He climbed into the boat and proceeded to pull stuff out of the grocery bag. He laid out a plate of cookies, a plate of brownies, a couple bags of chips and about 10 sandwiches wrapped in plastic. At that point, I was wondering if we were going squirrel hunting or if we were catering some big event at a campground located down river.

I said to him, "Are we camping out overnight or what?" He replied, "No, we should be done by noon." I said, "We already had breakfast, what possibly is all that stuff for?" He shrugged, "We might get hungry." I guess that's why we referred to him as Fat Boy.

He cracked open a soda from the cooler and handed me one, and we were finally drifting down the river looking for a squirrel. We no more than got started when we saw one, he then told me that this one was mine, and he would back me up if I missed. At the time, I had never hunted out of a moving boat or shot a shotgun from a sitting position. I had my Mossberg pump 20 gauge with me that day and I had it rigged so that it would hold seven shots instead of the standard five.

I started blasting away at the squirrel sitting in the top of a big hickory tree. I must not have been coming close to hitting it because it just kept running around in the top of the tree like it was having a good old time. There was bark flying off of the tree, limbs were raining down on the boat and into the water, while there were so many leaves floating down, you couldn't even see the top of the tree anymore.

I was empty, all seven shots had been fired and all I did was wake up the entire county, and strip that big hickory tree of its bark, limbs and leaves. I looked back at Chris, thinking, *wow, I can't believe Fat Boy missed too. He was used to this kind of hunting.*

To my surprise, there he sat in the back of the boat, grinning from ear to ear, a brownie in one hand, a sandwich in the other and his gun lying on the seat. He had crumbs all over him and he hadn't fired a single shot. I said, "What are you doing, you were supposed to back me up if I missed?" He snickered, "I was just enjoying the show, besides, I have shot a lot of squirrels along this river, but that's the first time I have ever seen anyone kill a hickory tree, and for that, you didn't need any help at all."

I reloaded and we continued down the river. I don't think we saw another squirrel the whole way. It may have been from all of the talking, sounds of potato chips crunching and pop cans opening, but I didn't care. The brownies tasted better than any I had eaten before.

I have to mention Coach Ondrus again. He would always play quarterback on the scout team offense when we were working on our defense against our upcoming opponent. He was a great athlete and fierce competitor, and gave it everything he had in those situations. He would call all of the plays from our scouting report and align the personnel accordingly. Whenever we were facing an opponent that used the option play as one of their weapons, he was in the height of his glory. He loved to carry the ball and try to fake us out. I think a lot of our defensive success was due to the fact that he ran the scout team offense so effectively.

You have to remember, we all had our full pads on and he was out there in shorts and a t-shirt without a helmet. This never stopped him, and it was a basic rule that none of us would actually tackle him, but just kind of wrap him up when he carried the ball.

One day, he was in an extremely competitive mood and when he carried the ball on the option, he would shake off our wrap ups and continue on down the field, high stepping, juking, and acting like he was Barry Sanders on 30-yard runs. He was really sticking it to us and taunting us the whole way. Coach McCord was even laying into us about that if we couldn't stop the scout team, how could we stop our opponent's first-string offense?

Finally, we were sick and tired of all of it, and started laying some pretty good hits on him, and at times, we actually tackled Coach Ondrus. His competitive nature stepped in even further, and finally he made his way to the sideline and started trying on helmets. He selected one with a decent fit, strapped it on and went right back to calling plays like nothing happened. At that point, it was time to stay to the side, and wrap him up, or he was going to run us over.

At halftime of every one of our games, there were always plates full of orange slices spread out for us to eat. Not only did we hydrate ourselves with water, but also with the sweet sticky juice of oranges. I particularly loved the oranges and always tore into a plate full of them at every halftime. By the time I was done, there would be juice dripping all down my arms and hands. I stopped washing it off after the first couple of games because I found it acted like a natural stick-em when it dried. I felt it gave me a better chance of catching passes, intercepting passes and made it easier to hold onto the ball in general. It also leant a helping hand to holding onto jerseys when I made a tackle. I knew it wasn't the purpose of them being there, but I found it an added benefit.

During a game, one of the officials touched one of my hands for some reason or another and inquired about why I had such sticky hands. I told him that we have orange slices in the locker room at halftime and I forgot to wash my hands before I came back out. He looked at me kind of strangely, then seemed satisfied, and turned his attention back to the game.

Brian Allen would later inquire about my sticky hands, and that in turn, sent his mind running in the direction of figuring out a way to make his hands sticky too. Brian was pretty innovative and figured it out rather quickly. He went to one of the managers' boxes and pulled out a spray can of tough-skin. Tough-skin was an aerosol spray that would be sprayed on an ankle before it was wrapped so the under wrap would stick better. He then proceeded to spray his palms to create some very sticky mitts. It wouldn't last long, and after a while, it kind of wore off, but Brian could be seen spraying his hands a few times a game. I am sure Coach McCord wondered why we were using so much tough-skin. I preferred to continue using the oranges, if anyone asked, I always had the perfect excuse of why my hands were so sticky.

A few players on the team seemed to have unique ways of celebrating touchdowns, sacks, or other great plays.

Aaron Roth of course had his sack dance that consisted of him jumping into the air and waving his hands in front of him like he was trying to kill a hundred flies.

Mike Wilson would run off the field after a touchdown with his head tilted back looking straight into the sky with his arms raised.

Phil Girlie after a great tackle would make a fist and pump his arm.

Tim Boals would race off the field on his toes, doing chop steps with his arms out after a touchdown

Denny Martin would thrust one arm out in front and point at the goalline when a touchdown was scored.

John Finn would slam his arm pads to the ground like he was making a statement when we scored.

Rob Giesige would spread his legs and arms and take a hop step after one of his sacks.

There was one player our sophomore year that made things interesting during our Monday game film viewing. That player was Kevin Gerschutz. He would always be in the middle of the action, and I think Coach Ondrus received great joy in hearing his response to certain events that took place during the game.

Kevin was a good player and he never missed an opportunity to put a hit on a guy. He had a humorous side that made him instantly popular with anybody around him. He was just a fun guy to be around.

During one film session, Gerschutz was defending a pass when the ball hit him square in the face mask. Coach Ondrus asked, "Gerschutz, why didn't you intercept the ball, it was right there?" Kevin's response, "I was getting ready to put a hit on the guy and I didn't see the ball." Coach Ondrus then asked, "It hit you right in the freaking face mask, did you have your eyes closed?" Kevin responded, "I might have coach; it was going to be a REALLY big hit."

On another instance, Kevin was carrying the ball and he broke into the clear. There was one guy between him and the goalline, and instead of putting a move on the guy, he just ran right toward him and ran him over. The collision was good, and he indeed ran the guy over, but stumbled and fell after the collision, well short of the end zone.

Coach Ondrus was shaking his head the whole time we watched the play on film. We could tell he couldn't wait for Kevin's response.

Rob Giesige recalled this moment, "Coach Ondrus asked Kevin Gerschutz why he did not juke the last guy to score a touchdown. Kevin said, 'I figured I would just run him over coach. Did you hear that CRUNCH?'"[40]

This incident was told to me by Coach Norman Beck. During the middle of the 1986 campaign, Coach Beck had to check into the hospital to have his tonsils removed. Coach McCord and Coach Beck kind of worked it out so that he could go in on Monday and not miss the Friday night game.

This is what Coach Beck had to say. "I am lying there totally out of it, and not really aware of too much going on around me. I am trying to shake it all off, when Fat Boy (Chris Schlachter) and (Denny) Martin come walking into my room with a pizza. They were carrying on and messing around. Finally, they put the pizza right on my chest and started digging into it. I was so out of it that I was just laying there with my mouth wide open. They proceeded to pick the mushrooms off of the pizza and fling them at my wide open mouth like they were playing basketball. They had a lot of fun at my expense, but it was really nice that they showed up with a pizza in the first place."[41]

We all parked our cars in the corner of the high school parking lot closest to the locker room. Now, in those days, you didn't see any cars that were less than 10 years old. We had quite an array of jalopies. The ones I remember the most, were of course the ones I spent the most time in. I drove an old stick shift faded red Monza, Giesige had a nice red Nova, Schlachter and Martin drove brown Chevette's, Carnahan drove a brown Pinto. Okuly had probably the nicest car, but that was from all the work he put into it. He drove a brown Cutlass, the car probably had more clear coat on it than any car I have ever seen.

George Schaffer drove the most unique car, that being a big black old thing that looked like it carried caskets to the grave yard. It was a dandy and looked just like a Hurst out of an old movie and must have weighed three tons.

George Schaffer talked about his priceless ride. "I drove a 1968 Cadillac ambulance for awhile. It was just huge and I wasn't allowed to park it at my house or across the street from my house because it looked like a Hurst from a funeral home. It was seven feet wide and 25 feet long. The thing weighed 7200 pounds, and had a 485 engine in it. I left it at the school for awhile because I couldn't park it anywhere else. Finally, Coach McCord told me I had to move it. I ended up selling it, but I sure wish I could have kept it."[42]

My most memorable ride in any of the cars, and a lot of them in Carnahan's Pinto would be really hard to beat was a ride in Okuly's Cutlass. Okuly, Schlachter and I were all present when the fuel filter plugged up and the Cutlass just quit running. Oak went under the hood, figured out the problem, cleaned the filter, and we were back on the road. Now Jeff was furious, he wasn't saying a word. Next thing we knew, he floored it. "This car doesn't quit on me," he snarled. It was dark and extremely foggy; we could barely see the road. He accelerated to a 100 miles per hour. Schlachter looked at me, then looked at him and said, "Jeff, you might want to slow down. We could barely see the road when you were doing 55." Okuly was not one to back down when he was mad, he kept it floored. I slowly reached down and put my seat belt on for the first time in my life. We survived, but as a passenger in a car, I have never been so scared, before or after that.

SEPTEMBER 12, 1986

EDON BLUE BOMBERS
HOME
WEEK 3

A "W" in week three would take Coach McCord and the Blue and Gold to uncharted waters with the Blue Bombers of Edon in town. None of Coach McCord's other teams had ever started the season off 3-0, so we could take him someplace he had never been before.

The week of practice consisted of some running, a little more running and a lot more running. Coach McCord was not at all delighted with the turnovers, penalties and mental lapses against Fairview the week earlier. On Monday, he told every back on the team to grab a football, take it home and never let go of it. When we had the football, it was not to be handed over to an opposing team. When we all filed out of the locker room after the Monday practice, the coaches were there to make sure every back had a ball to take home with them, which I didn't mind one bit. I had slept many a night with a ball tucked in my arms when I was growing up. It was nice to have that leather ball back in my arms all night long. Each night, I felt like a kid again.

During the Edon week of practice, Coach McCord started a little thing where if we were guilty of committing a penalty, we would be staying after practice for some extra conditioning. We had started the year off at 2-0, but we could tell he was not happy with the way we had been playing the game. Mistakes were not to be made like the ones we were making, that's why we had practiced all of those long hours in the hot summer sun.

Edon had a big strong fullback by the name of Bob Siebenaler. He would probably be the most punishing runner we would face all year. Even though Edon was 0-2 on the year, we knew they had some talented players and we would not be taking them lightly.

The game against Edon was Parents' Night, a night when every player, manager and cheerleader would walk down the 50-yard line with their parents. I always enjoyed Parents' Night because it was the one game where I could talk to my parents right before the game started. While we were in line waiting our turn, my Dad would be joking around and my Mom would be completely serious. She knew how serious I was on game nights and she always put a game face on for Parents' Night.

Without my parents, there would have been no chance for me to play football. I knew that, and on Parents' Night, I always appreciated them and what they did for me even more. My Dad would always look over at the other team and say, "They look pretty big."

He would always then pick out the biggest guy on the opposing team and say, "See that number 77 (or whatever number their biggest guy was), he looks huge, do you think you guys can take them?"

I think he knew this always got me going because I would just say back to him, "Yeah Dad, it doesn't matter how big they are, it only matters if they can hit hard." He would then reply, "I don't know, they all look pretty big, and it sure looks like they can hit."

Steve Deitrick and Mike Wilson were captains for the game and Steve didn't waste any time stepping up and delivering. On the second play from scrimmage there was no fumble, instead, Steve raced 53 yards for a touchdown. Our other captain, Mike Wilson, had sprung him with his patented trap block. The kick failed and we were up 6-0.

Our defense held the Edon offense in check and we began to drive the ball towards another six points. Chris Schlachter was still sidelined by the ankle injury and Travis Lewis stepped in and delivered a score from a yard out. The kick was good and we had the lead, 13-0.

Siebenaler was a beast and we were doing our best to gang-tackle him. Edon was just beginning to move the ball when the ball came loose on a sweep play and Todd Hanna scooped it up from his safety position and returned it 40 yards down the sideline for a touchdown. When we watched the game film on Monday, we could see him drop the ball just as he crossed the goalline. Coach McCord's take on it during film day, "That was really close to being a fumble before you crossed the goalline. Don't be trying any of that fancy crap, just hold onto the ball and hand it to an official. ACT LIKE YOU HAVE BEEN THERE BEFORE!" I think Coach McCord was sick and tired of fumbles.

We were up 20-0 with the addition of the extra point. We were only into the game one quarter and had a 20-0 lead when Edon finally struck like lightning in the second quarter with a 53-yard pass from Chad Hug to Mike Krausch. I was getting sick and tired of watching our secondary give up touchdown passes. Siebenaler blasted the kick through the uprights to make the score 20-7.

With 41 seconds left in the half, I took the play in from the sideline, and it was one of my favorite plays, pro-left Purdue. I would be split wide to the left and run a simple fly pattern right straight down the field. Denny Martin hung it up perfectly and there wasn't anyone near me. I caught it and ran the remaining five yards into the end zone for a 38-yard touchdown. The point after was good and we went to the locker room with a commanding 27-7 lead.

In the locker room at halftime, I called a defensive back meeting. Giving up touchdown passes had to end, we knew our assignments. We had worked on finding the receivers and covering them when they were in our zone. We could not allow teams to continue scoring through the air on us. We all were in agreement. We had to ratchet up our level of play and get the job done.

After the halftime intermission, Edon was driving the ball when Todd Hanna came up from his safety position and went head-to-head with the big fullback Siebenaler. He did bring the big bruiser down, but when he got up, his head was lying to the side and he was trying to go to Edon's bench. He had been knocked completely goofy. I thought he put a nice hit on him and I was proud Todd was a defensive back. He went head-to-head with the big hard-nosed fullback and wasn't afraid.

> Rob Giesige remembered the hit. "Todd put a great hit on him and shortly after that, Siebenaler was on his hands and knees on the Edon sideline trying to shake out the cob webs. Unfortunately, Hanna got the worst of the hit and he came off the field with a jelly head after the hit."[43]

The only score in the second half was a dynamic punt return by Denny Martin. We had a punt return middle on and Denny raced forward and caught the short punt. With all of his momentum carrying him forward, he just sailed right through the defense like a rocket on his way to a 40-yard touchdown. But wait, Denny was down in the end zone and he wasn't getting up. An Edon defender had fallen on him in a last ditch effort to stop him from crossing the goalline. I think the season flashed before Coach McCord's eyes because after Denny made it to the sideline, he grabbed me and said, "You need to start taking some snaps and working at quarterback in practice."

Oh, now wait a minute here! I was number 21 now and I didn't have a quarterback number. Todd Hanna wore number 10 and was the back-up quarterback. Unfortunately, Hanna had been banged up and he would be unable to play offense for a couple of games with a leg injury. My little number switch apparently didn't matter as much as I hoped it would. I instantly sought out one Denny Martin. "How are you feeling," I asked. "I was just shaken up a little bit," he replied. I shot back, "That's good because you can't get hurt."

He started laughing because he knew I couldn't stand playing quarterback. "Maybe it's worse than I thought. Maybe I will be out for the year. Maybe you will have to fill in for me like you did our freshmen year."

Before I walked away, I delivered a stern message to him, "Just shut up, and don't get hurt. If you do, you better just suck it up and play because I am not playing quarterback."

It wasn't just the fact that I didn't like playing quarterback. Denny Martin was the perfect guy to run our offense. It would have been a disaster if he went down with an injury. He had already been a first-team all conference quarterback in 1985. I was sure he would end up being a first-team all-conference quarterback for a second time as well. Those kinds of guys you can't replace.

When the clock finally ran out, we had won the game, 34-7. Overall, the statistics from the game would have made you think it was much closer. Edon had 109 rushing yards, 72 came from Siebenaler. Ayersville had 172 yards on the ground, with Deitrick picking up 102 of them. Martin threw for 101 yards, while Edon passed for 117 yards.

Both teams turned the ball over four times, and Edon had 35 yards in penalties to our 30. Once gain we had turnover troubles, only one of them was a fumble, but that was one too many in Coach McCord's book. We did make history by improving to 3-0, which was something no other team in Ayersville football history had accomplished.

Steve Deitrick continued the great play by Coach McCord's appointed captains and led the defense with 11 stops. Phil Girlie responded to our halftime defensive back meeting with a great game. He had 10 tackles, caused a fumble and made a great pass interception. Scott Kolb had an impressive game with 10 tackles, one caused fumble and a QB sack. Mike Wilson, our other captain for the game, played a significant roll from his offensive guard position. He made some great blocks, including a great trap block to vault the 53-yard touchdown on the second play from scrimmage.

STATISTICS

	Edon	Ayersville
First Downs	8	9
Rushing Yards	109	172
Passing Yards	117	101
Total Offense	226	273
Passes Attempted	22	17
Passes Completed	6	7
Had Intercepted	3	3
Fumbles	3	3
Fumbles Lost	1	1
Yards Penalized	35	30

Edon	0	7	0	0-	-7
Ayersville	20	7	0	7-	-34

AHS- Deitrick 53-yard run (PAT kick failed)
AHS- Lewis 1-yard run (PAT Schlachter kick)
AHS- Hanna 40-yard fumble return (PAT Schlachter kick)
EHS- Krausch 52-yard pass from Hug (PAT Siebenaler kick)
AHS- Groll 38-yard pass from Martin (PAT Dearth kick)
AHS- Martin 40-yard punt return (PAT Dearth kick)

SEPTEMBER 19, 1986

ANTWERP ARCHERS
AWAY
WEEK 4

We returned to GMC action in the fourth week of the season at Antwerp. The Archers were having a nice season with a 2-1 record and we didn't want them to derail our season, so we prepared very diligently for them.

The year before, a lot of our backs were complaining that there had been some less than desirable activities going on when they were tackled and lying at the bottom of a pile. The grabbing, poking and other stuff wasn't something our team ever participated in. I was pretty keyed up for the game and couldn't wait for the action to begin.

In the first quarter there was a whole lot of punting going on and Jerry Carnahan was getting a workout. Our defense was playing great, but offensively, we just couldn't sustain a drive. Finally, our defense got us on the board in the second quarter when Todd Hanna picked up an Archer fumble and returned it nine yards for a touchdown. Todd Hanna was becoming a touchdown scoring machine from the defensive side of the ball with his second score in as many weeks. The Schlachter kick was good, giving us a 7-0 lead. Nothing much happened for the rest of the half. Our defense was controlling the game and our offense was anemic.

Jeff Okuly was apparently having a tough go of it against the Antwerp offensive tackle he was facing. He had a very clear recollection of it when I asked him to name one of the better tackles he faced.

"The Antwerp game, I couldn't do anything with that offensive tackle," said Okuly. "He wouldn't let me push him back, I couldn't get around him, and he just frustrated the crap out of me the whole game. I was so frustrated, that even after we won the game, I just sat by myself completely dejected. Finally, Coach Beef came over and kind of kicked me into gear. It was a real gut check for me. I vowed to work as hard as I could the rest of the season so that it would never happen again."[44]

We went to the half with the 7-0 lead, and received another butt-chewing because of our horrendous effort to move the ball down the field offensively. The coaches got after the line, then they got after the backs, then I think they went all the way down the line and got after the managers for bringing us too much water.

Nobody was free of the disgust with our offense. I think one of our bus drivers, who happened to be in the bus listening to the radio at the time, even slouched down in his seat so as not to attract the wrath of the coaches for transporting us sorry bunch of players to the game.

Chris Schlachter was starting to get over the ankle injury he suffered earlier in the year and his role in the offense expanded. In the third quarter, Chris plunged in from a yard out and then nailed the extra point to give us 14-0 lead.

After a defensive hold and punt, our offense was rolling again. Finn, Wilson, Briseno, Boals and Hanna started to blow the Archer defense off of the ball. Our line was coming alive.

We continued to march the ball down the field when we faced a fourth-and-one from the Antwerp 37. The play came in and was a combo left blast left. I, as the blocking back, would line up on the left side of our fullback alongside Steve Deitrick and then blast through the guard hole and take out the linebacker while the guard double teamed the defensive tackle.

I don't know why it happened or if it just happened, but I did something on the play that I had never done before or that I would ever do again. We ran the play, and Steve and I blasted the linebacker, pancaking him on his back. We both ended up right on top of him, while Schlachter rumbled for 10 yards and a first down through the wide-open gap we created.

The big Archer linebacker was on his back and my face mask was right against his and I blurted out, "Eat it!"

We then got up and started back to our huddle as Steve Deitrick asked me, "Where did that come from?" I replied, "I don't know, after we leveled him, it just sort of came out."

We both then looked back at the big Archer linebacker who was slowly getting to his feet and he mumbled, "Screw you." Steve and I both busted out laughing simultaneously.

A few plays later, Deitrick danced into the end zone from seven yards out, the kick was once again good and we were in control of the game, 21-0.

Our defense continued to be dominant and the Archers continued to punt. We got the ball back and controlled the clock by running the ball until the fourth quarter finally arrived. We continued our march down the field when Denny Martin scrambled to his left, and I slipped and fell on the slippery field, I got up and started running back towards him from the curl route I was running. He hit me with a perfect dart and I curled back around and into the end zone for a 14-yard touchdown. The extra point was good and we had the game well in hand, 28-0.

From there, the underclassmen took over until the final whistle blew and we escaped not only with a victory, but with our first shutout of the year.

> Marv Andrews talked about the line play during the game. "I made one of the linemen from Antwerp cry. He said he had never been hit so hard in his life."[45]

The offense finally started rolling and we churned out 201 yards via the run. Phil Girlie picked up nine tackles and Johnny Armes had a huge game with six tackles, a fumble recovery and two picks. Our secondary was playing much better, as we allowed just 22 passing yards in the game. Our record was 4-0 and we definitely controlled our own destiny.

STATISTICS

	Ayersville	Antwerp
First Downs	14	4
Rushing Yards	201	92
Passing Yards	85	22
Total Offense	286	114
Passes Attempted	16	13
Passes Completed	7	4
Had Intercepted	0	3
Fumbles	3	2
Fumbles Lost	1	2
Yards Penalized	50	65

Ayersville	0	7	14	7-	-28
Antwerp	0	0	0	0-	-0

Ayersville- Hanna 9-yard fumble return (PAT Schlachter kick)
Ayersville- Schlachter 1-yard run (PAT Schlachter kick)
Ayersville- Deitrick 7-yard run (PAT Schlachter kick)
Ayersville- Groll 14-yard pass from Martin (PAT Schlachter kick)

SEPTEMBER 26, 1986

HILLTOP CADETS
HOME
HOMECOMING
WEEK 5

The final Friday of September was our Homecoming contest against the winless Hilltop Cadets. The week of school was filled with all sorts of festivities, but as players, I don't think any of us cared or became distracted by all of this. We basically didn't get caught up in it and just wanted to play the football game.

Thankfully, the homecoming dance was changed to Saturday night instead of after the game like it had been in years before. By doing so it enabled us to totally concentrate on the game and keep the dance separate from Friday night. Homecoming was a fun time and most of us would be going to the dance Saturday, but it was nice to have it on a day when we could relax away from football.

Even though Hilltop came in with a 0-4 record, we had a good week of practice and knew we had to play hard to get the victory. I think Coach McCord was always scared of the teams that we may overlook and increased the intensity of practices, so we would be focused when the time came. Nothing would be worse than to have our season ruined by a team we took too lightly, and before we knew it, let the game slip away.

On Friday, just before school let out, there was a pep rally, and everyone always got excited about the opportunity to be dismissed from class to go have some fun in the gymnasium. The high point of the pep rally was when John Finn was blindfolded and senior manager Amy Shinabery nailed him in the face with a bunch of shaving cream. John was always a fun-loving guy and took all sorts of things in stride with a laugh. We all enjoyed it and laughed right along with him.

> According to Amy, this wasn't the only prank she played on him. "I remember Saran wrapping John Finn's "Turbo Pinto" on a couple of Thursday nights before game days. John typically ran late and I usually had to pick him up because he couldn't get the wrap off in time for school."[46]

The evening started off with a fine mist of rain, which was perfect football weather. It dampened the pre-game Homecoming festivities a bit because of the girls in their pretty dresses and perfectly styled hair.

> Muddy conditions always wreaked havoc with our managers. "We had to wash all of the uniforms," explained Amy (Shinabery) Snyder. "We would let them soak overnight/over the weekend, then scrub all the dirt, mud and grass stains off those freakin pants! This is not one of my best memories, but certainly not forgotten!"[47]

We won the toss and elected to receive. After the kickoff, on the first play from scrimmage, Steve Deitrick took the ball on a 32 trap and raced 48 yards untouched for a touchdown. Great blocking up front by John Finn, Mike Wilson, Jaime Briseno, Tim Boals, Jeff Okuly and Tolly Hanna paved the way for an easy score. Chris Schlachter came on for the extra point and split the uprights to give us the early 7-0 lead.

Our defense suppressed the Cadets on their first possession and forced a third-and-long. The following third-down play didn't have much significance in the game but it sure gave us something to laugh about on film day. The pass was incomplete and when Todd

Hanna came up from his safety spot to defend, he was met by a huge Hilltop tackle that had made his way down field. Todd had basically stopped, and had his head down looking at the ball from the errant pass, when the tackle just continued right into him, delivering a crushing blow and leveling Todd right on the spot. Todd Hanna bounced right back up, but was a little shaken up for the second week in a row. On film day, Coach McCord kept running it back and forth to a bunch of chuckles and exclamation's of, "Ohhhhhh, you got drilled!" Coach McCord was snickering himself and on the final viewing, offered these words of wisdom, "You might want to keep your head up and quit standing around, if not, those big boys coming down field might knock your block off."

Once we had the ball back, we traipsed right down the field to the one-yard line. Earlier in the week during practice, we put in a play where we would line up in combo right, and then shift Schlachter to the blocking back on the other side of Deitrick and the blocking back would then shift back to the vacated tailback position. By doing this at the line of scrimmage, we would be switching our power formation from right to left, hopefully causing the defense to be out of alignment. It also enabled the bigger Chris Schlachter to become the lead blocker. I received the carry and barely made it into the end zone for the touchdown.

After the play, Schlachter approached me and said, "What are you doing? Get right behind me and I will lead you right into the end zone." He was right, I hadn't exploded into the line after taking the handoff, and a lineman had slid in behind him and almost stopped me short of the goalline. The kick was good and we had the lead, 14-0.

Our defense stopped them once again and forced a punt. We again advanced the ball right down to the Hilltop five. The same combo right, go combo left, blast left play was called and that time I stayed right behind Schlachter and blasted into the end zone untouched. Our line was totally controlling the game, and after the kick, we were cruising with a 21-0 first-quarter edge.

The second quarter was filled with a five-yard scoring strike from Denny Martin to Shelby Dawson, and with the successful point after, we were on our way to victory with a 28-0 lead.

From there, it was a lot of time on the sideline for the starters and the younger kids got some varsity-game experience. With the substitutes in, we managed a 31-yard field goal off of the foot of Chris Schlachter to take us to half with a commanding 31-0 score. Not much happened in the locker room other than the coaches getting the scout team and backups ready to play most of the second half.

Back on the field, our defense stuffed the Cadet offense once again and forced a punt. Our offensive line and Steve Deitrick took command as Steve capped off another scoring drive with a one-yard jolt into the end zone for a 38-0 lead following the PAT.

With the game being well under control, we knew we wouldn't be sending our first-team defense back out there, and the younger players began flowing into the game. The prior two games had been under control by the fourth quarter, so it was going to be the third week in a row a lot of seniors would be spending time on the sideline. As a senior, those kinds of games were bittersweet. We were winning, but yet missing the chance to play. It was difficult to sit back and watch, but nothing could be done about it and the guys running the scout team in practice deserved to play.

The game pretty much became a stalemate with neither team moving the ball much, when in the fourth quarter, I was told to get in there and take some snaps at quarterback. I thought to myself, *you have to be kidding me, quarterback? No, no, no. I was wearing number 21 now. I changed jersey numbers just so I would never have to take another snap in my life. Martin wasn't even hurt, he was fine, and he would stay that way, or I would operate on him myself if I had to.*

I ran onto the field, it was for the team, and as much as I was complaining on the inside, I could not act like I was upset about it or it would set a bad example for the younger players. You played where and when the coaches wanted you to play and you kept your mouth shut.

I went out there and took a few snaps, mostly handing the ball off and carrying out my fakes. We were finally faced with a third-

and-long from the Hilltop 31-yard line. The play came in and it was an I-right, waggle right. It was Denny Martin's favorite play and I tried to do my best Denny Martin impersonation. I took off around the end, and when I couldn't find anyone wide open, I tucked the ball and ran down the sideline. A few cuts, and stop and start later, I was in the end zone for a 31-yard touchdown. The kick was good to make it 45-0.

The game finally came to an end without anymore scoring. I didn't have to take another snap at quarterback after the touchdown run, which made me very happy.

I had scored three touchdowns in the game and none of them really had anything to do with me. All of them were blocked well and anybody could have scored three times on those plays.

Deitrick, on the other hand, had a huge night running the ball. He had 180 yards on just 10 carries. If we would have given the ball to Steve more, he would have undoubtedly broke the single-game rushing record held by Jeff Bauman of 264 yards in 1981. I am sure Steve didn't care at all, he wasn't into awards or stats, he was just a good, hard-nosed football player, and he did his job all of the time with out wanting any credit. He was so humble in his approach to the game that there were times when we didn't realize just how good of a game he had just played.

As a team, we rushed for 359 yards while our defense held Hilltop to 51 total yards. Our line blocked extremely well the whole game and deserved most of the credit for the win. Scott Kolb and Jerry Carnahan played great on defense, allowing us to get our second-straight shutout. Scott had eight tackles, a QB sack and a blocked pass, while Jerry registered seven tackles.

Coach Maag referred to our dominating offensive line. "Those guys that year played so intelligently. They would come off of the field and start making blocking adjustments early in the first quarter before Coach McCord or Coach Beef had a chance to say anything to them. They played so well together. Everyone on the team, linemen and backs included, knew what they had to do to win and they just did it. Everything was done with a team first oriented approach"[48]

We were halfway through the regular season and our mark stood at 5-0. I couldn't believe how fast the season was moving along. Our senior year was half over and we only had five games left if we didn't make the playoffs. I wanted to make the playoffs more than anything. Making the playoffs became my dream, my drive and my desire.

STATISTICS

	Hilltop	Ayersville
First Downs	5	13
Rushing Yards	9	359
Passing Yards	42	56
Total Offense	51	415
Passes Attempted	15	8
Passes Completed	4	6
Had Intercepted	1	0
Fumbles	3	4
Fumbles Lost	1	0
Yards Penalized	35	35

Hilltop	0	0	0	0-	-0
Ayersville	21	10	7	7-	-45

AHS- Deitrick 48-yard run (PAT Schlachter kick)
AHS- Groll 1-yard run (PAT Schlachter kick)
AHS- Groll 5-yard run (PAT Schlachter kick)
AHS- Dawson 5-yard pass from Martin (PAT Schlachter kick)
AHS- Schlachter 31-yard field goal
AHS- Deitrick 1-yard run (PAT Schlachter kick)
AHS- Groll 31-yard run (PAT Schlachter kick)

OCTOBER 3, 1986

HICKSVILLE ACES
AWAY
WEEK 6

At 5-0, we would be put to the test against a very talented Hicksville team with a record of 4-1. Hicksville had been a surprise and they were playing some great football. The Aces' defense was yielding only 6.2 points per game and we had to play them on their field.

On Monday as we watched film, it seemed like the coaches were extremely tough on their grading system. They just gave off a vibe that we weren't playing up to our potential.

> Rob Giesige had this to say, "We received a grade on each play when we watched film. A zero or #1 was a crappy grade, #2 meant you did your assignment correctly, #3 was a great play, and #4 was an outstanding play. Phil Girlie ran the ball on a counter, spun about three or four times, and broke what seemed like 10 tackles. Coach Ondrus said, 'Only a three!'"[49]

The week of practice was brutal. Coach McCord and Coach Ondrus must have sensed something in our attitudes because they were tougher on us that week than they had ever been before. Hicksville was obviously a huge game and with our blowout win, maybe we would slack off against an improved Aces' team. To make matters worse, the Ayersville Pilots were rated 12th in the latest

Class-A UPI Coaches Poll. We were a marked team with a bull's eye stamped on us.

Coach McCord started a thing that week which was referred to as the 14-14-14. Coach decided that we would have to play 14 games to be State Champions. He told us we would do the 14-14-14 each week to remember this. We did 14 push-ups, 14 sit-ups and 14 squat thrusts before we started practice, and we continued to do them throughout the season.

He had us drop down in a push-up stance and went on to say, "To get to the state championship, we need to play 14 games. We will do 14 push-ups before we start practice on Thursdays." Then added, "Down." We would count them off as he went until we were at the magic number 14. He did this with sit-ups and squat thrusts as well. Did Coach McCord really believe we could make it to state?

In our Wednesday practice, when we did our defensive team up against the simulated Hicksville offense, I was ready to get some hitting in. Our first-team defense didn't get to play much in the Hilltop game and I was starting to get anxious to tackle somebody. Actually, in our last three games our defensive line had played so well, very few ball carriers even made it through the line for the linebackers and rotators to tackle. It wasn't much different against the scout team offense. Andrews, Okuly, Roth, Burket and Giesige were smothering everything.

If a ball carrier actually got past them, Deitrick and Wilson were there to deliver the hit. On the other side of me was Phil Girlie and he liked to tackle just as much as I did, so it was like a bunch of hungry piranhas whenever the ball was handed off. I was crowding the line of scrimmage as close as I could. Phil Girlie was crowding it as much as I was and Coach Ondrus finally had enough of our blatant disregard to alignment. "Groll and Girlie, fence buster, and while you're running, think about where the rotators are supposed to line up."

Phil and I took off to touch the north side fence, not at all thinking about where we were supposed to line up, but instead whining and complaining about the freaking lineman making all of the tackles and we hadn't really got to hit anybody in three weeks.

At the north side fence, we turned and made our way back to touch the south side fence, once there, we turned and finally made it back to where we were practicing. Coach Ondrus let us sit out a little bit before he finally inserted us back in. Phil and I positioned ourselves correctly and tried to make some plays. I was just flying up as soon as the ball was snapped and laying a shoulder into anybody close to the ball. A few times, Steve Deitrick had the ball carrier wrapped up, and I just ran into him, and tackled him while he tackled the ball carrier. Finally he had enough of it and said, "Groll, quit hitting me in the back, I am on defense with you." I said, "Sorry Deek, I haven't hit anybody in three weeks and it's getting old, maybe we can switch spots." He said, "I don't think so, I am not running a fence buster."

That was the end of it, but I was sure getting sick and tired of the linemen in front of us being so dominating, and not only taking on all of the blockers, but making all of the tackles too. I know Phil Girlie was getting tired of it too, because on the last play of defensive team up, Rob Giesige strung a sweep out and made the tackle just before Phil could get there. We both ran to offensive groups and exclaimed to each other, "Linemen suck."

This was a real testament to our linemen that year, in the years past, all of the down linemen would be making their moves and taking on the blockers, freeing up the linebackers and rotators to make the tackle on the ball carriers. Andrews, Okuly, Roth, Burket and Giesige were taking it a step further and not only taking on all of the blockers, they were making the tackles too. I can count the number of times one of our opponents' offensive linemen actually made it down field to block me on one hand and that was for the entire year. Now that's what you call getting the job done up front. In the trenches is where football games were won and lost and our guys up front controlled the pits.

The practice went on to offensive team up and the coaches continued to be displeased with us. We continued to mess around and just had fun playing football. I don't know if we really knew what was at stake for our season. We had a chance to go 10-0 and make it to the playoffs, yet here we were not practicing like we were going to be winners. It was time for a wake-up call.

That wake-up call came in a form none of us had ever seen out of Coach McCord in the four years we had played for him. He called us together after offensive team up. You could tell he was disgusted and searching for the right words to inspire us. He opened his mouth to speak, hesitated, then just walked off of the practice field and took the other coaches with him to the locker room. He left us all just standing there huddled up with a look of shock on our faces. We had all seen him plenty mad before, but never so mad he couldn't even talk to us, or for that matter, yell at us.

> I don't ever remember just walking off and letting a team out there. I do remember in the late 70's walking off the field, but the whole team went in with me. Bob Lamb was playing nose guard and nobody could block him, so I said let's just take it in," recalled Coach McCord.[50]

We stood there in complete silence for quite a while not knowing what to do. Finally the seniors took over. It was our team and we weren't going to go down as one of the most disappointing senior classes in history. The harsh reality had set in, we weren't taking football serious enough and words were spoken to that effect. We pretty much challenged each other to step it up, practice harder and go down as the best senior class in Ayersville history. We were going to do it, we were 5-0, we were going to go 10-0 and make the playoffs. We decided right then and there, this senior class was going to come together, and this team was going to win.

We finished talking and a few of the underclassmen started heading for the locker room. The 16 seniors stopped them in their tracks with, "We haven't done our conditioning yet."

We decided, with or without the coaches, we were going to put in the work. We assembled in our class lines and proceeded to run 40-yard sprints. After running our sprints, Rob Giesige, who just loved the conditioning part of practice said, "How about we finish up with a cross country?" The other 15 seniors exclaimed, "Oh, what the hell, why not?"

So, the whole team took off on the hated cross-country run. We finished up the run and made our way into the locker room as it was getting fairly dark out. We showered, dressed and went home. Nothing was ever said, or needed to be said by Coach McCord about the incident. He had given us the wake-up call and we answered it.

Steve Deitrick had this to say. "I remember the Hicksville practice week thing too now that you bring it up. If I recall, it had to do with us not 'gel'ing' to Coach's satisfaction as a true team. Do you remember how he used to lecture us with the non-interlaced fingers thing that finally he acknowledged as interlaced the closer we got to the Edgerton game? Honestly, looking back, I think they had it all orchestrated to force us seniors to step up and make the team ours at that point. You know to get us to pull together by getting us mad at them for dogging some of us incessantly and unnecessarily. It definitely paid off for us (and them) in spades now didn't it? It's these exact lessons that I was referring to earlier when I said we were taught not just about football, but more importantly, about how to succeed in life."[51]

Thursday night brought on some heavy rain to the area and the Hicksville field was a turned into a quagmire. The only thing better than a football game, was a football game in the mud. What a night it would be, I had never seen our team so fired up to play.

My brother Lynn, who was six-years-old at the time commented on the wet conditions. "Before the Hicksville game, the family went to the TSC (Tractor Supply Company) Store and all bought boots because it was so muddy. All I cared about though was Mom and Dad buying me a little toy tractor."[52]

We opened the game with the ball and drove right down the field to the Hicksville three. The next play called was a combo right, go combo left, blast left. I got right behind Chris Schlachter and Steve Deitrick and raced into the end zone for a three-yard touchdown. Jeff Okuly and Tolly Hanna had great blocks on the play and we were off to a fast start. The snap was muffed on the extra point, so our lead stood at 6-0.

"I thought their offensive line would be a determining factor," said Hicksville head coach Robinson, whose team allowed 10.6 yards per play in the drive. It did a super job. Their whole offense is very balanced. They have no one to key on. They have too much balance."[53]

Our defense played like a bunch of ravenous wolves after sitting out most of the second half in our previous game. There were 11 guys flying to the ball on every play. Jerry Carnahan then intercepted a Jeff Doeden pass and returned it seven yards to the Aces' 38-yard line.

From there, our offense marched back toward the end zone. This time, Travis Lewis shot around the right end and scored on a nine-yard run. Our kicking game was taking a beating from the field conditions and the kick was no good.

Our defense went back in and continued to swarm the Hicksville backfield. I had never seen a defense play like our defense was playing in the game. Our coverage on pass plays was right on, and when they ran the ball, four guys were there to make the tackle.

Our offensive line was playing just as impressively, once we got the ball back, we again marched the ball right down the Aces' throats. This time it was Steve Deitrick's turn to get the goalline carry and he bounced his way into the end zone for a two-yard touchdown. The kick again failed but we were ahead 18-0.

During that drive, Travis Lewis was tackled along the Aces' sideline. It was a fairly decent hit, but when he went down it was right in the middle of a huge mud puddle. The tackle caused a huge SPLASH and the Hicksville side went crazy. It happened about two more times in the game. Apparently, the Aces didn't realize Travis was picking up good yardage on those plays and we were winning the football game.

Marv Andrews remembered the rain we received that week. "Coach Beef had us doing monkey rolls in the mud all week. I remember the bus ride to the game. The ditches were overflowing and we didn't know if they were going to cancel the game or not. Then Travis Lewis kept getting tackled in the water along their sideline and they kept going crazy even though we were drilling them."⁵⁴

On the Aces' next possession, Johnny Armes picked off a pass and we had the ball back once again. Chris Schlachter was almost fully recovered from his ankle injury and he was starting to run the ball with the authority we knew he could. He took off down the left sideline, lowered his shoulder into a defender and kept on trucking. He then stiff armed another guy, proceeded to run over another guy, and then stumbled over him, ending his reign of terror down the sideline.

It was a really nice run and finally our bulldozing tailback was back. Schlachter later capped the drive with a three-yard burst into the end zone. We decided to go for two and Denny Martin ran the option to perfection, and pitched me the ball as the defensive end converged on him. I high stepped into the end zone as a defender dove at my feet and we had put another two points on the scoreboard. We were in total command of the game, 26-0.

At halftime, the only talk was to not let up. For the first time all year, I don't think there was anything the coaches could complain about. We scored on almost all of our possessions, our defense was playing phenomenal and we weren't making any mental mistakes. Our extra point team was horrendous, but with the field conditions, it was overlooked.

We went back out for the third quarter and continued to exert our will on the Aces. Four different backs had already scored and it was time for a fifth to get in the end zone. Denny Martin took a muffed snap and broken play around the right end for a 13-yard score. Schlachter finally nailed the extra point, making the score 33-0.

When our defense returned to the game, Johnny Armes picked off his second aerial and we had the ball back. We finally had to punt the ball away on offense, but three plays later, I intercepted a long pass down the middle to get our offense back on the rain-soaked field.

We had to punt the ball back to the hosts, however. Our basic offensive objective at that point was to just grind out the clock.

Our swarming defense continued and we forced a fourth-and-long. Denny Martin was back deep to receive the punt and the play was punt return right. He caught the punt in the air and took off for the sideline in front of our bench. Seven Hicksville Aces were chasing Denny, but he made it to the safety behind a perfectly formed wall along our sideline. Each defender was picked off one-by-one and Denny raced down the sideline for a 67-yard touchdown.

On film it was such a pretty sight, watching Denny race to the wall, and then each of our blockers picking off the Aces individually. There were some really great hits thrown on those blocks, but our jerseys were so muddy we couldn't tell who was who. Again the kick failed but we were up 39-0 and it was time for the underclassmen to take over.

I was called on to take a few snaps at quarterback. I then attempted my only pass attempt of the year. I dropped back and threw to Jerry Carnahan, because I knew he had excellent hands and would catch it if it was close to him. He indeed caught the ball for a 20-yard gain.

We closed in on the end zone and I handed off to Scott Kolb, the first option on the 37 option play we were running, and he went into the end zone for the two-yard touchdown. I don't even have to say it by now, the kick once again failed, but our lead ballooned to 45-0.

When the final seconds ticked off of the scoreboard, we had made a resounding statement to the rest of the teams in the area. The Ayersville Pilots were for real. We had rushed for 331 total yards against the highly-touted Hicksville defense and held them to a measly 50 yards rushing.

> "It was a very big win league-wise," explained Ayersville head coach Craig McCord. "We continue to control our own destiny. Every game is like a championship game, because with one loss, you're out of it."[55]

The most glaring stat of the night was zero passing yards for Hicksville. To make that stat even more impressive, we picked off four Hicksville passes.

Denny Martin scored two touchdowns while five other backs got into the end zone for a completely balanced attack. Steve Deitrick had eight tackles. Mike Wilson was credited with four tackles, a QB sack and a blocked pass, while Johnny Armes played blanket coverage and had two picks.

It was a big game and probably the turning point of our season. We had finally put a complete game together offensively and defensively. Chris Schlachter was finally almost 100 percent and we had no other injuries to worry about. If we could continue to stay free of injuries, and stay focused without making mistakes, we would definitely have a shot at the playoffs.

STATISTICS

	Ayersville	Hicksville
First Downs	20	4
Rushing Yards	331	50
Passing Yards	61	0
Total Offense	392	50
Passes Attempted	8	6
Passes Completed	5	0
Had Intercepted	0	4
Fumbles	3	0
Fumbles Lost	1	0
Yards Penalized	40	35

Ayersville	12	14	13	6-	-45
Hicksville	0	0	0	0-	-0

AHS- Groll 3-yard run (PAT run failed)
AHS- Lewis 9-yard run (PAT kick failed)
AHS- Deitrick 2-yard run (PAT kick failed)
AHS- Schlachter 3-yard run (PAT Groll run)
AHS- Martin 13-yard run (PAT Schlachter kick)
AHS- Martin 67-yard punt return (PAT kick failed)
AHS- Kolb 2-yard run (PAT kick failed)

OCTOBER 10, 1986

HOLGATE TIGERS
HOME
WEEK 7

Our neighbor to the east, just across the Defiance County-Henry County line, made the short stroll to our place for week 7. Despite a 0-6 mark, the Holgate Tigers were just two years removed from a deep run into the playoffs and could stick a feather in their cap by ruining our undefeated season.

Even though Holgate had yet to find the win column, Coach McCord knew they were a talented team and had been missing some key personnel due to injuries in the prior weeks. The Holgate Tigers would have nothing to lose and everything to gain. They had a speedy halfback in Ron Tobias, who was finally back from an injury and ready to make a substantial contribution. The Holgate record was not a very good indicator of how good our opponent would be that Friday night.

Coach McCord ended many of his talks that week with, "We can have no let downs this week." When the game started, I think we did have a let down. We were in a slobberknocker right out of the chutes and Holgate was not just going to lie down for us. We would have to earn the victory if we wanted it.

At this point in the season, the managers started getting more superstitious than the players according to Kim (McCord) Engel.

"We always borrowed the players' varsity jackets for the games. When we started winning, we didn't want to switch to another guys jacket, so we stuck with the one we wore the game before. It even spilled over into the way we wore our hair. We wore it the same way because we didn't want to mess anything up."[56]

In the first quarter, we were unable to move the ball much, but our defense played strong and possessions were exchanged with a couple of punts before we finally mounted a substantial drive. We finally had the ball deep in Holgate territory, but the Tiger defense was holding, and forced a fourth-and-goal from the three-yard line. Coach Ondrus and Coach McCord decided to go for it and called an I-left blast left reverse. I would be the ball carrier and receive the ball after the fake and would hopefully have a clear shot into the end zone around the right end.

I took the handoff and tried to get around the right end for the touchdown. The line had the play blocked well, but when I turned the corner, Holgate cornerback, Tim Schumm, had not gone for the fake and he was in perfect position to make the tackle. I had two choices, try to outrun him into the corner of the end zone or cut back towards the middle and dive into the end zone. He had a really good angle on me, so I decided to cut back towards the middle and hopefully catch him off guard and make it into the end zone.

I made my cut and Schumm stayed right with me. I would have to lower my shoulder, and upon impact, spin to the inside and hopefully slash right into the end zone. I lowered my shoulder, felt the impact, and was ready to spin, when the unexpected happened. Buffard Butler, the big strong Holgate defensive end came pursuing down the line and lowered his helmet into my ribcage, delivering a great hit and stopping me a yard short of the goalline. It was a good, clean hit and it knocked the wind out of me a little bit, but I hadn't made it into the end zone, so I was rather displeased with myself and not really focusing on the pain in my side. I got back to my feet right away because I never wanted to stay down very long and give the opponent the feeling that they got the best of me.

Holgate took over on downs at their own one, much to my dismay. I was disgusted with myself for not scoring, and was having trouble breathing, when Phil Girlie made his way onto the field for defense. He must have sensed something, because he asked, "Are you all right?" I said, "Yeah, I am fine, I am having trouble breathing, but if we would have scored, I would be feeling a whole lot better."

Holgate ran a couple of dive plays to gain some breathing room, which brought up third down. I was trying like crazy to stop them because I felt like I had let the team down by not getting into the end zone. After each play, it became harder and harder for me to catch my breath. I had never had the wind knocked out of me like that before, but I was sure I could shake it off without heading for the sideline.

Holgate faced a third-and-six and Coach McCord decided to blitz. Our left defensive end, Eric Burket, was going to be crashing hard to the inside and I would be blitzing outside and have the responsibility of containment. Containment meant that under no circumstance was I to allow anyone to run around me on the left end. I would have to keep everything to the inside of me, and protect the sideline, so that our pursuit could catch up and keep Holgate from getting outside of us for a long gain.

The play unfolded and I blitzed hard, the Holgate quarterback faked to our right, and then he handed the ball off to the speedy Ron Tobias on a miss-direction play heading around our left end. This was where I was responsible for containment. He had a step on me, but I just couldn't let him get outside where there would be nobody at all to tackle him. I strung it out as far as I could until I felt he was obviously going to get outside and turn the corner. I then dove for his feet, hoping to trip him up and prevent him from breaking containment and racing down the sideline. When I dove, he retreated just a little bit, and I landed hard on my left side, while feeling my hands touch nothing but the dewy grass sprouting from the field. Tobias was outside and poised to waltz down the sideline. I was wondering *if Ayersville had ever given up a touchdown run of 95 yards* as I heard the roar from the Holgate crowd as Tobias burst into the open field.

I could not breathe at all since I had fallen hard on my left side. I could not stay down because nothing was worse than somebody screwing up then faking an injury as an excuse. Besides, I never wanted to be down on the field of play, and hold up the game, while they sent somebody out to work on me. I had always vowed that no matter what, even if my leg was busted, I would crawl off of the field before I would let them carry me off.

I made it to my feet just in time to see Tobias flying down the sideline. Then I saw No. 63 angling to cut him off. Mike Wilson was in hot pursuit and was maybe going to have enough of an angle to catch Tobias right at midfield. Sure enough, Mike made the great play to save a Holgate touchdown.

Thank you Mike Wilson, I thought the touchdown saving tackle would definitely make it easier for me to breathe. I was wrong, it was only harder, and I could not get any oxygen into my lungs at all as I ran off of the field. It felt like I was in a giant bear hug from an actual grizzly bear, I just couldn't expand my chest at all.

Once I made it to the sideline, I basically collapsed. The coaches came over to find out what was wrong, and I could only mouth the words, "I can't breathe."

Sensing the worst, they called on the Emergency Medical Personnel and they went to work on me. Something apparently wasn't right because the next thing I knew, I was being put on a board and the ambulance was pulling up. *No, no, no, this can't be happening* I thought. The game was just rolling on and there I was, looking at a possible ambulance voyage.

A couple of tubes were taped to the inside of my nose, and rich oxygen flowed easily into my lungs. That was what I had been missing, I had no trouble breathing then. In fact, I didn't even have to try and breathe. The tubes supplying the oxygen just forced the air right into my lungs without me even trying. Maybe a little oxygen and I could be back on the field. It wasn't to be, the ambulance lights started flashing and I was headed to the emergency room. All I could think about was, *how embarrassing, I was being hauled off in the meat wagon!*

Thankfully, Mike Wilson had made the stop, but Holgate rolled the rest of the way down the field and finally scored on a Tobias

17-yard run. The extra point was good and Holgate was thinking of a possible upset.

Our offense went to work and Chris Schlachter was running the ball with authority. The Pilots marched down the field and Schlachter blasted in for the score from two yards out, but missed the kick, which kept Holgate in the lead, 7-6.

Phil Girlie moved over to the left rotator spot and Jerry Carnahan moved into Phil's spot on our defense in my absence, and they played extremely well. The defense gave up nothing and we received the ball back.

> "I remember you getting hurt and leaving the game in the meat wagon. Okuly and I started yelling in the defensive huddle to get revenge for Groll. I think it was the motivation we needed," expressed Rob Giesige.[57]

With just 16 seconds left before the half, Denny Martin lofted a pass down the far sideline and Phil Girlie ran under it and dashed into the end zone for a 36-yard touchdown. The kick was finally good and we had the lead, 13-7, heading into the break.

I don't know what went on at halftime because I was at the emergency room, but I am sure Coach McCord was not happy with a slight 13-7 lead over a team that hadn't won a game all year. We had come out really flat and didn't have the intensity we had the week earlier when we buried Hicksville. I am sure the talk at half centered on picking up the intensity. We had allowed an opponent to score for the first time in four games and our defense would be called on to tighten up and play the way it was capable of playing.

The third quarter consisted of punts and turnovers with neither team scoring. The fourth quarter started with the Pilots still clinging to the 13-7 lead. The fourth quarter was always ours. Holgate had been ready for us and a single score could possibly ruin our entire season. It was gut check time!

Phil Girlie stepped front and center, he once again hauled in a long pass from Denny Martin in almost the same exact place he did to end the first half. The pass covered 42 yards for another touchdown. The kick failed again to keep our lead at 19-7, but at least we had a little breathing room.

> Tolly Hanna remembered an incident in the game that I was sorry to have missed. "I had to go in and play some defensive end for Rob Giesige. He came running off of the field screaming and yelling and I thought for sure he suffered some horrible injury. He was lying on the ground flopping around like a fish and his head was rolling from side to side as he screamed in agony. I thought for sure he was done for the year. He was diagnosed with … a cramp in his leg!"[58]

Chris Schlachter persisted to run the ball well, and he and our offensive line sat us up at the three-yard line. From there, the line blew Holgate off of the ball and Travis Lewis covered the three yards for the touchdown. The kick was good and the score inflated to 26-7. The defense continued to play great and when the clock ticked down to zero, the Ayersville Pilots had improved to 7-0 on the year. It was a hard battle and Holgate had played us very tough.

Chris Schlachter ran for 166 yards on 18 carries and paced our offense. However, Phil Girlie and Denny Martin made the huge plays with the awesome touchdown bombs. Phil Girlie played his heart out in my absence, and for that, I was very grateful. I was around Phil more than anyone else during practices since we played the same positions on offense as well as defense. To have him make plays like that while I was nowhere around, was bittersweet. I would have loved to have been there to slap a high-five when he caught those long touchdown passes, but at the same time, knowing that he had everything under control when I was unable to be there with him, showed how much heart and character Phil Girlie possessed.

I have to mention Jerry Carnahan as well, he stepped in at defensive back and the defense didn't miss a beat. In fact, Jerry Carnahan and Phil Girlie led the defense with 10 and nine tackles apiece. When I couldn't be on the field, to realize those two guys filled in for me and played great games, it was a great feeling. Phil had the responsibility of taking more snaps at blocking back, and he not only accepted it, but answered the challenge with a great game.

Jerry was thrust right into our defense and he played like he had been playing there all year. Jerry had actually played quite a bit at the safety position when Todd Hanna was banged up, but it was his first taste of the rotator position.

While the game was being played in my absence, I arrived at the emergency room and was wheeled in for x-rays once all of the paperwork was filled out. My Mom and Dad had followed the ambulance and were there to support me. After a long wait, the emergency room doctor came in and used a stethoscope to listen to my lungs and heart. He then pulled the x-rays out and clipped them to a thing on the wall, which illuminated the picture of my rib cage. He took a pen and pointed to one of my ribs and said, "Do you see that black line across the third rib from the bottom? That rib is broken."

My parents nodded and I asked the question, "What can you do for it, and when can I play again?"

The doctor, who must have been very cautious, said, "Rest is the only thing you can do for it, and you can't play since its broken and not cracked, if you're hit there, it could possibly be pushed right into your left lung and it could become punctured."

What was this guy talking about, it was my senior year, we were on the verge of making the playoffs, and my season WAS NOT OVER. I blocked it from my mind and didn't for one second believe it could be true. We had come too far, our team was undefeated, and it couldn't be over in a blink of an eye.

For many players it does happen, one day they are on top of the world playing the game they love, and in the next moment, their season, or even possibly their career is over. Leaving the solemn feeling of, you didn't know what you had until it was gone.

How many times do we take things for granted? We complain, or wish that we could be doing anything but what we are doing at the present time. Then one day something changes and we no longer have the opportunity to do the thing we were always complaining about. Oh, how we throw a fit then. Take it away and it becomes so much more important.

This isn't just a football lesson; this lesson can be applied to many of our life instances. How many times did we complain about some old junk car we owned when we were younger? Only to carry on like it was a fabulous race car when we no longer owned it. This can be said for pets and most importantly people when they were no longer a part of our lives. Whenever something is taken from us in a quick and unexpected way, it leaves us with a new found appreciation for what we once had. Sometimes we all need to step back and be thankful for all of the blessings in our life. Especially those blessings we take for granted. Should we really ever complain about a job? Take that job away, and things get a whole lot worse. Should we complain about the people in our lives? Not really, when they are gone, the complaints are washed away by tears.

After the news of the broken rib, I had a new-found appreciation for football. In one instant, anything can be taken from us leaving us to long for the days of old.

I received a brace to wrap around my rib cage, and they gave me some pain killers at the emergency room. Then my parents drove me back to the school. The game was over, and of course, my first instinct was to watch the movement in the locker room to see if we had won the game. Everyone was in a joyous mood, so I knew before anyone told me that we had indeed won to take our record to 7-0. I heard all about the game and went to find Phil Girlie and congratulate him on catching the two long touchdown passes. He didn't seem to care about it, and just gave me a gentle hug and wanted to know when I would be back. That was Phil, totally unaware of any personal gain, and just wanting all of us to be back together. I didn't say when I would be back, I just said, "I will be back." Not wanting to think about the news I had received earlier.

My journey continued through the locker room and not one guy cared about anything other than when I would be back. I must have been pretty hopped up on pain killers because they all told me later on that I was laughing and joking around with all of them. Under the circumstances, I guess I was just glad to be back in the locker room with the guys I spent most of my time with. The pain killers must have been doing the trick because I don't remember when or how I got out of my uniform that night.

STATISTICS

	Holgate	Ayersville
First Downs	5	14
Rushing Yards	75	294
Passing Yards	36	100
Total Offense	111	394
Passes Attempted	7	10
Passes Completed	2	5
Had Intercepted	0	1
Fumbles	2	3
Fumbles lost	1	2
Yards Penalized	20	50

Holgate	0	7	0	0-	-7
Ayersville	0	13	0	13-	-26

HHS- Tobias 17-yard run (PAT Gustwiler kick)

AHS- Schlachter 2-yard run (PAT kick failed)

AHS- Girlie 36-yard pass from Martin (PAT Schlachter kick)

AHS- Girlie 42-yard pass from Martin (PAT kick failed)

AHS- Lewis 3-yard run (PAT Schlachter kick)

Front row, from left: Jonathan McCord, Missy McCord, Kristen Bell, Tolly Hanna, Johnny Armes, Andy Groll, Rob Giesige, Denny Martin, Phil Girlie, Steve Deitrick, Kim McCord. 2nd row: Pam Roth, Deb Mansfield, Mike Wilson, Marv Andrews, George Schaffer, Aaron Roth, Tim Boals, Jeff Okuly, John Finn, Eric Burket, Jamie Briseno, Amy Shinaberry. 3rd row: Joe Florence, Dave Mack, Travis Lewis, Todd Hanna, Corey Ankney, Jerry Carnahan, Shelby Dawson, John Phillips, Randy Richard, Jason Guilford, Ann Shinaberry. 4th row: Don Andrews, Dave Delano, Denny Kuhlman, Chris Schlachter, Tim Kuhlman, Ron Leatherman, Erik McCoy, Scott Kolb, Doug Brown. 5th row: Terry Schlosser, Tracy Dockery, Scott Tyrrell Tim Wagner, Steve Briseno, Denny Dearth, Chris Schaffer, Chris Stiltner, Mike Jones. 6th row: Jeff Askins, Eric Waldron, Robert Temple, Scott Seigman, Matt Reineke, Lonnie Gershutz, Jeremy Stark, Aaron Giesige, Sean DeWolfe. Back row: Don Hammersmith, Bill Ondrus, Craig McCord, Norman Beck, Jeff Maag. (Photo courtesy of The Crescent News)

The infamous stealth raft at the July 4, 1986 raft race, piloted by (from left to right) Steve Waldron, Jeff Okuly, the author and Jerry Carnahan. Notice the size and thickness of our awesome war-club paddles.

Our offensive line controlling the line of scrimmage as Denny Martin carries out the Triple Option while I trail as the third option.

LETS GO BLUE!!! #63 Mike Wilson, #12 Denny Martin, #60 John Finn, #75 Aaron Roth, #76 Jeff Okuly, #25 Steve Deitrick and #84 Tolly Hanna lead our charge onto the field. (Photo Courtesy of Steve Deitrick)

My football locker sits between #12 Denny Martin and #76 Jeff Okuly's lockers. Our treats are in the football with our number on it. Our lockers had something new on them for each game.

Parents' Night with my Dad (Gary) and Mom (Pat) was one of my favorite games of the year. This one is from my sophomore year in 1984. The year I got to play linebacker and wear the awesome hand wrist pads. The pair I have on were brand new and given to me by Coach McCord just before the game.

Waiting to take in the play, I am thinking "Throw it long", Coach Ondrus (middle) is thinking "Sweep right", and Coach McCord (right) really wants to run the "32 trap".

Homecoming against Hilltop in the rain. My younger brother Lynn was the ball carrier. Leading him and crown bearer Andrea Brink off the field is the 1985 Queen Chris Batt. From left: Sophomores Darren Karcher and Katie Walz, seniors Steve Deitrick and (hidden) Bobbi McIntosh, the author and Queen Lisa Seigman, juniors Joe Weber and Ami Wilson, freshmen Scott Seigman and Beth Weisenburger.

Our managers' artwork on the locker room chalkboard, notice the P.S. Check your lavatory note. They obviously wanted to make sure we noticed.

Steve Deitrick looking to blitz, Jaime Briseno at the nose guard position, #76 Jeff Okuly, #64 Eric Burket, #25 Steve Deitrick, behind Okuly is Mike Wilson and #21 Andy Groll. (Photo courtesy of Jeff Okuly)

I am getting ready to be loaded into the meat wagon while Kristen Bell and Jonathan McCord look on during the Holgate game. (How embarrassing!)

The final play of the regular season, the jubilation is evident in our victory over Edgerton to run our record to 10-0. #60 John Finn and an unidentified player have Coach McCord in the air. (Photo Courtesy of Jeff Okuly)

The scoreboard at Ohio Stadium welcomes the Ayersville Pilots, notice the temperature.

Jeff Okuly and the author, notice the black glove. He didn't know it, but I would try his gloves on sometimes when he wasn't around and act like a big lineman.

The seniors with Coach McCord: #84 Tolly Hanna, #12 Denny Martin, #22 Phil Girlie, #25 Steve Deitrick, #73 Marv Andrews, #56 Jaime Briseno, #77 George Schaffer, #63 Mike Wilson, #64 Erik Burket, #75 Aaron Roth, #61 Tim Boals, #87 Rob Giesige, #76 Jeff Okuly, #60 John Finn, #21 Andy Groll, #85 Johnny Armes and Coach Craig McCord (Photo courtesy of The Crescent News)

The author scoring the first touchdown in the Hicksville game as #76 Jeff Okuly and #84 Tolly Hanna block. This was the first drive of the game and look how dirty the uniforms were already. (Photo courtesy of The Crescent News)

Steve Deitrick leading Chris Schlachter on the sweep during the Tinora game. (Photo courtesy of The Crescent News)

#12 Denny Martin on the option during the Woodmore game. #84 Tolly Hanna is destroying his guy. (Photo courtesy of The Crescent News)

Rob Giesige standing beside a sign in his yard. The sign said it all. "We had only one game to go." Rob's Nova is parked behind him and to the left of the picture.

Chris Schlachter coming up short on his dive for the end zone during the Mogadore game. (Photo courtesy of The Crescent News)

The captains meeting before the state final against Newark Catholic. #25 Steve Deitrick, #21 Andy Groll, and the Green Wave captains #32 Bill Franks, #15 Jeremy Montgomery.

Steve Deitrick scoring his touchdown against Newark Catholic in the state finals on a 32 trap. (Photo courtesy of The Crescent News)

The author defending against the Newark Catholic tight end delay pass. #32 Bill Franks made the reception for the first touchdown of the game. I and many others felt this frustration all game long. (Photo courtesy of The Crescent News)

The welcome home after the state championship game. The gymnasium was packed.

My senior farewell speech at the banquet. Seated, left to right: Coach McCord, Coach Beck, Coach Maag, Statistician Larry Green; Standing, left to right: Denny Martin, Jeff Okuly (laughing because he must have suspected I would say something stupid), Mike Wilson, Steve Deitrick, John Finn, Phil Girlie, Johnny Armes, Jaime Briseno and George Schaffer.

Coach McCord shaking the author's hand during our stretching exercises. Coach made his rounds and greeted every player before each and every game.

The Ayersville Pilots football team walks off of the field for the last time in 1986 after the State Championship. I can be seen towards the end of the line being hugged by an unknown Newark Catholic Green Wave player.

Amy Shinabery plasters John Finn at the pep rally before homecoming. Looking on from left to right: Marv Andrews, Rob Giesige, Kerry Temple, Mike Wilson, Deb Mansfield, Tolly Hanna and Phil Girlie.

Denny Martin back to pass against the Fairview Apaches. #76 Jeff Okuly and #60 John Finn seal off the middle, while #25 Steve Deitrick blasts the defensive end. (Photo courtesy of The Crescent News)

The Pilot defense defends the pass against Edon: #87 Rob Giesige, #76 Jeff Okuly, #64 Eric Burket, #22 Phil Girlie, #63 Mike Wilson and #21 Andy Groll.

Inside the Ayersville locker room sits the TV we watched all of our game film on. Coach McCord's record player is on the left side of the TV with The Ohio State Marching Band record set to play. On top of the TV is the GMC trophy amongst other awards.

OCTOBER 17, 1986

WAYNE TRACE RAIDERS
AWAY
WEEK 8

Our next Friday night opponent was the Raiders of Wayne Trace and their 3-4 record. Wayne Trace had a decent team led by a hard-running halfback by the name of Chris Sanderson. On Monday, I didn't go to school and stayed home all day, even missing practice to try and rest. I didn't get out of a chair all day, even though I wanted to. I was already planning to somehow get back on the field.

> Apparently, I did get out of the chair according to my younger brother, Lynn. "I thought it was great the day you missed school with the broken rib. I don't remember exactly which one of us got antsy to throw the football around in the dining room, but one of us did. Maybe I kept bugging you to throw the nerf ball around and you finally relented to my demands or maybe you got tired of sitting in that chair."[59]

I knew my Mom wouldn't let me play unless a doctor cleared me to play, so I stayed immobile, hoping to miraculously recover in a day and have a doctor clear me for Friday night. I talked to my parents and convinced them that if they were listening to a doctor that told me I couldn't play, they would have to listen to a doctor if they said I could play, just the same.

At school on Tuesday, I started my campaign. I asked anyone that had ever been injured before if they knew a doctor that was fairly lenient on allowing you to participate in an activity even though you were hurt. A fellow senior that I played baseball with, and was our fourth partner in the raft race that summer, Steve Waldron, told me to go to a certain doctor in Napoleon, a town about 15 miles west of where I lived, and he would let me play if I wanted to.

My plan to get back on the field was starting to unfold. I stayed for practice after school and then went home. I asked my Mom if she would make me an appointment to see this doctor in Napoleon because everyone referred me to him, even the coaches. It wasn't exactly the truth, but I felt like I only had one shot at it. My parents would not take me to more than one doctor, so I had to choose wisely.

The appointment was made for Friday morning in the hopes that I could play Friday night. I was still pretty sore, and when I ran even a little bit, it was hard for me to expand my chest and catch my breath. I didn't suit up for practice all week and I really couldn't have done much anyway because of the difficulty I had in breathing.

On Friday morning, we saw the doctor in Napoleon. He looked over the x-ray, listened to my chest, had me take some deep breaths and poked around on me. I tried to act like I was in no pain at all. My senior year hung in the balance, this man would decide when and if I could play again. He finally spoke, "I think if you wrap it up good, and use some good padding, you can play next week." Before I heard anything else I was up and ready to get out of there before he changed his mind, or my Mom could ask any questions.

He didn't say I could play in the game that night, but I was still fairly sore and couldn't breathe very well, so I probably wouldn't be helping the team much by not being able to go all out. I would, however, only miss the one game, and I could be back for week nine. I considered it acceptable and was ready to be on the sideline with all of my teammates.

The bus ride to Wayne Trace was much different than the bus rides when I was playing. I didn't have any assignments to think about or any reason to get myself psyched up to play. While we were in pre-game warm-ups, it still hadn't sunk in that I wasn't going to be playing in a game for the first time since I was a freshman. I was in street clothes and delegated to holding Chris Schlachter's gloves when he was on the field. When he came off the field, I was there to hand him his gloves so he could keep his precious paws warm. I guess Chris figured that since I wasn't going to be playing, I needed a worthwhile task to perform.

I asked him, "Who usually holds your gloves for you?" He replied, "One of the underclassmen," to which I replied, "Then why can't they do it?"

"Because I want you to do it, and make sure you wear them when I am on the field so that they stay warm," countered Schlachter.

I thought, *well, wasn't this going to be a great night at Wayne Trace? I was going to be glove warmer for the Fat Boy!*

Actually, I am glad he did give me the task. I don't know if he meant for it to distract me some from not being able to play, but it did give me something to do other than cheer and offer advice.

It didn't hit me that I wasn't going to be playing until we were in the locker room before the game and the starters were announced. They jumped around and got ready to play while I just stood and watched. Finally, they knelt on the floor, and Coach McCord said, "Seniors", and the rest of the seniors knelt down on their backs. He looked at me and motioned for me to follow suit. I did, and that's when it hit me. We were a team and I couldn't be out there helping our team against the Raiders. The rest of the team fell into place and Coach McCord offered up the prayer as tears rolled down one senior's face.

We won the coin toss and elected to receive. Coach McCord wanted a score to set the tone for the game. We marched the ball right down the field, keeping the ball on the ground and controlling the clock. Just 11 plays later, Schlachter plunged into the end zone from three yards out and we were off to a great start. Schlachter booted the extra point and we took a quick 7-0 lead.

The defense forced a three-and-out and the ball was punted and rolled dead on our 32. Six plays later, our punt team came on after we failed to pick up a third-and-long. Wayne Trace then took over and couldn't get anything going and was forced to punt after running three plays.

Early in the second quarter, the Pilot offense went on cruise control and marched the ball to the Raider one. Denny Martin then ran a sneak for the touchdown to put the Pilots up 14-0 with the addition of the PAT. That was how the score would stay as the first half came to a close.

The third quarter opened with Schlachter booting a high kickoff that came down in the awaiting arms of Chris Sanderson. He took off up the middle and BOOM! He was rocked by Schlachter and Phil Girlie. Sanderson stayed down for a few minutes and finally made it to his feet. Our defense once again forced a punt and our offense took over at our own 14.

The Pilot offense then went on a drive of three minutes and 30 seconds that was capped off by a Denny Martin to Shelby Dawson 56-yard touchdown pass. Dawson weaved and dodged his way past a number of Raider defenders after he caught the short pass, and with the extra point, the score was 21-0.

In the fourth quarter, our defense finally gave in and allowed a 20-yard touchdown pass from Chris Etzler to Eric Lyons. Our offense continued to grind out the clock until time expired and the Ayersville Pilots improved their record to 8-0.

> George Schaffer recalled it as the game he got to play the entire night. "The Wayne Trace game was the only game where I played the whole time at offensive tackle. Boals had hurt his back in warm-ups and I played the whole game at right tackle. I kept asking Mike Wilson what I was supposed to do on each play. Mike finally got sick of me asking and told me to just go hit somebody."[60]

It was a great win for the No. 10-ranked Class-A team in the state of Ohio. We had moved up a bit in the rankings, but I can honestly say at the time, none of us cared. We just wanted to win football games.

Deitrick and Schlachter carried an even load with 78 and 76 yards apiece. Denny Martin was 7-for-11 and 120 yards passing.

Efficiency had become Denny Martin's trademark. When we needed it, he could throw the ball accurately and timely, resulting in some great drives out of our offense.

Defensively, Phil Girlie continued his extraordinary play and had 11 tackles, a QB sack and an interception. Todd Hanna tallied 11 tackles and Mike Wilson had five tackles, including a couple QB sacks.

I had performed my glove warming duty for the game, and when Chris Schlachter came off of the field for the last time, I threw the gloves at him and said, "Find somebody else to hold your gloves, because I am back, baby!" My mind was on next week and arch-rival Tinora.

After the game, I did eat one of the sandwiches that were always waiting on us. For the first time, it didn't taste any better than a normal sandwich. I was done being a spectator; I couldn't wait for practice to start on Monday.

STATISTICS

	Ayersville	Wayne Trace
First Downs	16	9
Rushing Yards	184	103
Passing Yards	120	78
Total Offense	304	181
Passes Attempted	11	13
Passes Completed	7	5
Had Intercepted	0	1
Fumbles	1	0
Fumbles Lost	0	0
Yards Penalized	72	25

Ayersville	7	7	7	0-	-21
Wayne Trace	0	0	0	7-	-7

AHS- Schlachter 3-yard run (PAT Schlachter kick)
AHS- Martin 1-yard run (PAT Schlachter kick)
AHS- Dawson 56-yard pass from Martin (PAT Schlachter kick)
WTHS - Lyons 20-yard pass from Etzler (PAT Glass kick)

OCTOBER 24, 1986

TINORA RAMS
AWAY
WEEK 9

A donnybrook with arch-rival Tinora was on our slate in the next to last regular season game of the 1986 campaign. Although the Tinora and Ayersville rivalry was relatively in its early stages back then on the gridiron, it was sort of like the Hatfields and McCoys going head-to-head on a strip of grass 120 yards long by 53 1/2 yards wide.

The close proximity of the two school districts also helped kindle the friendly hostility between the two schools. Also, a lot of Ayersville and Tinora people worked together at area businesses and most Ayersville people knew someone from Tinora, either friends or in some cases family. The same could be said for Tinora people, so there was always plenty of banter back and forth between Ram fans and Pilots fans during the week of the annual Ayersville-Tinora skirmish.

With the Maumee River separating the two schools districts, the game was and still is appropriately called "The River Bowl".

Coach McCord even took a page out of Ohio State legendary coach Woody Hayes' playbook when referring to the school on the north side of the Maumee River. Much like how Hayes referred to Ohio State's top rival Michigan as "That team up north" or "That state up north", McCord referred to Tinora as "That team across the river".

They hadn't beaten us in seven years, but for some reason, Coach McCord would always get really keyed up for the game. I don't know if something had happened in the past, but we could always tell something drove him extra hard in the week of the Tinora game.

I was back in pads for Monday's practice. After standing on the sideline for one game, I couldn't wait to be back on the field even if it was just for practice. I was still sore and when I became winded, it was kind of difficult to breathe, but I didn't care. I wasn't going to let anything keep me out of Friday night's game.

I had received clearance from the doctor to play, and my parents had gone along with the doctor's decision, but there was one very important person that would have the final decision on if, when, and how much I would play. That person was Coach Craig McCord. He had always been in control of those things and I had just taken it for granted.

His decision was: I would be allowed to play, but only on defense. I would be taken off of all special teams, and I would not be allowed to play any offense. On defense, I would be moved from my left side rotator position to the right side. When we went to a 5-3 defense, I wouldn't be playing linebacker, but instead middle safety. I would be wrapped and padded up, then put on a pair of rib pads, with another pair of hard plastic rib pads over all of it. His last rule was there would be absolutely no contact or hitting for me during practice.

I couldn't believe it; I thought everything would just go back to the way it was before I got hurt. His decision was more painful than the injury itself. No offense, granted before the season started I would have been over joyous, but we were in week nine. I wanted to play offense too. I was taken off of special teams; I really liked special teams, most of the time that's where we got to deliver the biggest hits. I would be moving to the right side. I had played 17-straight games at the left rotator position. I would be moving to completely foreign territory. Finally, no hitting in practice, I thought to myself, *Coach has to be completely off his rocker, does he really expect me to stand around all of the time and play paddy-cake. The doctor said I could play, let's just forget about all of this horse crap and pretend like the injury never happened.* I flashed back to the emergency room when I was told that I was done for the year. My thoughts changed in a hurry, *I guess I can live with his rules, after all, I will be back on the field on Friday night.*

My move to the right side made one player in particular very happy. Phil Girlie would be playing on the left side and he always wanted to be the left rotator. In practices, he used to line up over there sometimes just to see if it was any different. Since most of the teams we faced had a right-hand quarterback, it was always assumed most of the plays would be heading to the left side of our defense. I don't know the statistics on it, but I didn't really believe much of that. I figured if a team was fairly good, they would be mixing it up all over the place.

I was welcomed to the right side of our defense. Aaron Roth, Rob Giesige, Steve Deitrick and Todd Hanna all shook my hand and said, "Welcome to the right side, the place the real men reside."

I was used to Okuly and Burket on the other side blowing everything up in front of me. It would be interesting to see what the right side was capable of.

In the years past, there was always one game where we seemed to be taunted by our opponent. There was the message left in the locker room in 1984, the marshmallows in 1985, and we would be receiving the 1986 taunting in week nine.

In the newspaper that week, there was a small ad that showed a picture of a tombstone. These words accompanied the tombstone.

Pilots

R.I.P

Rams

Are Waiting!

I don't know who took out the advertisement in the newspaper, sent the marshmallows, or left the note in the locker room, but I just don't know why another team would taunt us like that. It would stay unknown, as not once did I ever hear any rumor that it was someone other than our opponent. My feelings were that it had to be an Ayersville alumnus that wanted to see if it did anything to fire us up. Our attitude about the advertisement in the newspaper was, "On Friday night we will see who is resting in peace, and it isn't going to be us."

Tinora had a record of 4-4 coming into the game. They had a vaunted defense that was only allowing eight points per Friday evening and there was some hype of how they had nothing to lose and how it would make their season if they could destroy our perfect record. If they could beat us, it would take the limelight off of a week 10 showdown between two unbeaten teams with Edgerton scheduled to visit our place in the 1986 regular season finale.

Edgerton was surely going to win their week-nine game, setting up a GMC championship and playoff opportunity for the winner of our game against them in week 10. We were not looking past the Rams, but the Rams were looking at the possibility of beating us, and spoiling a much-hyped week 10 showdown between two unbeatens.

Our Pilot team was ready to show the Rams our defense, which was giving up just 5.63 points per game and an offense averaging 30.1 points per outing. We had won 17 straight games without a loss, dating back to week two of the 1985 season. The Ayersville Pilots were still the No. 10 ranked Class-A school in Ohio and we would be crossing the Domersville/281 Bridge over the Maumee River for our yearly fracas with the Rams of Tinora.

On Friday night, the buses loaded up and we took off across the river for the short 10 minute jaunt to Tinora High School. Steve Deitrick boarded the bus with a boom box and sat up front. I thought this was odd because under no circumstances would there be any music allowed on our bus. There was actually never a sound on our bus rides other than the high pitched whining of the transmission and the other sounds the bus made. On the way to away games, it was mesmerizing to just hear the sounds of the bus and nothing else. That is a memory that has always stuck with me, the sound of the bus and nothing else as we traveled to an away game. I don't think there is a sound that could compare with it. The sound of a football game waiting at the end of our journey, the bus transmission sound was priceless.

As soon as we crossed to the north side of the Maumee River (Ram Land as it's called), Coach McCord gave Steve a nod. Apparently, Steve had requested a little surprise for all of us. He then pressed the play button of his boom box and, "We Will Rock You", followed by, "We Are the Champions" by Queen blasted from the speakers. As the songs played, we all sat just listening to the words and feeling the beat. When we arrived at Tinora, our bus contained more serious and down-to-business faces than you would see at a World Summit Meeting.

After our inspiring bus ride, courtesy of Steve Deitrick, I was very glad I wasn't sitting out of the game. If I had been, I would have stolen somebody else's equipment, there was just no way I could have stayed out of a game when the stage had been set so beautifully.

> I asked Steve if he had this set up or he just went and did it on his own. "The bus event I only vaguely remember, so I can't tell you whether or not I got permission or figured that forgiveness would be easier to get than approval!"[61]

I was ready for the game, but with all of the padding I was forced to wear, I felt like I was wearing a spare tire around my rib cage. At least I was playing, so I couldn't complain. Halfway through the first quarter the Rams struck first and looked to be on their way to an upset victory. Steve Buttermore, the Tinora quarterback, scrambled on a pass play and covered the eight yards necessary for a touchdown with his feet. The extra point was good and Tinora led 7-0. The Ram defense was indeed good, forcing us to punt on our first few possessions.

Midway through the second quarter, we finally put together a nice drive and had the ball at the Tinora one. Chris Schlachter blasted into the end zone on the next play, and with his extra point, we tied the game at 7-7.

That's how the score stayed heading into the half. At halftime, the coaches were not pleased with our offense at all. We seemed to move the ball, but our drives continued to stall. We had to play harder in the second 24 minutes of action.

Denny Martin was having a difficult time throwing the ball, and hadn't completed a pass the entire game when he finally connected with Shelby Dawson on a short crossing pattern. Shelby caught the ball and sped away from the defenders for an 18-yard touchdown. The extra point was good and we were finally out in front, 14-7.

Our defense continued to quell the Ram offense, but the Ram defense continued to halt our charge for the end zone.

It was midway through the fourth quarter when Tinora began its journey to tie the game. Jaime Briseno was inserted for Marv Andrews at nose guard to give us more of a pass rush. I am sure the Tinora center was battered from having to take on the bruising 210-pound Marv Andrews the whole game, and with the quicker and fresher Jaime Briseno, he had his hands full.

Jaime became a one-man wrecking crew. He sacked Buttermore on second down, on third down and yep, you guessed it, again on fourth down for a total loss of 18 yards. I can remember being in pass coverage and thinking, *I wish Buttermore would throw the ball out here so we could pick it off,* but Briseno was getting to him pronto. Jaime Briseno made three outstanding plays and didn't waste any time doing it. He made those fantastic plays one right after another.

> McCord was pleased with Briseno's heads-up playing, as the senior stepped in at the nose guard position. "He (Briseno) rose to the occasion and did a fantastic job," praised McCord.[62]

Our offense gave us some insurance and put the game away when Chris Schlachter flipped into the end zone from four yards out with 19 seconds remaining. Schlachter missed the kick, but we would hold on for a 20-7 victory. The Ayersville Pilots were 9-0 and would face the 9-0 Edgerton Bulldogs in week 10 with the conference championship and a playoff berth on the line.

> "It was our inability to stop the run on crucial plays that was the key to the game. They had a successful rushing game the second half, but they earned every yard they got," said Tinora head coach John Graher.[63]

Chris Schlachter continued his great ground performances as he bulldozed his way for 175 yards on 23 carries. The yards could be contributed due to the great blocking up front by John Finn, Tim Boals, George Schaffer, Mike Wilson, Jaime Briseno, Aaron Roth, Jeff Okuly, Tolly Hanna and Shelby Dawson. Steve Deitrick, playing his unselfish role, had gone from primary ball carrier to lead blocker on Coach Ondrus' new favorite play, the sweep. I don't think Ayersville ever had a better blocking fullback than Steve Deitrick. Steve was so valuable because he could do any of the three things you ask a fullback to do with great success. He could run the ball, he could block and he was a great receiver out of the backfield.

Denny Martin only completed one pass, but it was the big one to Shelby Dawson. Our defense played fairly well, only allowing the one score in the first half. Jaime Briseno had a fantastic game, recording eight tackles and a quartet of QB sacks. Rob Giesige recorded five tackles, a QB sack and caused a fumble. Jeff Okuly rounded out our defensive line dominance with eight tackles and a QB sack.

I did manage to sneak into the game on offense for a few plays in the second half, which is hard to believe, considering I used to hide out on the sidelines when we had the ball the year before. I wanted to be a part of everything, and if there was anything I could do on the field to benefit the team, I was ready to play anywhere and at anytime.

I played through the game without any complications at all, my side was feeling better and breathing had become less and less strenuous. I was hoping to be fully recovered and back a full strength for our showdown with Edgerton. I did not want to be out there sissy-footing around against the tough kids from Edgerton.

Playing on the right side took some getting used to, but after a few plays it wasn't that much different than the left side. Playing behind Roth, Giesige and Deitrick was much the same as playing behind Okuly, Burket and Wilson. I did feel like it was easier to get a read on the play from the right side. I think it was because Deitrick played a little lower than Wilson, enabling me to see the snap and line movement better. Roth and Okuly at the tackles were pretty much mirror images of each other, while Burket was more active making an inside move. I think Giesige was very good at keeping containment to the outside.

Playing to my side and behind me was Todd Hanna; I think he was a little better at run support, while Johnny Armes, on the left side, was a little better at pass coverage. All in all, there wasn't a whole lot of difference between our left and right sides of our defense.

STATISTICS

	Ayersville	Tinora
First Downs	13	9
Rushing Yards	225	50
Passing Yards	18	104
Total Offense	243	154
Passes Attempted	8	29
Passes Completed	1	10
Had Intercepted	1	0
Fumbles	3	4
Fumbles Lost	0	2
Yards Penalized	35	18

Ayersville	0	7	7	6-	-20
Tinora	7	0	0	0-	-7

THS- Buttermore 8-yard run (PAT Higbea kick

AHS- Schlachter 1-yard run (PAT Schlachter kick)

AHS-Dawson 18-yard pass from Martin (PAT Schlachter kick)

AHS- Schlachter 4-yard run (PAT kick failed)

OCTOBER 31, 1986

EDGERTON BULLDOGS
HOME
WEEK 10

The long-awaited titanic encounter between GMC titans had finally arrived.

Week 10 was as good as it could get and it was for all the marbles. The victor would end the regular season with a spotless regular season record, an outright Green Meadows Conference Championship, and most importantly, a berth in the Division V playoffs. On the other hand, the loser would be ending its season in just about the most agonizing way possible.

At the beginning of the year, the first goal Coach McCord gave us was to win the Green Meadows Conference. We had done it the year before and I didn't care much about that part. I wanted the playoffs. Our final regular season game would pave the way for the playoffs if we could just beat the Edgerton Bulldogs.

But, what about my family's annual pheasant hunting trip to South Dakota? My parents didn't even plan one for 1986. If we lost and didn't make the playoffs, we would not be going anyway. I don't know what they based the decision on that year, maybe they hoped all along that we would make the playoffs and they didn't want to miss them either.

To say it was the biggest game us seniors had ever faced in our career would be an understatement. Two undefeated teams, meeting in the last week of the season for a conference championship and playoff berth was the perfect match-up. Everything in the papers had pointed to the match-up from the fifth week on. The media finally had the match-up and the buzz around the game was astonishing. Ayersville with their solid play and stingy defense, Edgerton with their stable of backs, wide-open running attack, and overall talented team, provided the fuel for the much-talked about contest. Edgerton returned 18 of 22 starters from the 1985 team we beat in a hard-hitting contest. The papers all gave the edge to Edgerton, the Bulldogs would just be too explosive for us to handle.

Watching them on film, all of the hype was believable. They had four backs that could carry the ball.

> "I think probably their (Edgerton) backs are a tad bit faster than ours," noted McCord. "Edgerton has got a wealth of backs. Most of their backfield has been to the state relays (In track)."[64]

#31 Joe Radabaugh (5-11, 170, senior) had been in their backfield since his freshman year in 1983. He was a strong runner and had the speed to get outside and go the distance. He had accumulated 757 rushing yards.

#32 Dave Weber (5-11, 160, junior) could possibly be the fastest guy we faced all year. Once he turned the corner, I doubt we had anybody that could catch him. He was the Bulldogs' leading ground-gainer with 818 yards.

#45 Jamie Herman (5-10, 165, senior) ran the ball very hard and stayed low on his carries. He had picked up 288 yards on the ground.

#40 Jeff Davis (6-0, 190, junior) the biggest of the Edgerton backs, and was a physical bruising runner. Davis had picked up 254 yards rushing and was a valuable receiver out of the backfield.

The Edgerton line was experienced and played well together. The center was Marc Traxler (5-9, 150); Guards: junior Randy Nihart (5-10, 155) and senior Ron Krill (6-2, 200); Tackles: junior Ray Leppelmeier (6-0, 170) and senior Butch Goebel (6-2, 210); Ends:

senior Dave Maugel (6-2, 200) and senior Mitch Malone (6-1, 175) rounded out the Edgerton line.

The quarterback was junior Tom Flegal (6-0, 150), who had completed passes for a total of 512 yards.

Edgerton was coached by Scott Thompson, who had turned the Edgerton Bulldog football program into one of the best in the area year in and year out.

Defensively, the Bulldogs played many of their guys both ways. The ends were Maugel and Nihart; the tackles were Goebel and Leppelmeier; nose guard was Herman; linebackers were Davis and Radabaugh; the defensive backs were Weber, Traxler, Malone and Flegal.[65]

Edgerton did not have a lot of depth, but with all of their talent, they didn't need much more than their starters. In practice that week, we worked on controlling the clock and grinding the game out so that we could use our depth to tire them out. We could not give up the big play and if our offense could keep their offense off of the field, it would be a great advantage for us, because their offensive guys would be out there playing defense as well as offense and hope-fully wear down.

We had a great week of practice leading into the Edgerton game. Everyone was focused and knew what was at stake. For the 16 seniors, it could be our last week of practice if we didn't come out victorious on Friday night. I was cleared to play offense again and I also returned to the kickoff team and the punt return team. The other special teams I would not be a part of anymore.

Coach McCord had also obtained a really nice flak-jacket rib protector that I would be wearing, instead of all of the bulky padding I wore the week before. I didn't have any pain anymore and my breathing was back to normal, so I was set to go as if the rib injury had never occurred.

The last week of the regular season was still conducted as if it would be our last. Coach McCord always had some special activities lined up for the seniors in their final week of practice. On Wednesday, at the end of practice, we conducted senior-hit day. Senior-hit day was an opportunity for all of the seniors to select an underclassman and perform a form tackle on them from about five yards away. The underclassman would have to stand motionless with his arm closest to the tackler raised and take the big hit from the senior. It was a riotous event and everyone cheered and laughed as the big hits were delivered. Nobody ever got hurt and it was almost an honor to be selected and tackled by a senior on their final week.

During the Wednesday practice, I fulfilled one of my life long dreams. I knew better than to try it during a game, so a brief moment in practice would have to suffice.

I somehow talked Jeff Okuly into letting me wear his big black gloves for a portion of our defensive team-up. I remember that he was very concerned about having to run a fence buster if we got caught, but I wasn't going to take no for an answer. He finally relented when I told him that he had to listen to me because I was a senior. He of course was a senior too, so he looked at me like I was a complete idiot.

He slowly removed the black gloves, shaking his head the whole time. I strapped those giant black gloves on and felt like the baddest of the bad. I don't think I even made any tackles with them on, but I felt like a WRECKING BALL running across the field with them flapping in the wind.

I was prepared to run a fence buster if I got caught, but nothing was said. Either the gloves were not noticed on my hands, or Coach McCord and Coach Ondrus let it slide, because they never said a word about it. Besides, I was more scared of what Okuly would do to me if he had to run a fence buster for handing them over to me.

There was another ceremony conducted on Thursday right before practice started. The ceremony was of the secret nature, and during the ceremony we all took a vow of secrecy to never share what it consisted of. I took that vow of secrecy, so I will not be allowed to share the details of the ceremony. It involved a selected junior wearing a big black top hat as he read from the sheets of paper given to him by Coach McCord. The seniors huddled closely on the football field while the other team members gathered around. The ceremony was conducted in complete silence, except for the junior running the meeting. There was a lot of laughter suppressed, but it was a very serious ceremony and every senior felt the finality of their high school football careers coming to an end. Once the ceremony was over, we were off to practice for possibly the very last time.

> I asked Coach McCord about the ceremony. "The ceremony was a secret. You don't reveal it do you? The ceremony was first done my senior year in high school. I then brought the tradition with me to Ayersville. Believe it or not, I still have the black top hat somewhere around the house."[66]

During school on Friday, we were already in game mode. Just watching my teammates in the hallways and during lunch, I could tell we were ready to play. Everyone was silent all afternoon and even while we got taped after school, the talking was at a minimum.

On game night, we all funneled into the locker room. Once we were dressed for the game, Coach McCord brought in a cassette tape and stuck it into the tape player. The tape proceeded to play, and one by one, all of the seniors' parents took their turn wishing us good luck and offering words of encouragement for the game. All of the parents gave excellent speeches; it was an emotional and moving experience. Tim Boals' Dad finished his speech in reference to the words I spoke in 1985 to Coach Ondrus when I wanted to carry the ball on the goalline.

He modified it to, **"WE WILL NOT BE DENIED."**

Hearing those words again, definitely inspired me. My Dad made reference to the trees I tried to tackle when I was a young boy, "Tonight imagine Radabaugh and Weber are the trees, and then they will be looking at the stars." I doubt anybody else understood it, but the message was loud and clear to me.

I cannot explain the feeling when we ran out onto the field for our stretching exercises that Friday night. It was a cool night and the air felt fresh and brisk. Everyone was ready to play. After we lined up and started our progressively faster clapping routine, the screaming and yelling was just out of control. I had never seen anything like it, everyone was so jacked up and ready to play I was hoping we didn't burn ourselves out before the game. I didn't want it to end, so

I waited a very long time before finally calling out "Pilot Jacks." We then proceeded to yell out the most emphatic Pilot Jacks in school history.

The captains for the biggest game in Ayersville football history were our standout tackles, Aaron Roth and Jeff Okuly. They made their way to the locker room after the coin toss and announced that we would be on defense first. Coach McCord's philosophy was to shut them down on their initial possession and send a statement that our defense was ready for them.

As we made our way to the field for the final game, we would play on our own field, win or lose; I looked around, and saw people everywhere. Both teams were undefeated and people had come from miles around to see the match-up everyone had anticipated all year long. The stands were full on both sides, the fence around the field was stacked two deep with people and they were still streaming in through the gate.

Halfway to the field, we heard what sounded like a giant semi blowing its air horn from the Edgerton side. Somehow they had an air horn rigged up, and its resounding roar echoed through the cool autumn night air. As cool as it sounded, and I don't think I ever heard a better noise maker at a game in my life, I did not want to be hearing from it much on that night. Surely that thing would blow like crazy when they scored a touchdown.

> After the game, I begged my Dad to come up with something comparable. "I couldn't get anything like that, so I obtained a fire siren from a volunteer fireman that I worked with," explained my father. "That thing was loud and really high pitched when I wound it up. I don't think many of the fans in the stands liked that high-pitch wailing."[67]

Once we were at the gate leading to the field, we stopped and stared in awe of the tunnel forming on the field for us to run through. It ran the entire length of the field and people were huddled so closely together to fit in that it actually appeared to be a real tunnel. We had to run about a 140 yards to get to the end of it and I remember thinking, *holy cow, we are all going to be so worn out from all of this pre-game activity, we will be sucking air before we can even kick off.*

Since it was the seniors' last game on our field, one-by-one they were announced and Coach McCord slapped them on their back and sent them through the tunnel. The rest of the team followed and finally we were ready to get the game under way. As much as I didn't want the night to end, I was ready to play some football.

Chris Schlachter boomed the kickoff, Joe Radabaugh received, and tried to get to the Edgerton sideline but before he could get there, Schlachter made the tackle at the Edgerton 25.

Our defense came on and anticipated the run. Radabaugh took the ball off tackle on the right side and Jeff Okuly just blew the play up for no gain. There was a penalty on the play, however, and the Bulldogs would face a first-and-15 from their 20-yard line. The Bulldogs ran the same exact play and once again Okuly made the tackle, but Radabaugh earned four yards. Edgerton tried the other side of the line with Jamie Herman carrying the ball off tackle left and he gained 10 yards before Phil Girlie and I could bring him down. On third-and-one, the handoff was on the left side to Jeff Davis, and Rob Giesige made a strong inside move from his defensive end position to make the tackle after a two-yard gain.

With a new set of downs, Radabaugh took the pitch on a sweep right and Eric Burket was all over the play, he was able to string it out, and cream Radabaugh for a five-yard loss. It was an absolutely perfect play by Eric from his defensive end position. Radabaugh again carried on second down, the play was a dive right. Phil Girlie came up from his rotator spot and put a big hit on him after a five-yard gain. Edgerton ran a trap left to Herman, and Steve Deitrick blasted him from his linebacker position after he gained one yard. Our defense had made the statement we hoped for. Eric Burket's play on the sweep emphatically sent the message we would be waiting.

Edgerton had to punt on fourth-and-nine following a strong first series from our defense. Davis kicked the ball away and Denny Martin caught the punt and raced to our sideline for a punt return right. He got to the corner and flew down the sideline for 33 yards before he was knocked out of bounds at the Edgerton 31-yard line.

The great return gave us excellent field position and our offense took the field.

Coach Ondrus opened the game with a blast left. Schlachter carried for six yards before he was brought down. Ondrus then turned to his new favorite play. Schlachter took the pitch on a sweep right, and cut it up as Shelby Dawson put a nice block on the defensive end. Tim Boals performed an excellent bear crawl block on the tackle to seal him off and the hole was there. Steve Deitrick led Chris into the hole and cleared the way for a 25-yard gallop into the end zone. The Pilots had drawn first blood. "The Ayersville Touchdown Bell" rang as the extra point sailed through the uprights, putting us ahead 7-0 with 7:09 left in the first quarter.

Schlachter kicked off, and Radabaugh received and returned the ball out to the Bulldog 26 before he was dropped by Jerry Carnahan. Play was halted as an Edgerton player was down on the field. Rob Giesige had sprinted down the field and blasted a blocker, who had to be attended to for several minutes. Giesige was great at delivering hits on the kickoff team and blasting into the blockers.

Edgerton opened their second series by running Radabaugh off tackle right and I made the tackle seven yards downfield. On second down, Davis carried up the middle on a trap and Deitrick made the stop after a two-yard gain. Radabaugh then carried on a power right and Burket crashed down hard on an inside move and made the tackle for a very short gain. The officials brought in the chains and Edgerton was short of the first down by just an inch. Big play time, it brought up fourth-and-inches. Edgerton hadn't thrown a pass yet and they definitely thought they could pick up the inch on the ground. After all, they had a backfield proclaimed the best in the area.

Without hesitation, they went for it. The handoff was to the big fullback Jeff Davis on the left side. Aaron Roth stayed low and stuffed the play at the line of scrimmage, the rest of us swarmed in like bees, but after the ball was spotted, the ball was just across the Edgerton 45, giving them the first down by mere inches.

Dave Weber finally took a handoff on an off tackle play left. Aaron Roth blew up the play and made the stop for no gain. Flegal finally dropped back to attempt a pass on second-and-10. Jeff Davis was the target but the pass fell incomplete which brought up a third-and-10. Once again Flegal dropped back to pass and looked to hit Dave Maugel in the right flat but the pass was once again off target, forcing the Bulldogs to punt the ball away.

The Davis punt was once again caught by Martin and Denny returned the punt five yards to the Ayersville 30. On first down, Deitrick took the ball on a quick pitch right and gained two. Deitrick again carried on second down for one as Edgerton stuffed the 32 trap.

Our offense faced third-and-long. Dawson brought in the play, and it was a newer play that we put in a couple of weeks prior where we ran play-action off of the blast play. I would be split out wide right and run a hook and go route. I told Denny after the huddle broke, "To throw it up, I would be open."

The play was executed well, the line gave Denny the time he needed to get the fake in and then drop back for the long pass. I ran the route, and just after I made my spin and headed up field, I looked up and the ball was thrown perfectly. I only had a slight step on the defender, but Denny had thrown the ball so well, that's all I needed. I tucked the ball away and sprinted as hard as I could because I knew the Bulldogs had some of the fastest kids in the area. None of them had an angle on me and I made it into the end zone 67 yards later for the score. The kick was good, and with the preemptive strike, our offense had struck like lightning and we had a 14-0 lead with 2:22 left in the first quarter.

Richard Baldwin, our Athletic Director, can be heard on the tape of the game saying, "What a pretty pass, everything was right there, we got to keep it going now."

I had never heard him so excited. Mr. Baldwin, as we all referred to him, was also our gym teacher when we were all in grade school. He had always told me that he wouldn't retire until after our class graduated. He said, "I have a feeling this class will do something remarkable and I want to be here for it."

"They (Ayersville) struck very quickly on a hook and go," recalled Edgerton head coach Scott Thompson. "Before you can look up we're down 14 points. It really hurt."

"I can't ask for any more on the Martin to Groll pass," said McCord. "But we knew with scoring quickly the game wasn't over."[68]

Chris Schlachter boomed the kickoff out of the end zone so the Edgerton offense was looking at a long field with the ball being spotted at the 20. Edgerton really got things going with a cross-trap-right to Radabaugh. Burket got sucked inside by the fake and Mike Wilson ran down Radabaugh after a 14-yard gain. Weber then received the hand back left and Marv Andrews made the tackle with Weber falling forward for five yards. Radabaugh then carried right up the middle for four yards with Andrews and Girlie bringing him down.

Weber then went off tackle left for three yards and a first down. Steve Deitrick made the tackle. A delay of game penalty on Edgerton then gave them the ball first-and-15 at the Edgerton 41. A cross-trap-left, with Weber carrying, gained nine yards before I finally pasted him, giving the Bulldogs the ball at the 50-yard line as the first stanza expired.

After the teams switched sides, Radabaugh carried up the middle with Wilson making the tackle after a gain of two yards. Edgerton was facing a third-and-five when Radabaugh took the handoff and went off the right tackle for half a dozen yards and a first down. Johnny Armes was there to make the tackle and prevent a longer gain.

Radabaugh then carried on a dive right and Okuly and Andrews stopped him after a yard gain. Weber received the next handoff on a cross-left and Scott Kolb, subbing for Deitrick, made the stop for no gain. Radabaugh then took off on a sweep right and gained six yards before Armes could bring him down.

This set up a fourth-and-two for the Bulldog rushing attack. Once again, Davis received the ball on short yardage and plowed into the pile for just the two yards needed. The measurement gave the Bulldogs a first down by a whisker.

After being lulled to sleep with the run, our defense was caught off guard when Flegal dropped back to pass. He found Dave Maugel open and hit him with a crisp pass. Maugel made the catch and was finally brought down by Kolb and Roth after he picked up 18 yards. Weber then took a pitch on a sweep left and gained three yards with me and Girlie combining on the tackle.

Edgerton faced a second down on our eight when Flegal rolled out right and found an open Weber in the end zone for the Bulldogs' first score. Davis kicked the extra point to slice our lead in half, 14-7.

The night air was riveted with the sound of a semi-truck air horn. Edgerton had found the end zone and that air horn blasted away into the night. As awesome as it sounded, there couldn't have been a worse sound on that night.

Davis kicked off and Travis Lewis fielded the ball on the 15-yard line and returned it out to the 22. We ran a quick pitch left and Schlachter was tackled hard by Maugel for a two-yard loss. Deitrick then carried up the middle on a 33 trap for no gain. The center-quarterback exchange was fumbled on third down, but Martin wisely fell on the ball.

Jerry Carnahan came on to punt and kicked the ball straight up in the air. It finally rolled dead at the Ayersville 27-yard line. Once again, the dreaded air horn blasted into the night air. Edgerton, after scoring its first touchdown of the night forced a three-and-out and was positioned only 27 yards away from knotting the game after the awful punt.

> "I had that punt all planned out. I was trying to catch Edgerton off-guard and kicked it straight up on purpose. I figured if it came down on top of one of their linemen, we could recover it and get the ball right back. Anyway, that's my story and I am sticking to it!" Jerry Carnahan admitted.[69]

The Edgerton faithful were on their feet, and Pilot fans were sitting in silence.

Weber took the handoff and dove right and Burket stopped him at the line of scrimmage for no gain. Radabaugh then carried on the same exact play. Deitrick stopped him after a three-yard gain. On third down, Flegal dropped back to pass but Phil Girlie was right there and almost intercepted the ball. Edgerton faced a fourth-and-seven and our defense needed to hold them as Radabaugh took off on a sweep right. Eric Burket stayed in front and strung the play out forcing Radabaugh to cut it up. Phil Girlie flew up from his rotator spot and tripped Radabaugh up after a short two-yard gain. Our defense held them on four straight plays and the only sound in the night air was coming from our side of the field.

Our offense took over on downs with 4:44 left in the half, with the hopes of chewing up a bunch of that time. A sweep right to Schlachter picked up five yards. Another sweep right with Schlachter netted another five yards and the first down. The clock was running and we were churning up field. Our workhorse back carried again on first down and picked up four yards on a 17 cross trap. Denny Martin then took off on his patented waggle and found Jerry Carnahan open, delivering a perfect pass that Carnahan converted into 11 yards and another first down.

Schlachter then carried on a sweep left for a couple of yards, but a flag was thrown on Tolly Hanna for holding which backed us up to our 40. Martin dropped back and tried to hit me on a fly pattern down the far sideline but the ball was either overthrown, or I was not fast enough, because the ball fell harmlessly incomplete a few yards ahead of me. A 16 cross trap, with Schlachter carrying, gained two yards. Martin then dropped back to pass again, but the ball was nearly picked off by Davis in the right flat which forced us to punt on fourth down.

This time, Carnahan hit the punt right on the nose. The coverage was good on the nice high kick, and Weber was tackled by Jaime Briseno, giving Edgerton the ball on their 36. With only a minute to go, Edgerton decided to keep the ball on the ground. Radabaugh dove right and Deitrick tackled him after gaining four. Edgerton then tried an option right, but Burket clobbered Flegal before he could pitch the ball for no gain. Edgerton ran the same exact play but this time Marv Andrews made the tackle for no gain as time expired.

We went into the locker room for the half with our 14-7 lead. Coach McCord told us in the locker room to keep up the intensity, prevent the big play out of the Edgerton offense, and for the line to hold their blocks because we were going to grind it out in the second half. He ended the halftime echoing the words of old. "Seniors, this is it, one more half of football. What will you be remembered for?"

I felt like something was wrong as I went through the gate for the second half. Something just didn't feel right, and I had an odd feeling all over. Then I realized what it was, where was the brown Carhardt coveralls guy? This was our last game on our home field. He wouldn't miss it for the world. As everyone else made their way onto the field, I waited at the gate. Finally, I saw him through the crowd. He came straight towards me, and this time instead of a slap on the back, we grasped hands and shared our first, last, and only hand shake.

I wanted to ask his name, but as if he sensed my question, he said, "It doesn't really matter, just get some good hits out there!" He then nodded, slapped me on the back and turned to walk away.

It was as if the swaying trees by our driveway that I tackled as a kid, and the swinging tire I ran into over and over as a child had sent him to watch over me during my playing days. He had been with me ever since I started my sophomore year, and as I watched him walk away and disappear in the crowd, I said to myself, *so long old friend.*

We received the ball in the second half. Travis Lewis made a nice run back on the kickoff, setting us up on our own 31-yard line. A 16 hand back to Schlachter netted nine yards. Schlachter then carried on a sweep left. I hooked the end along with my cousin, Shelby Dawson, and Schlachter got outside for a nice gain of 10 yards.

The ball sat at midfield and we ran an option to Deitrick for three yards. On our option play, the fullback was always the first option, as the quarterback, you kind of ride him into the line to see if he can pick up a few yards before you pull the ball out. If he can, you give him the ball and let him see what he can get. If the play isn't there, you pull the ball out and either run it yourself or pitch it to the trailing fullback.

Chris' brother, Brad Schlachter, had the best take on if you let the fullback keep the ball or not. He would say, "You put the ball into the fullback's belly and ride him into the line. If you feel him get crunched and he becomes limp, its time to pull the ball out and go to the next option."

Travis Lewis carried on second down with a sweep left for a loss of two. We faced a third-and-nine and Schlachter returned to carry on a 16 cross trap, but came up a yard shy of the first down. McCord and Ondrus decided to go for it on fourth down. I lined up beside and behind the tight end Tolly Hanna; we would double team the defensive end and hopefully allow Schlachter to pick up the first down on a sweep left. Tolly and I blew the end off the line of scrimmage and Schlachter rumbled for an eight-yard gain with Deitrick leading the way.

We had been taking all kinds of time off the clock with the drive, exactly what Coach McCord wanted. Edgerton even had to call timeout to try and stop our momentum. The timeout indeed subsided our quest for the goalline. I then carried on a 23 counter and picked up just one on first down. Martin faded back to pass on second down and the pass was incomplete intended for Tolly Hanna. On third down, Dave Maugel blew around Tim Boals for the sack on Denny Martin. Martin was shaken up on the play, but thankfully he shook it off and remained in the game.

The Carnahan punt then rolled dead at the Bulldog 19. Herman carried on a trap up the middle, but Deitrick made the tackle after only three yards. The next play, Flegal shuffled back to pass and tried to hit a streaking Joe Radabaugh down the middle of the field. Phil Girlie had good coverage and when he tried to intercept the ball, Radabaugh collided with him. The penalty was called on a distraught Radabaugh. The penalty put the Bulldogs back on their own 11. Our secondary loosened up, expecting a long pass play. I played way too deep at middle safety and a streaking Weber caught the ball across the middle for a 19-yard gain before I could come up and make the tackle. The result was a first down by inches. Just a horrible play by me, and I was disgusted with myself.

Radabaugh then carried on a cross right and Girlie flew up to make the stop after a one-yard gain. Flegal faded back to pass and found Davis in the right flat for a 10-yard gain before Armes could bring him down. Herman then carried on a power right and he picked up nine yards before Deitrick and I could smash him to the grass. Davis carried on a sweep right and was clouted out of bounds by Schlachter after a five-yard gainer and another first down. Edgerton was succeeding in marching the ball down the field to try and tie the score. Their fans were on their feet again, screaming for them to bust loose on a long run. The ball had been on the right hash for most of the drive, which was right in front of their bench, so the noise was becoming unbearable.

The ball was in our territory on the 48-yard line. Radabaugh dove right and he was tackled after getting four yards by me. Davis then tried the right side and Roth crushed him after a two-yard gain. Radabaugh then carried on a sweep right, he got the four yards necessary for a first down but was pasted hard by Girlie and I, and he was down. It was the workhorse Radabaugh's last carry, he suffered a foot or ankle injury on the double hit, and he did not return to the game.

Herman ran off tackle and Jaime Briseno made the tackle at the line of scrimmage. Flegal once again found Davis in the right flat for a 10-yard gain before I could drag him down. Edgerton had marched to our 26 where they started with a fresh set of downs.

The next play was an off tackle right with Herman carrying and he was stopped by Burket after two yards. Flegal then faded back to pass, he fired the ball into the end zone, but Johnny Armes was in perfect position and went high for the pick while wrestling the ball away from his opponent, giving us possession on the 20-yard line.

This may have been the biggest play of the game, Edgerton went on a long drive and just when they thought they had the ball in the end zone, it was snatched from them and they received nothing for the entire yardage they chewed up. Johnny Armes stepped up and made a big play when we needed it the most.

"That interception was a biggy ... wow!" admitted McCord. "I think it was a very big key."[70]

A 37 cross trap to Deitrick netted just one-yard and Schlachter then rumbled on a sweep right for six yards. We attempted the same play and picked up another pair as the third quarter ended. Everyone stuck four fingers in the air on our side of the field. We had to hold on for one more quarter.

We faced a fourth-and-one from our own 29. It would be a gutsy call to go for it. Coach McCord had confidence in his offensive line and he indeed chose to go for it. Schlachter got the call on a sweep left, behind the blocks of John Finn, Jaime Briseno, Jeff Okuly and Tolly Hanna while Steve Deitrick paved the way downfield for a jaunt of nine yards.

The next play was a 17 cross trap and Chris picked up six, Schlachter then picked up the first down with another four yards on a blast left followed by Deitrick's tote on a 36 for five yards. Our line continued their excellent job of blocking and Schlachter rumbled for a 10-yard gain on a sweep left.

Deitrick then carried on a 36 and bruised ahead for five yards. The line then did another excellent job blocking, springing Schlachter for a 10-yard gain on a sweep left. Deitrick then picked up two more yards on a 36. Our offensive line was doing the job and we continued to run the ball right down their throats with Schlachter carrying for eight yards and a first down with a sweep left.

Schlachter continued to keep the clock moving with an eight-yard gainer on a 16 dive. We faced a third-and-one after Schlachter once again carried on a blast left for one yard. Once again, the play was a sweep left and after Fat Boys nice carry of eight, we had moved the chains again.

With a new set of downs, Deitrick got back into the mix with a two-yard pick up on a 32 trap. We faced a second-and-goal-to-go from the Edgerton five. Schlachter advanced the ball even closer with four yards on a sweep left. The offensive line dug deep and Schlachter busted into the end zone from one-yard out to culminate the 80-yard drive. The point after was no good and we had a 20-7 lead with only 6:08 separating us from back-to-back GMC titles and the school's first-ever playoff berth.

Our offensive line had paved the way for a methodical, 16-play, 80-yard drive that kept the clock running the entire time. This was exactly the way Coach McCord liked to play football, as the offensive line came off of the field, he acknowledged every one of them.

The kickoff once again sailed out of the end zone, giving the Bulldogs the ball at their own 20. Davis carried on a power right and I made the stop after a nine-yard gain. Edgerton needed to score in a hurry and they elected to pass on second down. Flegal hit Davis for 15 yards before Wilson could drag him down. Once again, Flegal shuffled back to pass, he looked down the middle of the field like he did before, but this time I was not too deep and I intercepted the ball at our 40-yard line and returned it three yards.

We had the ball back with complete control of the game. Travis Lewis came on and ran a sweep right for one. Schlachter returned and blasted his way down the right sideline on a sweep left for 17 more yards. Deitrick threw a great block to spring him on the nice run.

Deitrick then garnered the carry on a 33 trap and advanced a couple yards. Lewis spelled Schlachter and fought ahead for two yards on a blast right. The Edgerton defense had become enfeebled by our power rushing attack and the results were becoming eminent. Schlachter then refreshed, returned to the game and made his way around the left end on a sweep. The blocking was great and he galloped 32 yards for the touchdown to put the game on ice. The kick was good with 2:48 remaining and the Pilots were on the smiling side of the scoreboard, 27-7.

The kickoff sailed through the end zone again and our defense went onto the field to hopefully end the game. We played loose and off the ball, knowing Edgerton needed to score three times to beat us. They moved the ball to midfield as the clock struck 0:00.

This was a great victory and classmates, parents and fans streamed onto the field. We shook hands with a great Edgerton team and gave them accolades on a great season. They were a good, tough team, and they played hard-nosed football. I know we all had a great respect for them and what they accomplished. I can't say any of us had any ill-feelings towards them. They played clean football and I don't remember any trash talk from any of them. For that, we respected them, and even wished they would have a chance to play in the playoffs too.

Even though we were victorious, it was hard to watch the dejected faces of those who would never play high school football again, especially a very talented team like Edgerton. They had worked hard and deserved to move on to the postseason with us.

> Marv Andrews credited the Edgerton interior line. "The two guards and center from Edgerton hammered me the whole game. All coach kept calling was blood defense. Those guys stood their ground, and it was just one big pileup in the center."[71]

For us, the dream had become reality. We ran through the regular season undefeated, and it was announced that we would indeed be playing in the playoffs the very next week. We were all so happy about our season continuing, that when the commissioner of the Green Meadows Conference carried the conference trophy onto the field, nobody went over to accept it. Finally, the announcer came over the loudspeaker and pleaded with us to accept the trophy. We were so caught up in everything else, we didn't even care about the trophy presentation. Finally, we came to our senses, and made our way over to accept the trophy. I for one didn't touch the trophy or even help hold it aloft. I wanted something more and I would not be satisfied until we had gone as far as we could go.

Our offensive line had played a fantastic game. John Finn, Tim Boals, Tolly Hanna, Jaime Briseno, Mike Wilson, Jeff Okuly, Aaron Roth, Eric Burket, George Schaffer and Shelby Dawson all did battle in the trenches. Chris Schlachter was free to rush for 199 yards on 26 carries, and was later named *The Crescent News* Player of the Week for his performance in the Edgerton game. I thought his booming kicks that went out of the end zone on our kickoffs were almost as important as his rushing yardage. This never allowed Edgerton to use its speed in the open field to pick up a big play. It also kept them firmly embedded on the 20-yard line to start their possessions.

Denny Martin only attempted five passes in the game, but one of them was the perfectly thrown 67-yard bomb to me that gave us our second touchdown and kind of put a dagger in the Bulldogs' hearts early in the game. Steve Deitrick didn't pick up a lot of yardage, but he was the lead blocker on most of the 199 yards Schlachter gained. Jerry Carnahan playing split end, did a fabulous job blocking downfield so that Chris could pick up extra yardage.

> "Every time I ran the ball, the hole was there. The line did a real good job blocking for me," Schlachter commented. "They make the holes then all I have to do is get past one guy and that's it. The whole team is doing a great job blocking and executing up front. They control the line of scrimmage so the backs can run through the holes. It makes it more fun for us," he added.[72]

Defensively, the Johnny Armes' interception was a key play. It came at a time when Edgerton was threatening to score and tie the game. The Bulldogs had put together a long drive and for them to turn the ball over in the end zone without getting any points was gut-wrenching for them. The line play of Andrews, Briseno, Roth, Okuly, Burket and Giesige was also a key, by never allowing the Edgerton backs an easy way through the line of scrimmage. Deitrick, Wilson and Kolb were there to make plays from their linebacker spots, and the secondary of Girlie, Hanna, Armes and me never allowed one of the Edgerton backs to get loose and crank off a long gainer.

Aaron Roth posted 11 stops, Phil Girlie had 10 tackles and I had nine tackles to go along with the late interception while Steve Deitrick picked up nine tackles as well.

After the huge celebration on the field, we made our way to the locker room where it continued. There had never been too many outsiders in our locker room, but after this game, there were fathers, classmates and other fans all over the place.

> "The senior managers were thrown in the showers with our clothes on because after all, we were all part of the team," recalled Kim (McCord) Engel.[73]

235

Coach McCord addressed us as a team and told us to stay hungry. We finally made the playoffs, but we couldn't be satisfied with just getting there. It would be a time to show more than northwest Ohio just what Ayersville football was all about.

STATISTICS

	Edgerton	Ayersville
First Downs	13	10
Rushing Yards	174	214
Passing Yards	81	79
Total Offense	255	293
Passes Attempted	13	5
Passes Completed	6	2
Had Intercepted	2	0
Fumbles	0	1
Fumbles lost	0	0
Yards Penalized	30	10

Edgerton	0	7	0	0-	-7
Ayersville	14	0	0	13-	-27

AHS- Schlachter 25-yard run (PAT Schlachter kick)
AHS- Groll 67-yard pass from Martin (PAT Schlachter kick)
EHS- Weber 7-yard pass from Flegal (PAT Davis kick)
AHS- Schlachter 1-yard run (PAT kick failed)
AHS- Schlachter 32-yard run (PAT Schlachter kick)

PART III:
The Playoffs

NOVEMBER 8, 1986

ELMORE WOODMORE WILDCATS
LOOSE FIELD
NAPOLEON, OHIO
FIRST ROUND PLAYOFFS
WEEK 11

Since we had never been in the playoffs before, none of us knew what to expect. With our win over Edgerton, we had picked up enough computer points to finish first in the Division V Region 18 standings. On Sunday, we found out we would be playing the Woodmore Wildcats at the neutral location of Napoleon's Loose Field, which was just a stone's throw away from the Maumee River.

None of us had ever heard of Woodmore before, but we understood they played some bigger Division IV schools and even a Division III school that enabled them to make the playoffs with an 8-2 record. Woodmore High School was located over by Lake Erie, southwest of Toledo.

With the football season extended, everyone was excited to be back in school on Monday. Coach McCord had obtained the game film from Woodmore, and he wanted us to watch as much of it as possible, since we were not familiar with them at all.

I don't think I had ever watched so much game film. I had a couple of study halls my senior year, so I would get a pass to go up to the locker room and watch the film every chance I had.

Our scouting report on Woodmore contained a lot of information on them. They had lost their starting quarterback, Steve Schmeltz, right before the final regular season game when he broke his collarbone in a car accident. They had shifted a halfback, Dean Epling, to quarterback in their wishbone power-rushing formation. They had some good backs and a big fullback, Andy Roe, to grind out their offensive attack. They had a good strong defense that allowed only eight points a game.

Later on that week when the final UPI football ratings came out, Ayersville had jumped in the Class A ratings up to the No. 6 spot. The top-ranked ranked team in Class A was Delphos Jefferson with a 10-0 record. Delphos Jefferson had played in the Division V State Championship in 1985, losing to Newark Catholic, who was rated No. 3 in 1986. Unbelievably, Delphos Jefferson had gone undefeated and did not pick up enough computer points to make the playoffs.

I can't imagine how devastated those seniors on that team must have been. They had lost in the state championship their junior year, only to come back for their senior year and go undefeated, but not have a chance to even play in the playoffs. I can't think of anything that could happen to a senior football player, barring an injury that could be worse. This must have been an unbearable feeling for them, and I wish they would have had the opportunity to showcase their talented team in the playoffs.

I am sure a lot of people would think along the lines of there being one less talented team in the Division V playoffs, therefore, we should have been happy. I for one, and I know the rest of our team would have felt the same way, would not feel any relief from this. Delphos Jefferson had a magnificent team and to deprive them of the opportunity to play in the playoffs was probably devastating, especially to the seniors on the team. My heart goes out to them; I wish they would have had the chance to play.

With the game being on a Saturday night instead of a Friday night, we would have an extra day to prepare for Woodmore. We had a really good practice that week and received a huge pep rally on Friday. It was a big event, and not only were the students there, but the parents, and even some other fans as well. At the end of the pep rally, coach McCord handed me the microphone after he was finished and I was totally caught off guard. One thing I hated more than anything else was public speaking. I figured he knew this and would never expect me to say anything at one of the events. It was too late, there I was with a microphone and I hadn't thought of anything to say. The crowd was silent, waiting for some inspiring words and uplifting message. What they got was something right out of a Bartles and James commercial. I finally said, "We'd like to thank you all for your support."

Jeff Okuly cornered me on the way out of the rally and he was laughing hysterically, "Groll, you sounded just like the Bartles and James commercial. We would like to thank you all for your support. What were you thinking? That was the worst pep rally speech of all-time."

It wasn't long before everyone was laughing and joining in with, "We would like to thank you all for your support."

Everybody was in a good mood as we headed to the locker room. I finally said, "Who cares about my lame speech, we are going to be playing some playoff football and we will let our actions do the talking on the field."

To that, there were cheers. I guess I should have said something along those lines when I had the microphone.

Woodmore's team was senior dominated, much the same way ours was, so we knew Saturday night would be a battle.

Offensively, they started: Senior quarterback Dean Epling (5-10, 165); junior center Fred Busdiecker (5-8, 180); guards, senior Ron Blausey (6-0, 195) and junior Robert Astle (5-10, 160); tackles, senior Keith Traver (6-1, 205) and senior Joel Sandwisch (6-1, 160); ends, senior Ken Sandrock (6-2, 185) and senior Tim Bock (6-0, 155); halfbacks, senior Todd Rothert (5-8, 170) and junior Erik Gronwall (5-11, 180); fullback, senior Andy Roe (6-3, 215).

Defensively, Gronwall and Sandrock were the ends; Blausey and Traver the tackles; Busdiecker at middle guard; Roe and junior Daren Cable (6-0, 220) the linebackers; Bock, Epling, Rothert and junior Todd Gardner (5-9, 165) were the defensive backs.[74]

Andy Roe was a big fullback, so we knew we would have to stay low to bring him down. Defensively, they had the two biggest linebackers we would face all year. Coach McCord was adamant about our line staying low. If we got in a wrestling match with them, he said we would have our hands full.

I had been dogging on Jeff Okuly all week about Traver. I had watched a lot of game film and noticed he was a pretty good player on both sides of the ball. Okuly would be going head-to-head with him from his tackle position.

I razzed him, "Hey Oak, Traver is going to blow you off the line Saturday night. He man-handled the tackles he faced in our film of him. You better make sure you have enough air in your helmet, I wouldn't want to see you get knocked out."

By the time Saturday night rolled around, I had him so angry, I didn't know if he would play hard against Traver or if he would borrow a Woodmore jersey and come after me.

On Saturday afternoon, we boarded the bus and took off for Napoleon, as we pulled out of the school, cars were lined up, people were everywhere, and car horns rang out as we left the school. The whole community was just as excited as we were to be playing playoff football.

My family contained my biggest fans and even though they had been there for the entire regular season, they ratcheted up even more support once we were in the playoffs. My support came from my Mom and Dad, my brother Lynn, my sister Teresa, her husband Mark Weddelman, and their newborn daughter Kristi. My other sister Tammy and her fiancé at the time Doug Johnston rounded out my favorite fans.

My sister Teresa confirmed. "Tammy, Kristi and I went on a trip to Florida right after the Edgerton game. We were hesitant about going because we didn't want to miss the playoff game. We ended up changing our return flight so that we could be back in time. We went right from the airport to the game. There was no way we were going to miss it."[75]

They were unbelievable and didn't miss a single game all year, even if it was raining.

> My brother-in-law Doug Johnston related, "I can remember during the Antwerp game when it was raining hard. We all held up plastic over the baby Kristi to keep her from getting wet."[76]

When we arrived in Napoleon, we got our first look at the Woodmore Wildcats. They were pulling up in their bus just as we collected our equipment from the Turbo Van. They were all wearing nice shirts, dress pants and ties. We looked like a bunch of slobs heading to a frat party. There were headbands, ball caps, sweats, ripped shirts, stained shirts, blue jeans and baggy sweat shirts.

Later on that summer, I met up with a couple of guys from the Woodmore team at an American Legion Baseball Tournament. They made reference to pulling up and getting a look at us for the first time. "We thought you guys were a bunch of poor undisciplined farmers the way you were dressed," they admitted. "We figured you would have no discipline on the field either, boy were we wrong."

During our warm-ups for the game, I was having some serious issues with my taped ankles. Since it was a Saturday night game, we taped ankles right before we left, not like usual for Friday night games when it was done right after school and we could go home. That was when I tore into the tape and made myself a whole lot more comfortable. Without the chance to free my ankles up a bit, I was going crazy. I know I was yelling and being a jerk to the managers, mainly Ann Shinabery, but I needed some tape cutters to free the tape up before the tightness short circuited my brain. Ann finally located a tape cutter and threw it in my direction without saying a word. Our managers weren't just our biggest fans, they were part of the team, and deserved our respect, and when they didn't get it, they let us know about it. Sometimes in just a subtle way, but the point was made. I did apologize to Ann after the game, for not being more patient while she tracked down the tape cutters.

It was a great night for football, cool and a little breezy, setting the perfect atmosphere for the first playoff game in Ayersville football history. Rob Giesige and I were the selected captains. We made our way to midfield, shook hands with the Woodmore captains, and listened to all of the normal official's rules, then awaited the coin toss.

Being selected as a captain for this game with Rob Giesige was one of the many highlights and memories I have of our senior year. Rob and I had been friends since the third grade. He was rabidly competitive in anything he did, so we did battle on the playground shooting marbles, playing all different sports in gym class, racing his hot wheels cars down the track when I spent the night at his house, and it didn't stop there. We even did battle in intellectual board games such as chess and stratego.

He was a great friend and I spent more time talking sports and football with him than anyone else. He was the one I turned to whenever I was down or things got rough. Rob would always have inspiring or encouraging words to uplift me. We had sat together on our bus rides to away games since the seventh-grade. To be standing next to him as the other captain for our very first playoff game was an honor and something I will never forget.

We won the toss and elected to receive, since that was the instruction from coach McCord prior to us going out on the field. The kickoff was a good one and Travis Lewis returned it to our 28-yard line. Our first play from scrimmage was a 37 cross trap with Steve Deitrick carrying. The play was successful and netted a handful of yards. Chris Schlachter then received the pitch on a sweep left that gained two yards. We faced a third-and-three and ran a waggle left. Martin elected to pass and Todd Rothert stepped in front of Phil Girlie and intercepted the ball at the Woodmore 41-yard line.

Woodmore ran their offense on the field as their fans cheered, while our's were silent. Rothert carried on a power left and was met by a huge hit from Steve Deitrick that spilled him for a yard loss. Eric Gronwall then carried on a power right and picked up the yard that was lost. Jeff Okuly tripped him up and Phil Girlie was there to finish him off. The Wildcats faced a third-and-10 and elected to pass. Dean Epling's pass was complete to Tim Bock in front of Johnny Armes for a nine-yard gain.

Woodmore's Coach Tom Peiffer elected to go for it on fourth-and-one. He called Epling's number on a quarterback sneak. The Wildcats picked up the first down as Epling slashed through for two yards before he was stopped by Aaron Roth. With the play being successful, Epling once again ran the ball up the middle on first down and picked up four yards before I made the tackle. Epling then dropped back to pass and hit Rothert on the right side with a perfect strike, gaining 15 yards before he stepped out of bounds.

Woodmore had the ball first-and-10 at our 33 and obviously this was not the start we wanted in our first playoff game.

Epling kept the ball on a quarterback sweep left. Roth, Giesige and I were there to make the stop for no gain. The big fullback Andy Roe then carried the ball right up the middle and picked up five yards before our linebackers, Mike Wilson and Deitrick could bring him down. Roe again carried on a dive left and Giesige and Roth made the stop behind the line of scrimmage for a yard loss. Woodmore faced a fourth-and-six and again elected to go for it. Epling dropped back to pass and had Ken Sandrock open down the left sideline but the ball was over thrown, which turned the ball over on downs to us.

Deitrick carried on a 32 trap for a yard gain, followed by a quick pitch right to Schlachter for another yard gain. Facing a third-and-eight, Martin dropped back to pass and tried to hit Tolly Hanna over the middle for a first down, but the ball landed harmlessly on the grass, forcing us to bring on the punt team. Jerry Carnahan got off a nice punt that landed on the field and didn't stop rolling until it was at the Woodmore 20.

Woodmore came right at us with their power rushing attack. Rothert sliced off tackle left and picked up 18 yards before he was tripped up by Todd Hanna. Roth had been double teamed, Giesige had been pushed outside, Deitrick got sealed off to the inside, and I had met the two leading blockers in the hole. Instead of staying low and making a pile, I stayed high and tried to make the lamest arm tackle of my career. Rothert ran by as I waved at him, thankfully Todd Hanna tripped him up, or it may have gone for an 80-yard touchdown. What was one of Steve Thieroff's basic rules of defense?

When you're taking on the lead blockers, stay low and create a pile. That was one of those times and I totally blew it.

Woodmore continued to feed the ball to Rothert. He carried again on a cross trap right and I wrestled him down after he picked up another nine yards. On second-and-one, the fullback Roe carried up the middle and Roth pasted him for no gain. Back to Rothert, he again carried on a cross left and picked up another eight yards before Deitrick and I could bring him down.

Woodmore was cruising down the field on the back of Todd Rothert. They had the ball at our 45-yard line and picked up another first down. Roe carried on a trap up the middle and picked up four yards before Marv Andrews and I could make the stop. On second-and-six, Rothert carried on another cross left and picked up half a dozen yards before Todd Hanna and I could bring him to the turf. Woodmore had been flagged for an illegal motion, however, and the play was nullified, leaving them with a second-and-11 on our 46-yard line.

Epling dropped back to pass, but overthrew his receiver on the right side. Johnny Armes was there for the second week in a row to make the huge interception. He returned the ball down the left sideline, but we picked up a penalty for clipping, and the Wildcats picked up a penalty for face masking. Our offense took over at our own 33-yard line after the officials walked back and forth to assess the penalties.

Denny Martin dropped back to pass on first down and delivered the ball perfectly to Phil Girlie across the middle. Phil took his eyes off the ball and dropped the pass, leaving us with a second-and-10. Schlachter then carried on a blast left and picked up nine yards. Chris then picked up the first down on a blast right that netted a pair of yards. The next play would finally get our offense going. Denny Martin kept the ball on a 37 option and raced 23 yards down the sideline before he was knocked out of bounds. Martin just accelerated on the play like I had never seen him do before. We had the ball in Woodmore territory at the 33-yard line.

Steve Deitrick then galloped 15 yards up the middle on a 33 trap shedding tacklers as he made his way down field. Deitrick had to come off the field after the play, apparently he suffered some kind of hand injury and he was quickly attended to on the sideline.

The first stanza ended as Travis Lewis toted the ball for three yards. We went back to the 37 option to usher in the second quarter and this time Martin elected to pitch the ball to Schlachter just as he got hit. Schlachter fumbled the quick pitch out of bounds, and thankfully we retained possession on the Wildcat 15-yard line.

Martin then rolled out on a waggle right and overthrew Phil Girlie standing in the back of the end zone. Schlachter brought his kicking shoe on to attempt a field goal on fourth down. He got under the ball and skied it straight up, leaving the score knotted up at 0-0.

Rothert carried again on a power left and the angling Marv Andrews made the big hit in the backfield for a one-yard loss. Epling dropped back to pass on second down, but Girlie raced in hard on the blitz and sacked him for a six-yard loss. Marv Andrews was there as well for the assist. Woodmore tried to catch us off guard with a quick trap up the middle with Roe carrying, but Andrews was right there to make the tackle after a two-yard gain. Woodmore would have to punt as they faced fourth and a cab ride.

The Woodmore punt was high and very short. Jerry Carnahan in a very smart and heads-up play sprinted forward and signaled for a fair catch. He caught the ball and was clobbered in the process by a Wildcat defender, giving us great field position once the penalty was assessed for fair-catch interference. It was a real fine job by Carnahan to stand in there and sacrifice his body, Jerry was always fearless, and his play on the field was always a direct reflection of that.

With the penalty, we had the ball first-and-10 on the Woodmore 14-yard line. Schlachter carried on a 17 and picked up a trio of yards. Martin then kept the ball on a 37 option for a meager one-yard gain. On third-and-six, Martin followed Mike Wilson on a waggle right, and just when it looked like Denny was going to run the ball, he pulled up, and hit Deitrick in the flat, Steve shook a tackler, and continued across the goalline for a nine-yard touchdown reception. Schlachter nailed the extra point putting us on the board first and out in front, 7-0.

The ensuing kickoff sailed out the back of the end zone and gave the Wildcats the ball on their own 20-yard line. Woodmore tried the right side with an off tackle play and Jeff Okuly was there to make the stop at the line of scrimmage. Rothert received the quick pitch left and Roth and I blasted him after he picked up four yards. On third down, Epling drifted way back to pass and tried to again catch us off guard with a middle screen to Roe. Andrews was there to make the tackle, but Roe moved the chains by gaining seven yards.

The big fullback Roe then blasted up the middle for 13 yards before Girlie and I could wrangle him to the ground. Epling then carried on a sweep left and was met by Scott Kolb after picking up two yards.

I don't know what was going on, but apparently Coach Beef was not pleased with the play of his tackles and Jeff Okuly was switched to the right tackle position. Whatever was going on, it was rectified shortly, because on the next play, Okuly slashed through the line and crushed Epling as he was trying to take the ball around the left end. Okuly just blasted him, causing the fumble to go shooting back about 15 yards. Rothert recovered the ball for Woodmore but the lost yardage had taken its toll, forcing Woodmore to punt on fourth down.

> "Aaron and Jeff were really good about letting me know what was going on out on the field," lauded Coach Beef. "If they were having trouble making their move, they weren't ashamed to tell me. If they couldn't handle the guy in front of them, we would switch it up and give a different guy a chance to see what he could do. They both played a little bit different, so what worked against one blocker maybe didn't work against another. By switching them it usually helped us."[77]

The punt was low and Martin couldn't get to it in time, allowing it to roll dead on our own 45-yard line.

Schlachter carried on first down for a six-yard gain on a hand-back trap right. I then picked up the first down on a 22 counter by picking up eight yards. On first down, Scott Kolb picked up one-yard on a 33 trap, subbing for Deitrick. On second down, Martin hit Shelby Dawson with a strike and he picked up 15 yards after the catch. The reception took the ball all the way down to the Woodmore 26-yard line.

Schlachter then picked up five yards on a blast left, before Lewis came in and picked up the first down with a six-yard gain on a sweep left. On first down, Schlachter picked up three yards on a 13 trap out of our pro formation. I then received another carry on a blast right reverse and picked up five yards. We had the ball at the Woodmore seven and faced a third-and-two. Schlachter then picked up the first down on a blast left behind Okuly, Briseno, and Finn after a run of four yards. It only took one more play to punch the ball in the end zone as Schlachter raced around the left end on a sweep and burst into the end zone for a three-yard touchdown with 1:13 remaining in the half. The point after was good and we were up 14-0.

Schlachter's kickoff sailed right out of the end zone, locking the Wildcats at their own 20-yard line again. Chris must have been eating a hearty breakfast, because he had been blasting kicks for two straight weeks. Andy Roe again tried the middle of our defense on the ensuing play and was met by Jaime Briseno after a pick up of two yards. Our defense was playing loose with not much time remaining in the half, and Roe again rumbled up the middle for 14 yards before Girlie and I could make the stop. Briseno from his nose guard position almost intercepted the ball on the next play when, Epling tried another middle-screen to Roe. Woodmore did not take any more chances and Epling sat on the ball to run out the half, which sent us into halftime with a 14-0 lead.

In the locker room at half, coach McCord talked to us about controlling the ball on offense and grinding out the clock with our running game. Our defense needed to tighten up on the running game, but not allow any quick scoring strikes by the Woodmore passing game. "We have 24 more minutes of football, play them like they are your last," were his final words at the intermission.

I don't know what happened and being a captain for the game, I should remember it, but for some reason we were assessed a penalty before we even kicked off in the second half. Kicking from our own 25-yard line, Schlachter couldn't get the ball to the end zone and to the delight of Rob Giesige, there was a return. Rob and Shelby Dawson combined for the tackle and Woodmore had the ball at their own 46 and decent field position to start their second-half attack.

Rothert carried off tackle right and Deitrick pummeled him after a three-yard carry. Rothert again carried off tackle right and picked up six yards before Hanna and Roth could bring him down. The Wildcats faced a third-and-one, and why we didn't see it coming by now I don't know. Epling sneaked the ball right up the middle for 5 yards before I could crash him to the grass. Epling had done this to us three times to pick up a short first down. Epling was very quick and if he hadn't been forced into the quarterback role, opposite Rothert in the backfield, we would have had our hands full.

Woodmore tried the right side and Deitrick dashed into the backfield and made the hit for a loss of three. Rothert then carried on a cross left and Briseno stopped him right at the line of scrimmage. The next play was a chance for Woodmore to get back in the game. Sandrock was wide open down the left sideline because he had about four steps on Todd Hanna. Epling threw a perfect pass, but Sandrock dropped the ball, allowing the entire Ayersville side of the field to breathe a sigh of relief.

Instead of an easy score, it was fourth-and-12 and the Wildcat punt team had to come on. Martin caught the punt and took off for the sideline in front of our bench. He turned the corner, kicked into overdrive and was finally brought down after a 20-yard return to our 30.

Just as coach McCord said we would do, we started to grind out the clock by running the ball. Schlachter carried on a 17 and picked up four yards. Coach Ondrus must have had a hunch, because he snuck in a pass play next. Martin's pass was complete to Carnahan across the middle, good enough for a pick up of 14 yards.

We went right back to the ground, with Schlachter picking up five yards on a blast left. Deitrick bounced ahead for the other five yards and the first down on a 33 trap. Woodmore then jumped offsides on the next play and we took the gift for another five yards.

Schlachter gained another two yards on a blast left. Tim Boals then pulled and led me down the line on a 22 counter. Tim delivered a crushing block and all I saw was daylight in front of me. It was short lived as I ran smack into a retreating official. I yelled out, "Get out of the way," as I slammed into him. The collision was enough to allow the Woodmore defense enough time to recover, and I got dropped after picking up 13 yards. As I got up from the grass, the official was right there to remind me of the proper way to address an official. We shared a laugh as I apologized and said, "Please accept my apology for running into you, sir."

Deitrick then picked up eight yards on a 37 cross trap. Travis Lewis then got totally blasted by the big Wildcat defensive tackle Traver on a sweep right after a yard. I wish it would have been Okuly blocking him, because I would have went right up to him and said, "I knew it Oak, Traver is just having his way with you, and before long, our entire backfield will be hurt because you cant get him blocked." Traver was good, but the majority of the time, our tackles didn't allow him to be a factor in the game.

On third-and-short, we got to run my favorite running play, combo left blast left. I would be lined up beside Deitrick, and we would bull rush through the area vacated by our guard who was blocking down on the middle guard. On that play, it was nothing about thinking or finesse; we just put our head down and blasted into anything in our path. With Deitrick at the side, I knew he would be right there to deliver the blow with me. We cleared out a good running lane and Schlachter burst through for eight yards.

The ball sat at the doorstep of Woodmore's goalline. Schlachter then carried on a regular blast left down to the one. Next, we ran one of my most hated plays, combo left blast RIGHT. This meant Deitrick would be doing all of the lead blocking on the right side while I faked into the left side. It was a nice miss-direction play and I can see why coach Ondrus called it, because the defense was expecting a blast to our power on the left side, but it didn't matter, I still hated it. The play worked just like it was supposed to, Deitrick cleared the way, and Schlachter went into the end zone on the right side as I cleared the way for absolutely nobody on the left side. The kick by Schlachter was good, making the score 21-0 with 2:31 remaining in the third quarter.

Epling caught the ensuing kickoff and decided to bring it out of the end zone. Schlachter sprinted down the field and made the tackle at the Woodmore 23. The snap was then fumbled and Rob Giesige darted in and fell on the loose ball. Coach Beck welcomed his defensive end, Giesige, back to the sideline with emphatic jubilation as our offense took the field.

Coach Ondrus again tried to catch the defense off guard by attempting a pass over the middle to Tolly Hanna, but the pass was incomplete. Deitrick then carried on a 33 trap and took a big hit after a two-yard pick up. We then received a delay of game penalty putting us back to the 26, and in a third-and-long situation. Denny Martin rolled out on a waggle right and found a crossing Shelby Dawson wide open. The Martin pass was right on target and Shelby raced the rest of the way to the goalline for a 26-yard touchdown. The extra point try was missed, making the score, Ayersville 27, Woodmore 0.

With 53 seconds remaining in the third, Schlachter again blasted the ball out of the end zone on the kickoff. Epling then passed to Rothert in the left flat for a five-yard gain before Girlie made the tackle. The next Epling pass was intended for Sandrock on the left side, but the ball was overthrown out of bounds. On third down, Deitrick applied the pressure up the middle, and Kolb hit Epling just as he released the ball and it fell incomplete.

Denny Martin caught the punt that followed and was dropped immediately. Jerry Carnahan took a shot in the back after the play was over, and apparently Jerry had enough of being hit on our punt return team, because he kind of took off after the guy that put the hit on him. I was close enough, so I grabbed onto Carnahan to hold him back before he did something he would later regret. I personally did not want to see Jerry in trouble with Coach McCord, so I settled him down and sent him to the sideline. Yet again, there were offsetting penalties on the play, clipping by Ayersville and a personal foul on Woodmore.

Our offense took over at our own 32 and ran one play before the time ran out in the third quarter. The play was a 37 option with Martin keeping for a two-yard gain. After changing sides, Eric Burket took over from his guard position. He led Martin around the right side on a six-yard pick up on a waggle right. He then picked up not one, but two blocks, as Deitrick blasted up the middle for a 36-yard run on a 32 delay trap. Deitrick hammered it out on the ground for another five yards on a 33 trap, before Burket got another great block on a blast left by Lewis for a 10-yard gain.

We had the ball first-and-goal at the nine-yard line. I received the handoff on a 23 counter and picked up five yards, taking the ball to the four. Travis Lewis then went around the left end and hit paydirt. When Burket left the field and made his way to our sideline, his great blocking effort did not go unnoticed, as coach McCord was right there to deliver a smack to the helmet and nod of approval. This was the most cherished type of praise we could receive from our respected head coach. The extra point try was successful, making the score 34-0 with 9:35 to play.

Rothert caught the kickoff at the five and brought it right up the middle. Rob Giesige, flying down the field like the head hunter that he was, delivered a huge hit at the 24. Roe then carried up the middle and was stopped by Roth for two. Woodmore made a switch at quarterback and Gardner carried on a quarterback sweep around the right end for seven yards before Carnahan and I could make the tackle. Rothert tried the left side on cross trap and was reintroduced to Giesige after a short gain. Jeff Okuly strung a sweep right out and made the stop after a four-yard gain leaving Woodmore with a second-and-six. The next play was a hand back right to Rothert and he rumbled for 11 yards before Todd Hanna could make the stop. Rothert then pounded the center of our defense, but Scott Kolb was there to make the tackle after a short gain.

The Rothert carry brought the ball across midfield to our 49 where Woodmore faced a second-and-eight. Rothert again carried on a power left and once again Kolb was there to make the stop after a minimal gain. On third down, Gardner attempted to pass, but the ball was short of Sandrock and fell incomplete. On fourth down,

Gardner kept the ball on a sweep left and was stopped just shy of the first down.

Our scout team then took the field, since we were so close to the end of the season, I would no longer be taking any snaps at quarterback during a game. I would still take some snaps in practice, but it was time to get a healthy Todd Hanna ready for next year.

We received a delay of game penalty trying to get all of our personnel set up, but once they got set up, they were eagerly awaiting their chance to play in an actual playoff game. Corey Ankney received the ball on a blast left and picked up two yards. Hanna then dropped back to pass and hit Carnahan for a 12-yard pick up. Scott Kolb received the ball on a 37 option and rambled nine yards. Corey Ankney then slashed outside on a 16 and picked up nine yards.

The scout team's march to the end zone was temporarily halted by a Hanna fumbled snap, but they got back on track with a blast left for five yards. Jason Guilford then carried on a 22 counter and picked up nine. Kolb again took the handoff on a 36 option and gained just one-yard. Corey Ankney continued his fine running with an 11-yard gain on a blast right.

The ball was on the three as we scrimmaged with a first-and-goal. Coach Ondrus then called Ankney's number once again, and he went into the end zone for the touchdown. I felt this was a very classy move by coach Ondrus. Corey Ankney ran more scout team tailback than anyone else on our entire team. He got blasted in practice repeatedly, but he never gave up, he never complained, and he never whined about it. When nobody else wanted to carry the ball against our first-team defense, Corey Ankney always stepped forward, even if he was hurting from the last hit he received. For him to get into the end zone in a playoff game after all of the hits he received in practice, hopefully that made it all worth it to him. Denny Dearth came on for the extra point try and failed to get the ball through the uprights, leaving the score at 40-0.

Dearth then kicked off and Carnahan made the tackle. Don Andrews then made the tackle on a dive up the middle that netted six yards. Roe, who was still in the game, blasted up the middle for a 10-yard gain before Lonnie Gerschutz, a second cousin of mine, made the tackle. Woodmore turned to the passing attack and lofted a pass deep down the middle that fell incomplete. They again tried the same play on second down but Jaime's brother, Steve Briseno, was there to make the interception and return it 15 yards before he was tackled. Hanna came on to down the ball, and the first playoff football game in Ayersville history was a 40-0 win as time expired.

Our offense featured a very balanced attack with many different backs carrying the ball. Our line dominated, and allowed us to run through the Woodmore defense after the half. Denny Martin had a great game running the option and tossing for a pair of scores. A handful of Pilots found the end zone, with Schlachter rushing for two scores.

The defense made some key plays, especially the interception by Armes, and also delivered some big hits courtesy of Giesige, Okuly and Deitrick. Phil Girlie recorded seven tackles and a QB sack, while Steve Deitrick was credited with eight tackles. Holding the Woodmore team scoreless was of course beyond our wildest dreams.

Even though the score appeared to be a blowout, I didn't feel like we just overpowered them. We caught some breaks, and I felt Rothert was a really fine running back. Epling was a victim of playing out of his normal position, and I felt he too was a good ball carrier. If he would have been able to play the other halfback position on the other side of Rothert, I feel like the game could have been a real dogfight. Especially if Woodmore had their normal and very talented quarterback, Steve Schmeltz, calling the signals. Losing Schmeltz to the car accident injury took its toll on the Wildcats. If he would have been playing, I am sure the final score would have been a lot different than what it was.

We didn't have a long bus ride home, but when we did get into Ayersville, there were cars lined up all along the road while fire trucks ushered us into the parking lot with blaring sirens. This was something I had always heard about, but I had never seen. I thought it was reserved especially for State Champions. I guess the Ayersville community was so excited about playing playoff football, they couldn't contain themselves and they went all out for us. It was awesome to see and all of us stared out the windows in awe of the huge reception we received.

Coach McCord greeted the screaming fans and closed with this, "Tonight we won number 11 on our way to 14. This was just fantastic, we don't know who or where were going to be playing, but we go for number 12 next week."

For the night, we would enjoy the victory, but soon we would have another opponent to prepare for. All of the unknowns of playoff football sure made things exciting.

STATISTICS

Woodmore	Ayersville	
First Downs	11	16
Rushing Yards	124	274
Passing Yards	33	75
Total Offense	157	349
Passes Attempted	12	10
Passes Completed	4	5
Had Intercepted	2	1
Fumbles	2	2
Fumbles Lost	1	0
Yards Penalized	40	60

Woodmore	0	0	0	0-	-0
Ayersville	0	14	13	13-	-40

AHS- Deitrick 9-yard pass from Martin (PAT Schlachter kick).

AHS- Schlachter 3-yard run (PAT Schlachter kick).

AHS- Schlachter 1-yard run (PAT Schlachter kick).

AHS- Dawson 26-yard pass from Martin (PAT kick failed).

AHS- Lewis 4-yard run (PAT Schlachter kick).

AHS- Ankney 3-yard run (PAT kick failed).

NOVEMBER 15, 1986

TIFFIN CALVERT SENECAS
LIMA STADIUM
DIVISION V REGION 18 CHAMPIONSHIP
WEEK 12

Our second playoff venture took us to Lima Stadium for the Division V Region 18 Championship with our adversary being the Senecas of Tiffin Calvert and their 9-2 record. The Senecas had blanked Fostoria St. Wendelin 8-0 the previous week to keep their playoff hopes alive. Obviously, with their shutout in the previous game, we knew we would be facing another strong defense.

By then we were all caught up in playoff football and the atmosphere at school and practice was unbelievable. Everyone was excited and we didn't want it to end. The entire community was behind us and many signs started to appear in front lawns. Family, classmates and the cheerleaders made their rounds decorating all of our homes. My sister, Teresa, had even taken it a step further and started decorating my bedroom. There were times I could hardly make it to my bed because of all of the streamers she had running across the room. I could not believe how much passion and emotion our playoff run was generating throughout the Ayersville community.

The week of practice was cold and there was even some snow flying during the week to add even more excitement. None of us had ever played late enough in the year to have snow flying around us while we practiced and it seemed to make us work even harder.

> Tolly Hanna remembered. "Coach McCord recommended that we wear panty hose in November (playoff season) as the days at practice were getting very chilly. I admit ... I wore panty hose."[78]

> I asked Tolly if I could use his quote in the book. He responded back with, "Feel free to use what you like, no problem. Just for the record and to avoid any confusion ... I have not worn panty hose since."[79]

The enthusiasm was running rampant and the practice sessions seemed to be more enjoyable than they had been before. Everyone knew what was on the line and we were determined to continue playing football as long as we could. A loss and we would be done, a win and all of this would continue. None of us wanted it to be over for us as players, or for the community that was following along with us.

During practice that week on Tuesday, I suffered a minor setback. During defensive team up, I made a tackle and my left leg got tangled up with the ball carrier. When I went down, my left knee bent in an awkward position and the result was a strained knee. It wasn't unbearable, but hurt a bit when I ran and remained sore for the rest of the week. I didn't have it checked out, because I felt there wasn't any serious damage and it was decided that I would just tape a brace to it and play like there wasn't anything wrong. That's what I did, and nothing really happened to agitate it any further, so it was basically forgotten other than the brace taped to it for the remainder of the season.

The Tiffin Calvert Senecas featured the wing-T offense under the guidance of Coach Bob Olwin. This was a power rushing formation, but the Senecas could pass if they had to. Coach McCord was familiar with Coach Olwin because Olwin had coached the Antwerp Archers from 1979-1982, and the Pilots had the Archers on their regular season schedule in all of those years. Coach McCord had a record of 3-1 against coach Olwin with his single loss occurring in 1980, when Antwerp picked up the victory, 7-6.

The Calvert attack featured a pair of 800-yard rushers. The fullback was junior Brad Adelsperger (5-9, 188), the halfback was junior John Fabrizio (5-4, 148) and the wingback was senior Kevin Shelt (5-9,165). The quarterback position featured junior Todd Warnement (6-1, 176). The receivers were senior tight end Jim Kirchner (5-11, 160) and split end was senior Tim Henige (5-9, 140). Up front, Calvert went with senior center Rich Brodman (5-7, 170), senior guards Chuck Clouse (5-9, 177, senior) and Larry Seifert (6-1, 198). They were flanked by senior tackles Greg Smith (5-10, 196) and Darin King (5-8, 175).

Defensively, most of those guys were going both ways with the additions of senior tackle Jim Distel (6-4, 206), senior end Tom Larkins (6-3, 173), junior linebacker Tony Fronk (6-2, 185) and junior safety Rick Demith (5-10, 139).[80]

When Saturday afternoon rolled around, it was freezing cold. We rolled out of Ayersville on our bus in the early afternoon, as bundled up fans lined the parking lot screaming and cheering for us to bring home a victory. After we arrived in Lima, we made our way to the locker room and I wasn't impressed. It was dark and not very warm in there. I would have much rather been at Ayersville in our nice locker room, but we had a game to play and it was quickly a non factor.

Many players chose to wear some type of long sleeved undershirt amongst other things to stay warm during the cold evening game. I decided I wasn't going to change anything; I still only wore my blue surfer half shirt under my pads, and left my arms and legs bare. I did have a big pair of brown gloves to keep my hands warm during pre-game and warm-ups. My hands were the only thing I cared about keeping warm; I knew the adrenaline and excitement of the game would do the rest.

Coach Ondrus had worn shorts for every game, he had done this ever since he started coaching, and even when it was cold, he continued to wear shorts. Coach Beef and Coach Beck had honored the tradition with him, and even on this freezing night, they all three had shorts on. If they could stand it, so could I.

> Coach Beck remembered that as the coldest night he ever experienced in shorts. "We went along with Billy (Coach Ondrus), he was going to do it, and so we said we would do it as well. Whenever anyone tells me it's too cold to be wearing shorts, I think back to that night in 1986."[81]

After our pre-game warm-up, we were all in the locker room sitting around and waiting for coach McCord to begin his pre-game pep talk, when coach Ondrus called a defensive backs meeting and told us to all get into the shower room. All of the defensive backs clambered into the dreary shower room that consisted of a bunch of moldy brick and took a seat on the floor. What could we possibly be in trouble for now? It was almost game time, why didn't he address whatever the issue was before? He had a serious and mean look on his face, so all of us were worried about why he was calling the meeting. He came in, sat down on the shower room floor with us, looked at us with a super intense face, and ripped off the hugest fart I had ever heard. Then he laughed his wicked laugh and said, "That was just a little something I wanted to share with you guys before the game started."

Slowly, we all began to smile, and the laughter began softly until we were all bursting out laughing. Next thing we knew, there was another fart from somebody else, then another. Coach Ondrus continued his onslaught as 17 other defensive backs tried to keep pace. Soon the sound was echoing off of the shower room walls, and a resounding fart song formed. I don't know how everyone kept from seriously crapping their pants because everyone was straining as hard as they could to be a part of the action.

Finally, Coach McCord called the team together and we went back out with the rest of the team, and tried really hard not to laugh. I am sure some of the other guys sitting closest to the showers heard it, because they were trying to suppress their laughter as well. Coach Beck must have not heard it because he was shaking his head and complaining something fierce about the dim lights, the cold, and the locker room from hell that smelled like crap. What can I say about Coach Ondrus? He was always full of surprises when we least expected it.

Coach Ondrus was a very intelligent person. I completely doubt that he was just performing some sort of funny prank to amuse himself. I am sure he saw something during pre-game that led him to believe one or more of us defensive backs were feeling the intense pressure of playing in this big game. He used his little stunt to create a loose and relaxed atmosphere, so that when we got on the field, we could play the way we were capable of playing.

Phil Girlie and Mike Wilson were the selected captains for the game and it didn't take long before they made a huge impact. Chris Schlachter kicked off and Jim Kirchner returned the ball out to the Seneca 43-yard line before Steve Deitrick made the tackle.

John Fabrizio received the first handoff on a sweep and Phil Girlie rocketed up out of nowhere and performed a perfect no-handed tackle on him, dumping him for a three-yard loss. Girlie went into his elbow pump action as he got up and Fabrizio slammed the ball to the turf in frustration. If the Tiffin Calvert offense was already frustrated after the first play, it would be a long night for them.

The tackle Girlie made, I felt, was the biggest play of the game. We couldn't start the game out much better. A highlight reel tackle that resulted in a loss and very frustrated ball carrier was the perfect way to start a game. Phil could make those no-handed body tackles where you took the ball carriers legs out from under them. I tried it once during a scrimmage our junior year and the ball carrier bounced off and continued on for a long touchdown run. On film, it was not pretty and I was blasted openly about not wrapping up after I made the hit. It was considered very poor tackling to not wrap up, but Phil could do it and it sure looked good when he did. Coach McCord's philosophy on hitting and then wrapping up the ball carrier was very effective. I don't remember very many missed tackles from our defense in 1986. It was the most sure-tackling defense I had ever seen on film.

The Senecas faced a second-and-13 and tried a dive left. Aaron Roth was there to stop Fabrizio for a yard loss to send them back even further. On third down, Kevin Shelt fumbled the handoff on a reverse. Calvert recovered, but it forced them to punt on fourth-and-long.

Denny Martin caught the punt in the air but was tackled immediately at our own 35-yard line. Chris Schlachter went to work picking up six yards on a blast left. Schlachter then carried on a 16 cross trap but was met in the backfield and dropped for a one-yard loss. On third-and-five, Coach Ondrus went to his favorite third-down play, the waggle right. Martin got outside and kept the ball picking up 10 yards and the first down. The next play sent the Seneca bench into jubilation and got their fans on their feet. Schlachter fumbled the ball on a sweep right and Calvert recovered at midfield.

Back on offense, Coach Olwin continued to feed the ball to Fabrizio. On a dive left, I stopped him after he picked up two yards. Fabrizio continued to try and break one loose by carrying on a dive left but he was met by Deitrick after a two-yard pick up. Brad Adelsperger tried his luck up the middle and he got blasted by Jeff Okuly after picking up one yard.

The Seneca punt was a low one and Martin couldn't corral it, putting us back at our own 15-yard line to start our drive. Deitrick carried on a 33 trap and picked up four. On the next play, I followed the pulling Aaron Roth down the line of scrimmage on a 23 counter, took the handoff from Martin and turned up field to find absolutely nothing between me and the end zone but the frozen tundra of the field. The one guy standing there was obliterated by my pulling left tackle escort, Aaron Roth. It was like a bomb went off and cleared the entire area. I couldn't hear anything, and it was like I was all alone on a desolate playground. I snapped back to reality and realized I better run as fast as I could because it was a fence buster to the end zone and I surely wasn't the fastest guy on the field.

There was a bomb that went off on that play. The bomb was in the form of our offensive line. Aaron Roth, Jaime Briseno, John Finn, Mike Wilson and George Schaffer had cleared the area of the entire Senecas defense. Everybody on our team, including the coaches and managers could have scored on the play, that's how well it was blocked by our linemen.

Two weeks before in practice, we had really worked on our 22 and 23 counter play. In the years before, it was one of Coach McCord's best weapons. It hadn't been run with any success for the last few years, and during practice one day, I approached Coach Ondrus with the reason why I felt it wasn't as successful. When I was playing on the scout team, the quarterback faking the pitch for the sweep, and the tailback acting like he was catching the ball was what really made the play work. The play looked like a sweep all the way, and it was too late to recover when the blocking back came sprinting through the line in the opposite direction with the ball. For some reason, the fakes had been taken out of the play, and I felt like it was a lot easier to read the play when the quarterback and tailback didn't really sell the sweep.

Coach Ondrus agreed and took the concern to Coach McCord. It was decided to put the fakes back into the play for the Woodmore game and the results were immediate. The play was once again being run with great success as three different blocking backs had nice runs during that game.

In the Tiffin Calvert game, the counter play sprang me on an 81-yard touchdown run and got us rolling early. The Schlachter kick was good and we enjoyed the early lead, 7-0.

Chris Schlachter booted the kickoff out of the end zone and our defense took the field to try and keep the Senecas offense at bay. Adelsperger carried the ball on first down up the middle and Marv Andrews made the stop after a short gain. Todd Warnement then kept the ball on a bootleg left and Rob Giesige was right there to make the tackle for no gain. Fabrizio then tried a dive right and was smashed by Jeff Okuly after he picked up just two yards. The Tiffin Calvert punt rolled dead at our 36-yard line and our offense was back in business. A quick pitch to Deitrick on the left side netted two yards, followed by a 37 cross trap with Deitrick again carrying for another seven yards.

We faced a third-and-one and executed just enough to get the first down with Schlachter carrying on a blast left for two yards. Deitrick carried on first down and got stuffed at the line of scrimmage on a 36. Coach Ondrus was setting up the option and on the next play Martin pulled the ball out and pitched it to Schlachter for a gain of eight yards. Schlachter again carried on third down and picked up 10 yards and a first down on a sweep left.

We had the ball first-and-10 at the Senecas 29-yard line. Deitrick went up the middle on a 32 trap and picked up nine yards. Another 36 option with Martin pitching to Schlachter gained another 10 yards. Schlachter then slammed the ball into the right side on a blast right picking up four yards. Tiffin Calvert had been lulled to sleep with the run and on the next play, Martin caught them off guard when he dropped back to pass and found a wide open Shelby Dawson in the end zone and another six points. Schlachter blasted the kick through the uprights and we increased our lead to 14-0.

Rob Giesige and Jerry Carnahan shot down the field like missiles and made the tackle on the kickoff at the Senecas 35-yard line. Coach Olwin's Senecas found themselves in a hole and they came out passing. Warnement's pass in the left flat fell incomplete on first down. On second down, Phil Girlie came hard on a blitz and stripped the ball just as Warnement brought the ball forward to complete the pass. The call was an incomplete pass and Tiffin Calvert faced a third-and-10. Warnement completed his next pass to Shelt but it only gained half the needed amount before Girlie made the tackle, forcing Calvert to once again boot the ball away.

Martin fielded the punt but it squirted away and he wisely fell on it so that we could maintain possession. Deitrick took the handoff on a 32 trap and picked up 30 yards before the Senecas defense could recover and spill him. Deitrick made a nice run dodging and eluding tacklers on his 30-yard jaunt down the field. Schlachter tried to keep the ball moving on a blast left, but he picked up only three. Scott Kolb had come on for a winded Deitrick and carried for just one yard on a 36.

Coach Ondrus called the usual waggle right on third down and this time Calvert was ready. They almost intercepted Martin's pass attempt and forced us to punt. Jerry Carnahan dropped back and struck a punt that rolled dead all the way down at the Tiffin Calvert 10-yard line.

Fabrizio tried to finally get things going but Mike Wilson made the tackle on a dive right that netted just one. Fabrizio then raced outside on a sweep, but big Marv Andrews lumbered down the line, all the way to sideline, and made the tackle after a pick up of five yards. Tiffin Calvert faced a third-and-four and elected to try the same play. Phil Girlie and Okuly made the stop of Fabrizio a yard shy of the first down. Tiffin Calvert couldn't take the chance and they punted the ball away. Denny Martin let the ball roll dead at our own 33-yard line.

> "On that sweep play, I was hit harder than I had ever been hit before," explained Jeff Okuly. "I was going out, and Phil Girlie was coming in. The ball carrier hit the dirt and me and Phil collided. That was the hardest hit I took all year."[82]

On first down, Coach Ondrus changed it up a little bit and ran a waggle right. The pass was tipped and a concentrating Jerry Carnahan leaped and snagged the ball for nine yards. We picked up another nine when we went back to the ground with Schlachter and a sweep right. Schlachter again carried and picked up four yards on a blast left. Travis Lewis came on for a carry and gained three yards on a sweep right. Deitrick was stopped just short of the first down on a 33 trap on the third-and-three. Instead of punting, we elected to go for it and Schlachter made the decision pay off by sweeping right for an easy first down with a gain of eight.

Phil Girlie then tried his luck on a 22 counter and he picked up six yards before he was brought down. Schlachter picked up another first down on a blast right for eight more. Girlie showed his grit and determination on another 22 counter when he broke tackles and shook off defenders on his way to the one-yard line and 19 more yards. I was really hoping Phil would make it into the end zone and get himself a score, but it was still an excellent run.

Schlachter came on and covered the last yard on a sweep right. The one-yard plunge came with just 34 ticks remaining in the half. The extra-point try was good making the score Ayersville 21, Tiffin Calvert 0.

Jason Wenner fielded the kickoff and Schlachter made the tackle, giving the Senecas the ball and not much time to work with. Warnement dropped back to pass and Jeff Okuly swatted the ball out of the air just after he released it. Warnement then connected with Shelt underneath against our loose coverage and Phil Girlie made the tackle as the first half came to an end.

The halftime was pretty uneventful, as our offense and defense were basically playing as well as they could be. The only point of interest was there could be no let downs. We needed to finish the game off and not take anything for granted.

> George Schaffer had moved from his right tackle position to the left tackle position so as to free Okuly and Roth up even more for defense. "When I moved over to the left side, I had Jaime Briseno at guard instead of Mike Wilson," stated Schaffer. "Jaime hadn't heard me asking all year long about what to do on certain plays. So when I asked him, he looked at me like he couldn't believe I didn't know all of my blocking assignments by the time we were in the playoffs. I didn't start playing football until my junior year, while everyone else had been together since junior high. It was just an awesome experience for me."[83]

Travis Lewis received the second-half kick and didn't make it very far before he was tackled. Our offense began the second half on our own 19. Coach Ondrus caught the defense sleeping when Martin delivered a crisp pass to Jerry Carnahan, who made no move to get open because they were playing so far off of him. This was called a zero route, when the receiver just stayed right where they were lined up and the pass was delivered immediately upon the ball being snapped. Carnahan took off across the field and picked up 13 yards before he was tackled. The next play we dodged a bullet when Martin's pitch on the option went off of Deitrick's shoulder pad and out of bounds after a 10-yard pick up.

Deitrick took a more secure handoff on the next play and gained three yards on a 37. Schlachter could only pick up a pair on a sweep right, leaving us with a third-and-five. Martin dropped back to pass, but the ball was under thrown to an open Shelby Dawson and we had to bring the punt team on. Carnahan got off the nice punt and the ball rolled dead at the Tiffin Calvert 10 again.

Marv Andrews must have been working on his speed all week because he once again chased down a sweep to the right sideline, and made the tackle on Fabrizio after he picked up a handful. Jeff Okuly stuffed a dive by Adelsperger and the Senecas faced a third-and-four. Jeff Okuly once again got in Warnement's face and swatted his pass away just after he released it. The Tiffin Calvert punt was a wobbly one and the Senecas downed it at their own 45.

Deitrick carried on a 33 trap and picked up six yards, before Schlachter picked up another three on a blast left. Schlachter converted the third down into a first down when he rumbled five yards on a sweep left. Martin again found Shelby Dawson open and hit him for another first down and 10 yards. Lewis then picked up two yards on a sweep left, followed by another Phil Girlie 23 counter that netted another six.

The ball was sitting on the Tiffin Calvert 12, and the yards to gain were two. Schlachter barely picked up enough yardage on a blast left but it was all we needed for a new set of downs. Martin covered the final 10 yards when he kept the ball on a 32 option and crossed the goalline for the touchdown, high stepping his way across the chalk. Schlachter missed the extra point, but we had a firm lead of 27-0.

Kirchner returned the kickoff and was tackled by Girlie and Carnahan at the Senecas 39-yard line. The Tiffin Calvert offense then had their chance to put some points on the board with the next play. Warnement ran a play-action pass and the receiver was wide open and in the clear, but dropped the pass, saving us defensive backs a real butt chewing by Coach Ondrus. Actually, I don't think it mattered that the pass was dropped, we still heard him on the sideline yelling at us to keep everyone in front of us.

Warnement tried the same play, but Okuly slapped the pass out of the air once again. Warnement finally got a pass over Okuly and to one of his receivers on third down. Girlie and I made the stop, but not until Kirchner covered the needed yardage and picked up the first down. Warnement then attempted back-to-back passes in

Shelt's direction, but both of them fell harmlessly to the ice cold grass.

Tiffin Calvert once again converted a third-and-10 when Shelt caught the next pass and gained 18 yards before Roth could make the tackle. On first down, Jeff Okuly once again slapped a Warnement pass to the grass. I don't think I had ever seen a defensive tackle block so many passes at the line of scrimmage in one game. This was Okuly's fourth blocked pass of the game. He was getting a good push up the middle and then when he saw Warnement release the ball, he just went in the air and knocked the ball to the ground.

I had never seen anything like it before. He looked like King Kong on the top of the Empire State Building swatting airplanes as they buzzed by. It was another great play by Okuly, and even though I wasn't there to see it, I am sure he received the helmet tap and nod from Coach McCord when he made his way to the sideline.

> I asked Jeff how he could do such a great Kong impersonation. "I really just had the quarterback timed. He would take a short three-step-drop, and after I got a good push on the tackle blocking me, I would jump up and introduce Mr. Black Glove to Mr. Pigskin.[84]

On second-and-10, Eric Burket, who had been quiet all game, sacked Warnement for a seven-yard loss. After an illegal motion penalty, a screen pass to Kirchner was incomplete, sending the Tiffin Calvert punter deep to lay a foot into the pigskin.

The ball rolled dead at our 12 and our offense took the field to see if they could put together a long drive and eat up the clock. Deitrick picked up seven yards on a 32 trap before Schlachter gave us another first down by picking up four yards on a sweep right.

I got another carry on a 23 counter and earned a hard six yards. Martin then lost the handle on the snap and wisely fell on the ball to force a third-and-four. The next play found Tolly Hanna covered over the middle and the Martin pass sailed by, forcing Carnahan to drop back and await the snap for another punt. Jerry continued to boom his punts out there and this one wasn't downed until it covered 47 yards down to the Tiffin Calvert 24.

Warnement then repeated the Martin play and wisely fell on his fumbled snap. Scott Kolb then blitzed on an excellent call by Coach McCord and drilled Warnement for a sack and loss of 10.

Warnement continued to try and pick up some yardage via the pass, but Deitrick was there and almost intercepted his next attempt.

Once again Tiffin Calvert would have to punt, and the short punt rolled dead at Calvert's 42-yard line. Kolb slammed into the line on a 32 trap and picked up two yards on first down. This set up Martin for a 32 option on which he kept the ball and made a nifty move to register a gain of 11 yards. Coach Ondrus called the same play, but this time, I popped the safety right under the chin for my best downfield block ever, and Martin waltzed into the end zone untouched for a 29-yard touchdown. The extra point was good by Schlachter and we had increased our lead to 34-0.

On the kickoff, Giesige busted through the blockers and made the tackle at the Senecas 40. Warnement immediately went back to the passing attack and hit Kirchner over the middle for eight yards before Wilson made the hit. An illegal procedure penalty on Tiffin Calvert backed the ball up five yards, giving the Senecas a second-and-seven yards to go. The next pass was intended for Wenner but it fell incomplete. Another incomplete pass forced Calvert to go for it on fourth down.

With the lead, our secondary was playing deep and very loose, and I allowed the ball to be caught down the middle right in front of me for a 26-yard gain. I wasn't real happy about allowing the long pass play, but I guess keeping the Calvert offense in check was better than risking a long touchdown to ignite their team.

It worked out okay because on the next play, Jaime Briseno dropped Warnement for a sack and loss of nine. Followed by another great Coach McCord defensive call, Scott Kolb blitzed and tallied another sack, causing a fumble that Eric Burket pounced on.

With the game in the bag, the scout-team offense came onto the field for the second week in a row. Kolb carried on a 32 trap and picked up a yard. Lewis then swept around the left end for another five. Jason Guilford then picked up three yards on a 22 counter, but didn't quite make it to the end of the chains, causing us to punt. The Carnahan punt was fielded but dropped and covered quickly by the Senecas at the Calvert 26.

The Pilot second-team defense was in the game to try and preserve the shutout. John Letterhos received the first carry around the left side. He broke free and covered 20 yards before Carnahan could make the stop. Letterhos tried the left side again but Jason Guilford was there to drag him down after he obtained seven yards. Letterhos then fumbled the pitch on the next play, but Tiffin Calvert recovered. The next play was a pass and the ball fell incomplete forcing another fourth-down play. Coach Olwin went back to his last successful fourth-down play and was successful again, when Terry Wright caught the ball over the middle and picked up 20 yards before Guilford could spill him.

The Calvert offense was on the move and Letterhos caught the next pass and went 15 yards before another cousin of mine, Doug Brown, made the hit. The next pass play was successful as well and Young made the catch for another 10.

Somehow Aaron Roth got back on the field and sacked the quarterback with just 37 seconds remaining in the game. I think there was some excitement amongst the starters when Calvert started to knock on our goalline door. They had advanced the ball right down the field and had the ball at our 19-yard line. We all wanted the shutout, but Coach McCord wisely called a timeout, and got anyone that wasn't supposed to be on the field, off of it. Randy Richards then flew around the outside of the blockers and sacked the quarterback to back the Senecas up even further. On the final play, Calvert tried a reverse and Matt Lloyd was there to make the tackle, ending the game and the scoring threat. We were Division V Regional Champions, beating Tiffin Calvert by a score of 34-0.

This wasn't the first time Coach McCord had dealt with starters running back onto the field to preserve a shutout. In 1984, our Athletic Director, Richard Baldwin, gave a pep talk before the Tinora game. He was full of fire and brimstone, and at the end of his talk, he said, "I don't want you to just win, I want you to shut them out. In fact, if you shut them out, I will buy all of you pizza."

We had some kids that really liked to chow down and the thought of free pizza was enough to get everyone all charged up. I only played in the first half of the 1984 Tinora game because it was the game I received the gash in the chin, and I had to spend the second half getting stitched up in the emergency room.

However, I heard later on, that late in the game, Tinora was threatening to score and our starters ran out onto the field to try and preserve our pizza party. Coach McCord was trying to get them off of the field, but the allure of free pies was causing all sorts of trouble. The score just happened to be the same as the score in the Tiffin Calvert game, 34-0. The shutout did indeed get preserved, but I am sure Coach McCord was not happy about the chaos on the field.

Richard Baldwin did make reference to this incident when he spoke at the end of the year banquet.

Stated Baldwin: "A couple of years ago against Tinora, I told the guys that if they would shut them out, I would buy them all pizza. This got me in all kinds of trouble, because late in the game, Tinora was threatening to score and the varsity was running back onto the field when they had the game well in hand, 34-0. The Tinora crowd was wondering what was going on, why would our varsity be going back onto the field? Then they found out, oh, Baldwin is buying pizza if they shut us out. It was a sticky situation and everybody was mad at me, but it was the best 100 bucks I have ever spent on pizza."

After we defeated Tiffin Calvert, there wasn't a whole lot of celebration going on, our fans must have been cold because they headed to the warmth of the heaters in their cars in a hurry. We headed to the locker room and thankfully we had won, because it would not have been any fun at all showering in that nasty shower room if we had lost. I can remember heading out of the locker room on our way to the bus and our wet hair was freezing to our heads. Coach McCord was yelling, "Cover your heads up with something or you will all be sick next week."

For the first time all night, I finally felt the frigid temperature as we boarded the bus for the trek north back to Ayersville.

My brother-in-law Mark Weddelman remembered the cold. "We had some air horns with the canisters attached to make some noise at the game. We would have to be careful, or the whole can would freeze up if we held the trigger on it too long."[85]

This may have been the best overall performance of our team all year. Chris Schlachter ran for 100 yards, I picked up 87 yards on only two totes, Steve Deitrick picked up 86 yards while Denny Martin rushed for 57 yards.

All of those yards were picked up behind our stellar offensive line of Tim Boals, George Schaffer, John Finn, Mike Wilson, Jaime Briseno, Eric Burket, Jeff Okuly, Aaron Roth, Tolly Hanna and Shelby Dawson.

Defensively, Phil Girlie set the tone with his big hit to start the game. The Pilot defense reigned supreme that night. In the first half, Tiffin Calvert mustered just 13 yards rushing, 14 total yards through the air, no turnovers, no yards in penalties and zero first downs. For the game, Calvert finished with negative five yards rushing and a measly 127 yards passing. I had seven tackles and Jeff Okuly led his reign of terror in the pits with five tackles while also swatting four passes out of the air with his big paws.

The entire line of Marv Andrews, Rob Giesige, Eric Burket, Jeff Okuly, Aaron Roth and Jaime Briseno controlled the line of scrimmage so effectively, that I can't remember a game where I had less contact with ball carriers and blockers. After the game, it felt like I had just participated in a Thursday walk-through practice. Defensively, the plays were whistled dead before I could even get out of my read step (that I was now taking on every play, thanks to Coach Ondrus).

"Their defense is quick and gets to the ball," praised Calvert head coach Bob Olwin. "They defended our running game."

"Our defense is designed to stop the run," said McCord. "If we can contain the run we're going to be in the ballgame."[86]

When we arrived back at Ayersville, it was late and with the temperature being so low, I wasn't expecting anybody to be there. I couldn't have been more wrong. There were cars lined up everywhere, and once again, the sirens of fire trucks led us into the parking lot. The excitement was so intense, we couldn't have asked for better fans.

After Coach McCord thanked everyone, he ended the night with, "We have Mogadore next week in Berea, it's going to be a little drive, but we'll show up!"

STATISTICS

	Tiffin Calvert	Ayersville
First Downs	8	18
Rushing Yards	-5	371
Passing Yards	127	41
Total Offense	122	412
Passes Attempted	22	8
Passes Completed	9	4
Had Intercepted	0	0
Fumbles	2	1
Fumbles lost	0	1
Yards Penalized	10	0

Tiffin Calvert	0	0	0	0-	-0
Ayersville	7	14	6	7-	-34

AHS- Groll 81-yard run (PAT Schlachter kick)
AHS- Dawson 6-yard pass from Martin (PAT Schlachter kick)
AHS- Schlachter 1-yard run (PAT Schlachter kick)
AHS- Martin 8-yard run (PAT kick failed)
AHS- Martin 29-yard run (PAT Schlachter kick)

NOVEMBER 22, 1986

MOGADORE WILDCATS
BALDWIN-WALLACE COLLEGE'S FINNIE STADIUM
BEREA, OHIO
DIVISION V STATE SEMIFINAL
WEEK 13

The state semifinals had become our next obstacle. We had come so far and needed only one more win to advance to our ultimate goal, The State Championship.

State power Mogadore was all that stood between us and a title tilt at Ohio State's Ohio Stadium two days after Thanksgiving.

Be that as it may, this obstacle was unlike any that an Ayersville team had tangled with before. If we had any ideas of playing in the next weekend's crown jewel of high school football, it was time to tighten up our chinstraps a few extra notches and get ready for a back alley brawl with one of Division V's biggest toughies.

The Mogadore team definitely loomed large. There was Division I college quarterback prospect, Richard Pierce, who had led the Wildcats to the state semifinals just the year before. Head Coach, 13-year veteran, Norm Lingle, had won the regional four consecutive years. In fact, Mogadore had played in the state semifinal in 1979, 1980, 1981, 1983, 1984 and 1985. In 1979, they advanced to the state championship and won the Class-A title, when there were only three divisions in Ohio high school football.

It could definitely be said that Mogadore was a major force in the Buckeye State and they were obviously very well coached to achieve that kind of success year in and year out. With no playoff experience, and our team of overachievers, we went into the game as colossal underdogs. We would face the best quarterback and passing attack of any opponent in Ayersville gridiron history.

> "If you look at their (Mogadore) points scored (419), you see they can put points on the board," reminded McCord. "They are a fine offensive team."

> "They say some major colleges are looking at their quarterback (Pierce)," continued McCord. "We're going to have to have a good week of practice with our secondary."[87]

To make matters worse, we would be playing them on turf instead of our normal natural grass. Their high-octane passing attack on turf against our grind-it-through-the-mud rushing attack would certainly be to their advantage.

On film, they looked as good as they did on paper. During film sessions, I could see that our secondary would have their hands full. They even had some very nice running backs to compliment their aerial assault. Their line played low and had great technique, it was no wonder they had enjoyed so many fine seasons. Defensively, they stayed low, flew to the ball and were a bunch of sure tacklers. It was going to be a real fracas on Saturday night, and our week of preparation needed to be top notch or the Wildcats would knock us all the way to the Pennsylvania-Ohio border.

We were willing to work hard because all of us wanted nothing more than to give Coach McCord the opportunity to coach a football game in the Horseshoe down in Columbus. Coach McCord was a big Ohio State Buckeyes' fan and even though he never mentioned anything about it, we knew it had to be one of his dreams to stand on the sideline and coach at the "Shoe."

Coach McCord did a great job keeping everything low key that week, there wasn't a whole lot of hoopla going on, and we just went about our business preparing for Mogadore. On Wednesday, he had obtained permission to get us some practice time on some real turf. We got out of school a little early to travel to Toledo, Ohio to practice on the University of Toledo Rockets' football field.

The practice was conducted just like a normal one and everything was the same except for our shoes. Our cleats would be of no use on the artificial turf and a lot of our parents had bought us turf shoes. A few players wore some loaners that Coach McCord had obtained.

I was one of the lucky ones and my parents purchased me a new pair of white Adidas turf shoes. My grass cleats were black, but I couldn't find any black turf shoes, so I would have to adjust and wear white ones. I really liked my black cleats, and hated the fact I couldn't wear them on Saturday night. The new shoes worked fine on the turf and I slowly got used to them.

Practicing on turf felt a lot like practicing on carpet, it just didn't feel the same as natural grass. The smell was different, the feel against my feet was different, and when I fell on it, the feeling was different. As much as I noticed those things when I was running through drills and stretching, once we teamed up and went live, I didn't notice the difference at all. On Thursday and Friday, we practiced back home at Ayersville and felt like we were as prepared for Mogadore as we could possibly be.

While we went about our business and concentrated on football, friends, cheerleaders, families and anyone living in Ayersville decorated the town. Houses all over the Ayersville School District had huge signs, banners and lights. The players' homes were hit the hardest, and yards were full of all sorts of stuff to cheer us on. My sister continued her barrage and I couldn't believe how excited everyone was. The football game on Saturday was all anyone was thinking or talking about.

We didn't pay much attention to who was playing in the other semifinal match-up, but we were aware of the other two teams still involved in postseason play in Division V. The Newark Catholic

Green Wave would be playing another team from northwest Ohio, the St. Henry Redskins. Their game was very similar to ours in the fact that St. Henry had minimal playoff experience and Newark Catholic was the exact opposite. They had a storied playoff history, including the past two state championship titles in Division V. Since they had squared off so many times before, I am sure everyone in the state suspected a Newark Catholic vs. Mogadore finale.

On Saturday, we did not travel all the way to Berea on our normal bus. Instead, a really nice roomy charter bus was our mode of transportation. When I woke up Saturday, it was my birthday. All I wanted for my birthday was a win against Mogadore. My parents' birthday present for me was a really nice am/fm cassette player with headphones. I would be able to listen to the radio on the long bus ride to the game and even be able to listen to "On the Dark Side" right before the game.

A lot of other guys had utilized headphones on our bus trips, but I never had any, so it would be my first experience at the good life. I always sat with Rob Giesige and he didn't have any either, so we just watched the scenery roll by and concentrated on being ready for the game. Since we had such a long bus ride, and it was the week of the Ohio State/Michigan game, it was nice to have the opportunity to listen to the game on our long trip east to Berea.

At 11:00 in the morning, we met in the school cafeteria for a nice lunch before we boarded the bus, and started off for the biggest game of our lives. The parents had all pitched in and we had a great buffet-style lunch in the cafeteria before we went to the locker room to grab our gear. Something about the atmosphere of that lunch struck me as odd. It was so quiet, and not one person was loud and rambunctious. It was as if everyone knew what was at stake, and even at that hour, we were prepared to play the game.

Coach McCord gave a small talk before we left the locker room to board the bus. He concluded with this, "We know all about how good Mogadore is supposed to be, but I can guarantee you one thing, they put their pants on one leg at a time just like we do."

Before we went out the door, he made one final statement, "Make sure you have your cleats in your bag, I don't want anyone leaving their cleats in their locker."

I don't know if it was a superstition, or if he wanted to make sure we had our normal shoes if we didn't like the turf shoes. I know I wondered about it, but I never asked. Whatever his reason, my cleats were in my bag just as he asked.

When we pulled out of the parking lot, we were once gain sent off by our adoring fans. Signs adorned our path out of Ayersville, and right at the crossroads of town hung three sheets or pieces of cardboard with big block letters painted on them. The sign said: THE LAST ONE OUT OF TOWN TURN OFF THE LIGHTS.

This sign appeared later in many newspapers and also on the evening news. Our fans were the best, and apparently, everyone was going to be traveling to the game.

The bus ride to Berea was pretty uneventful except for the fact that Michigan beat Ohio State at the Horseshoe in Columbus. I remember thinking, *if we can just win this game, Coach McCord will be coaching in that same exact stadium next week.*

Apparently another ride to the game was somewhat eventful according to my Dad. "We got together and all rode up to the game in a camper. There was a whole mess of us in there and it must have thrown the balance of the camper off because it was a scary ride. That thing was rocking and rolling and it felt like we were on two wheels most of the way up to Berea."[88]

We arrived fairly early to find the stadium securely locked up. Finally, someone found somebody to let us in, and we made our way to the turf to check out the field. It was a nice stadium, but the turf seemed to be older than the turf at Toledo. It was kind of worn down and even appeared to be matted in one direction. Running towards our bench seemed to be better traction. Running away from it seemed to be a bit slippery. The coaches all gathered and spent some time checking out the field and how the different aspects of it would affect our game plan.

We knew we could not completely shut down the Mogadore passing attack, so we hoped to contain it, and make them nickel-and-dime us to get the ball downfield. If we could keep the Mogadore receivers in front of us, and force Richard Pierce to throw short passes, we would have a much better chance of defending the Wildcats.

Richard Pierce (6-2, 185) was a major concern of ours at quarterback. He was tall, strong, had a good arm and was a great leader on the field. He had thrown for 2,324 yards and 28 touchdowns. We had never faced a quarterback of his caliber.

His main targets were ends, junior Eric Barker (6-1, 185), who caught 63 passes for 990 yards, and junior Ronald Pierce (6-2, 192). Ronald was Richard's brother, so without a doubt they definitely knew each others tendencies. Ronald Pierce had been hurt with an ankle injury and missed eight games, but he came back strong and caught 24 passes for 297 yards.

The Mogadore backfield featured senior fullback Doug Sharpless (6-0, 173), who had picked up 749 yards on the ground. He was a hard runner and fought for every yard he could get. The halfbacks were junior Andy Adolph (6-1, 185), with 434 yards rushing, and sophomore Todd Meighn (5-10, 150), who had hauled the ball for 539 yards rushing.

Up front, the line did a very nice job of blocking and consisted of junior #53 Brian Kapper (5-11, 175) to go along with senior guard #59 Mike Morris (5-9, 170) and sophomore #65 Eric Acord (6-1, 165). The tackles were senior #61 Charles Martin (5-9, 170) and junior #55 Doug Straight (5-11, 180)

The Mogadore defense was led by outside linebackers Sharpless and sophomore #44 Jerry Owens (5-11, 165). The inside linebackers were junior #58 Steve Shannon (6-1, 220) and sophomore #30 Robert Christy (5-11, 175). The tackles were Kapper and junior #50 Jeff Pastva (5-11, 155), the ends were Martin and Straight. The secondary consisted of Richard Pierce, Eric Barker and sophomore #17 Jeff Meighen (5-9, 150).[89]

During our pre-game warm-up, something happened that would never be forgotten. Our band director, Scott Fisher, directed the Ayersville Pilot Marching Band in the playing of "Happy Birthday".

The fans in the stands sang along, and the player in the #21 jersey couldn't help being overwhelmed at the spectacle taking place. On my birthday, having a real live marching band play the song, while avid football fans sang to me, and there I was playing the great game of football in an awesome stadium. To play the legendary Mogadore Wildcats on my birthday, with the winner getting a berth in the Division V Ohio State Championship, was a dream beyond anyone's birthday wishes.

Our captains for the game were Aaron Roth and Jeff Okuly, and we elected to receive the opening kickoff. Soon both teams were lined up for the kickoff and the biggest game of our lives was set to get underway.

Travis Lewis muffed the kickoff and fumbled it along the Mogadore sideline. The Wildcats came down the field like a bunch of hungry lions and pounced on the ball before he could retain control of it on our 10.

Wow, Mogadore was fast and aggressive. It was not the start we needed. Doug Sharpless received the first carry of the night and Marv Andrews angled right into his legs, while I flew up from my rotator spot and cleaned Sharpless up for a loss of one. On second down, Richard Pierce started his passing assault, but the ball intended for brother Ronald was overthrown and fell incomplete. The Wildcats were then penalized five yards for an illegal motion call, sending them back to the 15. Pierce dropped back on third down and had Todd Meighen open along the right edge in the end zone. Phil Girlie was right there in man coverage as Meighen hauled in the pass out of bounds.

Our defense had held, but the Mogadore field goal unit came onto the field to get the Wildcats on the board early. Mike Wilson got a great jump around the left end and flew in to block the field goal. It was an awesome block and a perfect way for us to atone for the fumbled kickoff.

Denny Martin kept the ball on first down when he found a seam on a 32 option and garnered a gain of four. Steve Deitrick got involved in the offense a play later by picking up one-yard on a 37 cross trap. We faced a third-and-five and Martin dropped back to pass on a 32 pass and tried to hit Jason Guilford over the middle. Guilford was bumped before the ball arrived allowing our drive to continue after the pass interference penalty was walked off.

The Mogadore defense stiffened as a 33 trap by Deitrick and blast left by Schlachter were absolutely stuffed, forcing a third-and-long. Coach Ondrus went to the waggle left. Denny Martin slipped on the turf and went down before he could get outside, forcing Jerry Carnahan back deep to punt. The Carnahan punt was kicked out of bounds at the Mogadore 32.

Pierce and company lined up to try and get some points on the board. Sharpless was met in the backfield by Eric Burket and dropped for a three-yard loss on a sweep right. Then Mogadore ran a play that was designed very well and gave us trouble all night. It was some sort of counter trap, with misdirection, and a slicing ball carrier coming through the line in the opposite direction of the initial backfield flow. I really liked the way the play was designed, and if I ever became a football coach, I would put that play in my arsenal.

Andy Adolph carried the ball on the counter trap and picked up 19 yards before I could make the tackle on the right sideline. Phil Girlie had dove at his legs and missed, Johnny Armes tried an arm tackle, and it was apparent that we better buckle our chin straps and hold onto our jock straps if we wanted to make a tackle on one of the Mogadore backs. Speaking of jock straps, apparently Steve Deitrick forgot his and had to borrow one for this game. He thinks he borrowed one from Coach Ondrus.

> "Mogadore game I forgot my jock strap! Pretty sure I got a loaner from Coach O there if memory serves."[90]

A trap up the middle, run by Sharpless, was stuffed by Jeff Okuly for no gain. Richard Pierce then showcased his quarterback skills with a ball pump, allowing the receiver to clear our defense, and then delivered a perfect strike to Todd Meighen. Johnny Armes and I brought him down after a gain of 11 yards. Adolph then carried on the counter trap play again. Adolph gained 13 yards before Armes and I could combine on the tackle. Jaime Briseno checked in at nose guard, while Coach McCord called the perfect angle defense, stopping Todd Meighen on the counter trap play for a loss of a yard.

Pierce dropped back and delivered the ball to Eric Barker across the middle but he couldn't hold on to force a third-and-11. Richard Pierce then dropped back and delivered the ball across the middle but nobody was there.

With the ball on our 26, it forced head coach Norman Lingle to take a shot on fourth down. The Pierce pass was delivered across the middle for Barker, but it went through his hands and doinked Phil Girlie on the helmet, giving Denny Martin and our offense possession on our own 26.

On a sweep right, Tolly Hanna made a nice hook block, but the Mogadore defense swarmed Schlachter and tackled him after grabbing two yards. Martin dropped back to pass on second down but then tucked the ball and took off when he saw an opening. Denny picked up 10 yards before the ball came loose. The play was whistled dead, however, and a nice bouncing pick up by Deitrick for 10 yards was negated by the officials.

Schlachter bruised his way for three yards on a sweep right, before he picked up the other seven yards and a first down running the same play behind a battering lead block by Deitrick.

Deitrick was rewarded with a carry on first down and picked up four yards on a 33 trap. The next play, a hand back right, shook Schlachter loose and he rumbled for 21 yards before he slipped and fell trying to cut back. Either we didn't have very good shoes, or the turf wasn't very good, because our players were having trouble cutting on the damp carpet.

With the ball resting first-and-10 on the Wildcat 23-yard line, Coach Ondrus elected to pass and called a delay left pass. During film that week, the coaches noticed something about the Mogadore linebackers and this was a new play put in for this game. I, as the blocking back, would line up outside the tackle on the left side, take a few steps towards the sideline, and then release and run straight down the field. The pass was supposed to be delivered within five yards after the linebackers had cleared out. Martin threw me the perfect pass and I was hit immediately, I remembered my days playing in the yard when I hit and spun off of trees, so after I took the hit, I spun to my outside. The spin had shaken the tackler, but I was wobbly and stumbled to the ground after a gain of 11 to earn a new set of downs.

With the ball on the 12-yard line, Deitrick picked up three yards on a 33 trap. Schlachter then picked up another four yards on a sweep right. On third-and-goal from the six, we aligned in combo right, and on our shift to combo left, the Mogadore defense was flagged for an encroachment penalty. From a yard out, we then ran the combo right with Schlachter carrying on a blast right. Deitrick shot through and into the end zone, while I met the big linebacker in the hole. I was low enough and stood him up, allowing Schlachter to slam into the end zone. The Schlachter kick was good to put us out in front 7-0 with 1:58 left to play in the first 12 minutes of action.

On the kickoff, Schlachter ran down the field and made the hit on Todd Meighen, causing him to fumble, but the Wildcats quickly recovered the ball.

The Mogadore offense then took over at their 35-yard line. Sharpless carried on a sweep and Girlie made the tackle after five yards. Adolph then carried on the counter trap and Mike Wilson pasted him after two yards. On third-and-three, Phil Girlie read the play perfectly and dropped Meighen for a loss on a quick pitch.

We knew special teams would play a huge part in the game, and we worked hard on them all week in practice. As Mogadore dropped back to punt on fourth down, special teams play became an evident part of this football game.

Sophomore Don Andrews split the up backs, and with perfect technique, blocked the punt. Eric Burket was right there to scoop up the loose ball and he sprinted the 22 yards to the end zone. The Pilot players went wild, the fans went wild, and after the kick, we had a 14-0 lead with 12 seconds remaining in the first quarter.

At that point in the game, there was a fumbled kickoff that was recovered by Mogadore to open the game, a blocked field goal by

Mike Wilson, a blocked punt by Don Andrews and a touchdown return of it by Eric Burket. Special teams were without a doubt playing a huge role in the game. That's why we had worked so hard in practice, when game time came, we were more than prepared.

On the kickoff, once again the Mogadore ball carriers proved to be hard runners. Meighen received the kickoff and took off for the Mogadore sideline. Rob Giesige was in pursuit, but he dove and missed. Then Shelby Dawson gave an arm tackle a try and was promptly shrugged aside. Jerry Carnahan finally made the tackle at the 32-yard line.

Richard Pierce came out slinging on a pass to brother Ronald right over the middle for 12 yards, before Girlie could make the stop. An illegal procedure penalty backed the Wildcats up five, but then Mogadore ran another one of their plays that I was envious of. Richard Pierce would drop back to pass and after he was behind Doug Sharpless, he would reach around and stick the ball in an awaiting Sharpless' belly on a wrap around draw play. We had seen it on film, and knew it was usually a very successful play for the Wildcats, but seeing it live was a whole different aspect. Even the cameraman was faked out. Sharpless rumbled for 16 yards before Deitrick and I could make the sandwich tackle.

Richard Pierce then went right back to the air, and found Barker over the middle for a pick up of 10 yards before Girlie and I could smash him to the turf, as Scott Kolb piled on.

On a pass to the left sideline, Ronald Pierce made the catch and stutter stepped for 10 yards before Todd Hanna could bring him down. Johnny Armes was then beat deep for 23 yards, when Pierce connected with Todd Meighen down the right sideline. Meighen was too close to the sideline and he stepped out of bounds after the catch, putting the ball at the Ayersville five.

Unbelievably, Mogadore was whistled for another illegal procedure call, backing them up to the 10-yard line. Pierce tried to hook up over the middle with a receiver, but Deitrick was there to defend, and the pass was incomplete.

We switched from zone coverage to man-to-man on second down. Jerry Carnahan lost track of Ronald Pierce on the next play and Richard hit the wide-open target in the end zone for a Mogadore touchdown. Adolph converted the PAT and the Wildcats had trimmed our lead in half, 14-7.

Scott Kolb fielded the short kickoff on a bounce and returned it 15 yards out to our 40-yard line. Mogadore was then hit with a 15 -yard face mask penalty and our offense had great field position at the Mogadore 45.

As Denny Martin pulled the ball away from Deitrick on a 32 option, he lost the handle and fumbled the ball. Chris Schlachter was in the right place and fought a couple of Mogadore defenders for the ball. Schlachter came out of the pile a winner, and Ayersville retained possession.

Tolly Hanna was shaken up on the play and had to be walked off of the field.

> "I tripped and the Mogadore linebacker's knee hit me square in the helmet." Tolly Hanna remarked. "I was totally out, and didn't remember anything until I saw the trainers' light shining in my eyes on the sideline. He told me I had a mild concussion and that I was done for the night."[91]

Schlachter then carried on a blast left and picked up half a dozen. A sweep left by Schlachter was then called back for holding and we faced a third-and-long. This was a key point in the game and we should have driven the ball right down their throats and got our seven points back, but poor execution put us in a long yardage situation.

The pass on the right side was bobbled and finally dropped by Shelby Dawson (his only drop of the year), forcing the Pilot punt team onto the field. The Carnahan kick was nice and high and a fair catch was called for on the 14-yard line.

Giesige then strung a quick-pitch left to Adolph all the way to the sideline and I made the tackle after a two-yard gain. Richard Pierce then went back to work. He found Ronald Pierce open over the middle and delivered a perfect strike. Todd Hanna and I finally made the drag down along the sideline, but not until Pierce had covered 21 yards.

A hand back to Sharpless on the left side chewed up another nine yards before I could slam him down. I then had to meet Sharpless head on for a pad cracking hit after he broke through the middle for another six yards. The Pierce connection tried their luck with another crossing route over the middle, but that time I was there to make the hit as the ball arrived, causing an incompletion.

Scott Kolb then made an excellent play on the wrap around draw to Sharpless and dropped him for a two-yard loss. I guess Kolb was paying attention when we watched the game film of Mogadore because he wasn't the least bit faked out by the tricky Wildcat play.

The tricks continued for the Mogadore offense as Pierce dropped back and fired a long pass that was considered a lateral to Jeff Meighen, who was behind him along the right sideline. Meighen then delivered a long pass down the middle of the field into the awaiting arms of Ronald Pierce. The play resulted in a 27-yard gain that shouldn't have happened, but it could have been worse.

Before the ball was snapped, there was some confusion on who was supposed to cover Pierce. Rob Giesige, our right defensive end, was pointing and motioning for somebody to cover the split-wide Pierce, and since we were in man coverage, Todd Hanna should have had the outside man. I don't know what happened or if it was indeed Todd Hanna's man or not, but luckily, Rob Giesige sensed the confusion and sprinted down the field and was there to drop Pierce right after he hauled in the pass. A real bad play by our secondary, but a nice heads up play by Giesige saved the day.

Aaron Roth then slapped the first down pass attempt out of the air at the line of scrimmage, but Pierce found his brother across the middle on the next play and picked up the 10 yards and a first down before Todd Hanna could make the stop. The counter trap to Adolph was then sniffed out by Briseno, but there was a holding call against Mogadore to wipe out the play.

Mogadore faced a first-and-15 from the Pilot 18-yard line and elected to allow Richard Pierce to show off his arm. The result was a 17-yard pass to Eric Barker down the middle with Hanna and Kolb making the stop.

Mogadore elected to use the strong fullback Sharpless from the one, our entire defense swarmed like pesky horse flies and made the stop for no gain. Richard Pierce then tried to sneak the ball into the end zone and he was met full force by just about everybody again. Sharpless then tried to dive into the end zone and once again the entire defense was there, but one of the officials signaled touchdown. We had given it everything we had, but it just wasn't quite enough to keep the Wildcats from making the score tantamount at 14-14 after the kick was good.

Travis Lewis returned the kickoff out to our 27-yard line, where our offense took over. A quick pitch right to Schlachter netted three yards. I then carried on a 23 counter and picked up six yards. Schlachter then picked up a first down with a nine-yard run on a sweep left.

On first down, Martin overthrew Girlie before Deitrick mustered only one on a 37 cross trap. Another pass over the middle attempted for Shelby Dawson was once again incomplete and we had to punt the ball back to Mogadore.

The Carnahan punt was caught by Jeff Meighen, but Deitrick and Burket were right there to cause a train wreck and make the tackle. On the play, Jaime Briseno needed help off of the field. Either the turf or a hard-hitting Mogadore squad was taking its toll on our injury-free roster.

Todd Meighen carried on a hand back left on first down. Giesige was there to make the stop after a gain of one-yard. Sharpless picked up nine yards on a dive left before Deitrick and I could bring him down. Another dive left by Meighen picked up four yards before he was stopped by Todd Hanna.

Even with the ball on their own 38-yard line, Mogadore called a timeout to allow enough time for the strong arm of Pierce to possibly do some damage. With only eight seconds remaining, Rob Giesige broke through and sacked Pierce before we could see how far Pierce could throw it. The half was over and the Ayersville Pilots were in a stalemate with the Mogadore Wildcats, 14-14.

Rob Giesige had been flying all over the field in the first half and he was jacked up from making all of those plays. It may have been Rob's best half of football all year, and he couldn't have picked a better time for it.

We all ran in for halftime, the talk centered on containing the Mogadore passing attack and controlling the clock by sustaining our offensive drives. With 24 minutes of football left, it was put up or shut up time. We knew what we had to do, and if we didn't do it, we would fall just one game short of reaching the finals.

We would have to kickoff to start the second half and our defense would have to make a stand and get the ball back for our offense.

Todd Meighen received the kickoff and was blasted by Schlachter and Giesige at the 24-yard line. It took just one play for our defense to make the statement we had been waiting for. On a quick pitch left to Adolph, Deitrick made the hit on the inside, just as I crunched a hit right on the football. The ball came loose and Todd Hanna tried to fall on it, but it squirted away. A Mogadore player then tried to fall on it, but once again the ball had a mind of its own and it squirted away. During the process, I had made it back to my feet, and the loose ball was like the Holy Grail to me. I just had to get my hands on the football. I sprinted by a Mogadore player and slid around the ball, cradling it like it was a valuable antique. I got to my feet, and in a rare form of celebration, held the ball aloft. I was never one to show any form of excitement after a touchdown or other great play, but this game was special.

Our offense took over at the Mogadore 24-yard line. Chris Schlachter carried on a sweep right and picked up six yards to start the possession. Martin then dropped back to pass, but the ball was under thrown, and Deitrick didn't have any chance of catching it. We then went with a power formation left, and Dawson and I sealed the outside to send Schlachter around the end for nine yards to move the chains.

On first-and-10, Schlachter carried on a sweep right and was somersaulted into the air on a nice hit after picking up three yards.

Denny Martin then rolled out right and couldn't deliver the strike to Shelby Dawson, forcing a third-and-long. A 17 cross trap with Schlachter carrying could only net one-yard, forcing Coach McCord to make a decision on fourth-and-six at the Mogadore 10 .

He elected to send the field goal unit onto the field. Chris Schlachter then promptly put the ball through the uprights to give us the lead back, 17-14.

The Schlachter kickoff was then fielded by Todd Meighen and he picked up some good yardage before Deitrick could make the tackle at the Wildcats' 37-yard line.

Richard Pierce went to the air and connected with Ronald Pierce for eight yards before he was brought down by Deitrick.

On second-and-a pair, Sharpless took the quick pitch around the right end and was met by Girlie, Carnahan and Deitrick after picking up four for the first down.

Sharpless then got the call on first down, but Jeff Okuly totally blew up the play for a loss of two. Pierce then went back to pass and found Todd Meighen open on the left side, but I got a good read on the ball and arrived just as the ball did, and put a hit on Meighen to force the incompletion.

On the next play, Coach McCord called for a blitz and I got to Pierce just as he was releasing the ball. The pass wobbled to the ground incomplete and forced Mogadore to punt.

Denny Martin fielded the punt at our 19-yard line and ran for five yards before he was hauled down.

Deitrick slammed into the line of scrimmage on a 32 trap and fought for a handful of yards before Schlachter carried on a 16 cross trap and was demolished in the backfield for a loss of four.

On third-and-nine, the wheels fell off. Martin dropped back and pump faked to the right side. He then turned and slipped as he tried to get the ball over to Schlachter on the left side where we had a screen set up. As Martin slipped, his pass was delivered short and right into the awaiting arms of Jerry Owens. Owens snagged the ball and had nobody between him and our goalline. The result was a 20-yard interception return for a Wildcats' touchdown. Adolph again blasted the kick through and Mogadore was back out in front, 21-17.

Once again the slippery carpet had cost us. It was the same for both teams, so there could be no whining about it. The sad thing was the screen was set up beautifully, and if Martin wouldn't have slipped, it would have been nice to have seen how far that play would have gone.

Stated by Steve Deitrick, Coach McCord was not one to let conditions be used as an excuse. "Coach M's words of wisdom still get plenty of use out of me to this day," remarked Deitrick. 'I don't want to hear excuses about the conditions (weather, field or otherwise); both teams have to play in the same elements so suck it up.'"[92]

On the kickoff, we received a break as the ball squirted out of bounds just outside the end zone marker to cause a penalty. The Wildcats had to kick again, and since they were backed up, we should have gotten the ball with decent field position. That didn't happen, however, as Kolb muffed the kick and Lewis had to fall on it at our 30-yard line. Coach Norman Lingle had his guys flying down the field on kickoffs, and if we didn't execute perfectly, they were right there to make the stop.

A 33 delay trap was blown up by the Mogadore line and Deitrick lost three yards on first down. Finally, Martin connected with Shelby Dawson across the middle and Dawson took off across the field and down the sideline for a pick up of 29 yards.

Shelby said this about the success of his crossing routes. "Those plays were always set up with our running game. After awhile, the linebackers would just suck up on the run and it would be wide open across the middle."[93]

Deitrick then picked up nine yards on a quick-hitting 33 trap. Phil Girlie was then stopped for no gain on a 22 counter, forcing a short third down.

Schlachter then slammed into the line on a blast right to pick up the necessary yardage to give us a first down. Martin elected to pitch the ball back to Schlachter on a 33 option and he picked up three on the play. Travis Lewis then gave Schlachter a breather and picked up five yards on a sweep left.

Schlachter returned and rumbled for three yards to give us another series of downs on a blast right.

Tim Boals then got anxious on our long snap count for a five-yard false start penalty. We ran a lot of long snap counts later in the season when we went in motion, and this was the only time I can remember one of our linemen jumping offsides.

A pass thrown out to Schlachter in the left flat fell incomplete, setting up a second-and-15. Coach Ondrus decided to go back to the ground and see if we could catch the Mogadore defense napping. That didn't happen to a team the caliber of Mogadore, they stuffed Deitrick on a 33 trap for just a yard. This brought us to a third-and-14 at the Wildcats' 25.

I know I was on the sideline standing right next to Coach Ondrus begging him to throw it deep. I know this because there wasn't a game that went by where I wasn't begging him the whole time to throw the ball deep. I would keep track of which cornerback I felt we would have the best chance of beating and would relay the information to him.

Most of the time when I was waiting to take the play in from the sidelines, we had Coach Ondrus thinking sweep, Coach McCord in his one ear saying a 32 trap would work, and me on the other side of Coach O saying I could beat them deep if he would just call a long pass play.

This was no secret and Coach McCord made reference to it at the end of the year banquet, while Coach Ondrus just nodded his head and thought to himself, "Thank God, Groll is graduating, I will never have to listen to him on the sidelines to throw the ball deep ever again."

The whole play calling scenario was always a hot topic of the players standing on the sideline. When I wasn't on the field or waiting to take in a play, I would usually stand next to Rob Giesige who liked to play offense even less than I did. We would go back and forth with what the play would be. "Did you see that?" Giesige would ask. "McCord whispered something to him right before he called the play. This has to be a 32 trap."

"Oh whatever," I'd shoot back. "Ondrus has fallen in love with the sweep. I guarantee the play will be a sweep."

Then we would both nod and agree, "Maybe he called a waggle, they both are in love with that play."

It was also no secret that Coach McCord's favorite play was the 32 trap. It was always the first play we put in each year and as Coach McCord would always say, "It's our bread and butter."

It was a really nice play and we picked up tons of yardage on it. Opponents would even say to us after the game, "Keep running that fullback trap, it's hard to stop."

When he called the offense in the years before, he was so confident in the play that he would even call it if we were faced with a third-and-long.

He would think for a little bit and look like he was coming up with a special play for the situation, but would then lean down and whisper to the player taking in the play to the field, "Flanker right, 32 trap."

We all got a big kick out of it, but we couldn't argue with the plays success.

> "We ran so many 32 traps during practice, that our fullbacks' Bob Froelich and Steve Deitrick would have 200 yards rushing in each practice, just practicing the 32 traps," said Denny Martin.[94]

Back to the game, we faced a third-and-14 from the Mogadore 25. Both of Mogadore's corners were good, so it wouldn't matter which side we ran it to, but I finally won out and Coach Ondrus called a pro right Purdue. I took the play in and relayed it to Martin.

The first option on the play was for Martin to hit the tight end on a delay across the middle. As the blocking back, I would be lined up wide right and run straight down the field and be the second option. When we broke the huddle, I looked at Denny and said, "Throw it deep, I will be open."

We ran the play and I really wasn't open. The defender was right with me and I thought to myself, *oh great, I should never have said anything about throwing it deep.* It was too late, Martin chucked it long and it appeared it was going to be out of my reach. Somehow, I found another gear and the ball dropped right on my fingertips and stuck as I fell forward right into the end zone.

I got up, held up the ball, and pumped a fist in the air one time. I never did anything like this after a touchdown before in my life. I was mostly relieved to have caught the ball and that was where the excitement came from. The credit needed to go all to Denny Martin and our offensive line. The offensive line gave him the time needed to throw the high, long pass and Denny threw it just far enough that the defender couldn't get a hand on it, and I could just get my hands on it. Just an inch either way and it would have been an incompletion. Schlachter lined up and split the uprights with the extra point and we had taken the lead back, 24-21.

Scott Kolb made a nice tackle on Todd Meighen after the kickoff and the Mogadore offense was back in the saddle with the ball on their 37.

Steve Deitrick went to the sideline with helmet trouble after the kickoff return. During this game I had never seen so many guys with helmet trouble. Rob Giesige had it right at the beginning of the game, Jaime Briseno had it right before half and Deitrick was coming off the field holding his helmet. I guess the Wildcats could lay a lickin' on their opponent.

Richard Pierce went right to work and hit Barker over the middle for 10 yards before I could make the tackle. Adolph then picked up six yards before Todd Hanna could drag him down on a quick-pitch left. Pierce dropped back to pass, but our line pushed the blockers right back into him, and as the pocket collapsed, Pierce went to the turf. On the play, the third-quarter horn sounded, setting up the most exciting quarter of football ever played in Ayersville football history.

With the loss of two, Pierce tried a pass over the middle to Sharpless, but the ball sailed harmlessly to the turf, forcing Mogadore to punt.

The punt was absolutely perfect, and the Mogadore punt team surrounded the ball, and let it roll right to the edge of the goalline before they downed it. Alarmingly, we took over from our one-inch line.

The next play was late coming in and we had to call a timeout. The coaches talked about it and decided to try a short pass out of our combo formation to see if we could get the ball away from our goal-line. Martin dropped back, it looked like I was open in the right flat, but then Richard Pierce flashed between us, and with his height, he plucked the ball out of the air and returned it seven yards for another pick-six.

Unbelievable, this game was so full of ups and downs it had to wear our fans out. The Adolph kick was good making the score, Mogadore 28, Ayersville 24.

Travis Lewis then nearly broke free on the kickoff down the left sideline, but a clipping call backed us up to the shadow of our own goal post again.

A 16 cross trap carry by Schlachter netted three yards and Coach Ondrus followed that with a sweep right call. Schlachter picked up another three yards on the play, setting up a third-and-four. Schlachter continued to come up threes when he picked up another trifecta on a sweep right.

Decision time with a little less than nine minutes to play in the game, Coach Ondrus talked with Coach McCord and decided it was now or never. We had to go for it on fourth-and-one from our own 16. I felt like this was an extremely gutsy call, but our offense usually picked up short yardage plays, and it was nice to see the coaches have confidence in us.

The call was a sweep right into our power formation. Finn, Wilson, Boals, Dawson and I sealed off the inside, while Deitrick led Schlachter to the outside for a first-down gain of five yards. Deitrick then bulled his way for four yards on a 32 trap, but then was stuffed for no gain on a 33 trap. The third-and-six call was a waggle left. The pass for Dawson fell incomplete, forcing us to punt the ball away.

The punt by Carnahan was caught, dropped by Robert Christy, but Christy then fell on it giving the Mogadore offense possession at their 49-yard line. A power left with Todd Meighen carrying gained six yards before Roth and Hanna could make the stop. Adolph then picked up three yards on a dive left with Kolb and I putting the crunch on him. The Wildcats were facing a third-and-one with the opportunity to chew up more of the clock and continue their drive.

With them being ahead, and needing only a yard, I figured it was now or never. I decided to crowd the line and forget about taking a read step, if I did, it would be too late and Mogadore would get the first down. Our defensive line occupied all of the blockers and I was free to make the stop on the diving Andy Adolph. BAM! I made the hit. It was going to be close, they brought out the chains for a measurement, and the ball was short by inches. Not taking a read step had paid off.

Mogadore brought the punt team on and assumed we would be rushing the punt. They then tried to draw us offsides with an extremely long snap count. They let the play clock run out and accepted the five-yard penalty to give their punter more room to work. It didn't work out that way, as the punt was still too long, and rolled into our end zone for a touchback.

With less than five minutes to go, we had 80 yards to go, or our season would be coming to an end. Coach Ondrus called a blast left, mostly to set up his second-down play. Schlachter picked up two yards on the blast play, but Coach Ondrus had a plan. We hadn't ran a blast reverse in a very long time and it was time to bring it out. I received the handoff from Martin on the reverse and the line had it blocked well. There was however, one Mogadore player right there at the line of scrimmage. As I dodged him to get around the end, he grabbed right onto my face mask and proceeded to wrap me up. Well at least we would get the 15 yards from the penalty.

Not on this night, it was indeed my birthday and he fell right off of me. I took off down the sideline like I stole a radio, but Eric Barker was fast, and he took a nice angle on me, finally knocking me out of bounds after a gallop of 38 yards.

The face mask penalty would still be assessed to the end of the run, giving us the ball all the way down on the Mogadore 25-yard line, with a total net of 53 yards on the play. After the run, their wasn't much cheering from our stands and sideline because they all gasped at the dreaded flag and thought it was a holding call against us. When I made my way to the sideline, I was shocked to see everyone just staring onto the field and not going crazy. I kept grabbing my face mask to let them know the penalty was a face mask on them, but they were all so worried about a holding call wiping out the run, they were expressionless.

I made my way to where Coach Ondrus and McCord were standing, and even after I told them it was a face mask against them, they didn't get excited until the officials walked off the 15 yards. Finally, the Ayersville side went bonkers. I was beginning to think I took off in the wrong direction or something, because there wasn't one happy face on our side until that face mask penalty was revealed.

Now we were cooking and had the ball right down where we wanted it with time running out. Our offense could punch it in with not much time remaining and we could get out of there with a victory. A blast right with Schlachter carrying picked up the first four yards and a Schlachter sweep right then picked up five more to set up a third-and-one.

A 33 trap to Deitrick looked like it would get the first down and maybe go the whole way, but Erik Barker grabbed his jersey, and held on to ride Deitrick down after a gain of eight yards. We faced a first-and-goal to go at the Mogadore eight.

Schlachter picked up half of those yards on a sweep right. Coach Ondrus then tried to stick it in the end zone with me carrying on a quick-hitting 23 trap out of our combo formation. I could only get two yards, however, to bring up third down from the six-foot mark.

Schlachter carried on a blast right and dove for the end zone. It looked like he was in and we all raised our arms.

The ones with the arms that mattered didn't raise theirs and the officials spotted the ball at the two-inch line. The ball sat just a smidgen away from hallelujah land.

The season came down to this, fourth-and-inches. We lined up in a combo left and got ready to blast it in left. Mogadore called a timeout to set up their defense. The coaches huddled and talked about what play we should run. They changed the call to a combo left sweep right and tried to catch them off guard. At the time I was furious and thought to myself, *our combo blast play hasn't been stopped for less than two yards all season long, why can't we just slam it in there? I don't care if they know its coming.*

As I slammed into the line on the left side, the Mogadore defense swarmed there as well. The sweep right should have been wide open with Deitrick leading. Doug Sharpless then made an outstanding play from his left outside linebacker position. He knifed in and tripped up Chris Schlachter just as he was headed for the end zone. Schlachter had been dropped a foot from the goalline.

Mogadore took over on downs with only 1:19 to play and our season was all but over. Mogadore was jubilant, they had stuffed us on the goalline, and we were devastated. The evidence of defeat was looming straight in our faces, but we pressed on.

"I didn't think we had the game won," recalled 13-year Mogadore head coach Norm Lingle. "I have been at it too long to know the game is not over until the whistle blows."[95]

Richard Pierce tried to sneak ahead for some breathing room on first down, but we all crashed hard and stopped him at the one. Mogadore let the play clock run all the way out, taking more precious time off of the clock. The penalty would only back them up half the distance to the goal, which was barely anything.

Pierce again tried to get away from the goalline on second down, but we once again crashed with everybody.

Coach McCord then called a timeout to stop the clock with 33 seconds left. On third down, fearing a fumble or stripped ball, Pierce took off through the end zone on the right side. We gave chase and he promptly ran out of the end zone to give us two points and a safety. The score was Mogadore 28, Ayersville 26.

Mogadore had to punt the ball away on a free kick after the safety, according to the Ohio High School Athletic Association football rules. Pierce kicked the ball away and I caught it along the right sideline. Since the ball wasn't kicked off, and they had to free kick it from their own 20-yard line, I was able to return it back to their 35-yard line before stepping out of bounds.

Our chances were slim, but we were still alive with 23 ticks left on the clock.

A waggle right found Jerry Carnahan open on the right side-line and he hauled in the pass, but more importantly, Jerry got out of bounds after a gain of 12. Martin then rolled out right, double pumped, and delivered a pass that was tipped and fluttered into the end zone. I was sort of close to the ball, so I ran and dove. I thought I cradled the ball right off of the carpet, but an official was there to wave it off as incomplete. I thought our season was over, so close to the catch and now we had lost.

There would never be another chance like that. I slammed my hands to the turf before I got up and started to head back to the huddle. On my way back, #9 Eric Barker, sensed my dejection, and in a show of respect and good sportsmanship, came over, took my hand, and gave me a nod. This was the kind of sportsmanship only true great teams possessed.

We only had 12 seconds left to make some kind of miracle happen.

Martin once again dropped back to pass and hit Phil Girlie as he was falling out of bounds for 10 yards. The ball rested on the artificial turf at the 13-yard line with just eight seconds remaining. AWESOME THROW DENNY MARTIN AND GREAT CATCH PHIL GIRLIE!

I don't think any of us except for Chris Schlachter wanted to try a field goal. Coach McCord called our final timeout, even though we all wanted to run another play. He decided it was time to let Schlachter have a shot at it. It would be a 30-yard field goal attempt.

I think everyone in the entire stadium was holding their breath as we lined up for the kick. An entire seasons worth of sweat, pain and desire came down to just this one moment. The game had been back and forth and was probably the most emotionally draining game I had ever played in. Yet, here I was holding my breath on the sideline while a ball had to be snapped accurately, held properly, kicked straight, and with enough force to go over the uprights. This all had to happen while eight other guys performed their blocking assignments so the ball wouldn't be blocked.

Coach Beck was on the sideline when Schlachter was stopped on the fourth-down play earlier in the waning minutes, "He came to the sideline and immediately grabbed his kicking shoe and said,

'I am going to get another shot.' So he was ready to kick that field goal," remarked Coach Beck[96]

John Finn made an accurate snap, George Schaffer, Tim Boals, Jeff Okuly, Aaron Roth, Tolly Hanna, Shelby Dawson, Phil Girlie and Steve Deitrick made their blocks; Denny Martin sat the ball on the tee and Chris Schlachter put his right foot into the ball. Everyone else held their breath, and while some watched, and others covered their eyes. The ball took flight, end over end, and when it lost its momentum, started to tumble on its downward path. The uprights were just ahead, it was going to be accurate, but it was falling so fast it might not make it.

My mind flashed back to *the summer heat when we were all tired, and Coach McCord made us line up for endless field goal attempts. We were tired and it was getting so monotonous but he kept pressing us,* "*When the game is on the line, and you're tired, we can't afford to make mistakes. Practice is what separates winners from losers.*"

The plummeting pigskin continued its downward stroll as John Finn leaned and raised his hands, Tim Boals followed, and Deitrick slowly began to raise his. The ball fell just on the far side of the crossbar, barely making it across safely. The officials' arms shot straight up as the Mogadore players dropped to the turf one-by-one.

The Ayersville stands erupted in pandemonium and bedlam. It was pandemonium 1986 and it was crazy … crazy as it could be. The Mogadore stands collectively gasped. Coach Ondrus did a cartwheel right onto the field. With five seconds still showing on the clock, I made my way to the huge pile of Pilot players on top of Chris Schlachter and started dragging them off one-by-one.

This game had more turning events than a soap opera and I wasn't going to be ready to celebrate until the clock showed zeroes. I faced a number of players that thought I was being a real prick to break up the happiness on the field, but I had seen enough crazy final-second kickoff returns go for touchdowns, that I hardly thought the game was over. I didn't want the field shortened by 15 yards for excessive celebration.

Once everyone was finally off of the pile and back to the sideline, we huddled the kickoff team up. While we did this, the announcer came on and repeated, "We request that all fans stay off of the field when the game is over, I repeat, stay off of the field."

> Our fans in the stands had us winning all along according to my sister Teresa. "When they stopped us on fourth down, all of the fans around me started trying to figure out a way for us to win. They added points up for a safety and a field goal and decided we did indeed have a chance to win. They were all talking about it before it even happened. It happened exactly how they had it planned out, except they took the safety on third down instead of fourth down."[97]

I didn't know what to expect from the Mogadore kickoff return team. Maybe they would try to get out of bounds and let Richard Pierce throw one deep for the end zone. Maybe they would try some sort of trickery and lateral the ball all over the field. I only knew that I was the safety on the kickoff team and I needed to be on my toes and ready for anything they might pull out of their bag of tricks. Schlachter kicked a bouncing ball down the middle of the field. Doug Sharpless, who had moments before saved the game for Mogadore, fielded it. After a short run, he was hauled down.

THE GAME WAS OVER, WE HAD PUNCHED OUR TICKET TO THE DIVISION V STATE CHAMPIONSHIP GAME!

> "You can't instill that type of quality into the kids," said an emotionally drained Ayersville head coach Craig McCord. "It's the kids' ballgame, they won it. I'm just so proud of them. I guess it's never over until it's over."[98]

Our fans did not stay off of the field, they did the exact opposite. They charged the field in a swarm. The announcer finally gave up saying, "Will the Ayersville fans please get off of the field?"

> My brother Lynn related what was going through a six-year-old's mind. "At the Mogadore game, all I wanted to do was run around on that great looking turf since I'd never seen it before. It looked beautiful to my six-year-old eyes. I was trying to find a way onto the field around a gate before the game when someone was talking to Mike Wilson. I hoped someone would just lift me over the

fence into Mike's arms and I could do whatever I wanted on that field. I was bound and determined that before the night was over, I was going to get onto that field and see what this amazing surface felt like. Then that darn announcer got on the PA system near the end of the game and said that all fans MUST stay off the field after the game. I was like, yeah right buddy, I'd like to see you stop me and the rest of the Pilot crazies. I was not going to be denied in my quest for that green carpet and hoped like crazy you guys would come back and win that game so I could run out there and celebrate. I think all the Ayersville fans had the same idea that I had because the announcer kept screaming for the Ayersville fans to get off the field after you guys won that game. I remember telling my mom or dad or whoever was with me, what's the big deal we're out on the field, my big brother and the Pilots just earned a trip to the state finals … we aren't going to hurt this precious turf and we had a good reason to be out there."[99]

My thoughts immediately turned to the team we had just done battle with for 48 minutes. I found the fine quarterback Richard Pierce, shook his hand, and told him he was a great player. I then sought out the great warrior Doug Sharpless, to him there were no words that would do justice. He was a hard-nosed player and played his heart out. A nod and bump was all that was needed to acknowledge that respect. Finally, I looked for Eric Barker, he was the player that had picked me up when I was down by coming over when the long pass was ruled incomplete. He was only a junior, so unlike Pierce and Sharpless, he would have another season to play. I shook his hand, but I don't remember what I said to him.

The Mogadore Wildcats were a class act. Their players played hard, never trash talked, and they played with a perfect code of conduct. The style of football they played was completely admirable. This had to be a direct reflection of Head Coach Norman Lingle and his assistants. I had a great respect for the Mogadore football program after playing against them. It was truly an honor to have played them. Mogadore had such a tremendous football tradition and winning attitude that on that night when the score went back and forth and they finally came up one point short, it was truly a "Point of Sorrow".

As the Wildcats made their way off of the field and their fans walked to their cars in disbelief, we celebrated right on the field. The hugs I received that night would more than surpass the amount of hugs I had received in my entire life. Finally, after they had enough of all the celebrating and disregard to staying off of the field, they just turned the lights out on us. The celebration then spilled over into the locker room.

The game was dubbed, "The Pilots fly back for a Miracle Victory".

What a game it was, there was even birthday cake right outside of our locker room courtesy of my Mother. It just didn't get any better than that. It was a festival of elation at the highest level for Ayersville football.

It took half of the bus ride home before I realized what it all meant. The following week we would be playing in Columbus for the Division V State Championship. How did a bunch of eighth-graders that finished 1-4 become good enough to play for the State Title? The answer was simple, COACH CRAIG MCCORD.

He was our commander and he had led us to that point in the season. He of course had help from Coach Ondrus, Coach Beef, Coach Beck and Coach Maag. Our parents that supported us so dearly helped, along with everyone that was there to support us. We didn't have any real superstars, or flashy players, all we had was a bunch of football players.

When we got back to Ayersville it was very late and all of us were tired and completely emotionally drained. The way the game went back and forth, with the highs and the lows, it took its toll on our minds as well as our bodies. Mogadore had been a very physical team and we were battered, bruised and sore.

The next day, my cousin, Shelby Dawson, took Steve Deitrick, Phil Girlie and me with him to his parents' pool and spa business (Defiance Water Recreation). We sat right in the showroom and soaked in a spa to ease our aching muscles while talking about the game of a lifetime we would play on Saturday.

While the unimaginable triumph over Mogadore on that November night in Berea would be cherished forever, the Ayersville football program had achieved the right to play on the biggest stage of them all for a high school football player in the state of Ohio, THE STATE CHAMPIONSHIP.

The Mogadore game had everything in it that I ever dreamed of. I got to catch a long pass, carry the ball on a long run, block on short yardage, blitz the quarterback, cause and recover a fumble, tackle some strong, physical runners, and defend against a great passing attack. Even if we hadn't won, it would have been one of the most enjoyable football games I had ever played in. I can say that because we won, if we would have lost, I might not have felt that way.

Statistically it was pretty much a team effort. Absolutely everyone had something to do with the victory.

Back-to-back defending state champion Newark Catholic had beaten St. Henry in the other Division V semifinal, 17-7. We had to get ready for J.D. Graham's vaunted Green Wave outfit. It was going to be a stirring week.

STATISTICS

	Mogadore	Ayersville
First Downs	14	15
Rushing Yards	107	207
Passing Yards	175	87
Total Offense	282	294
Passes Attempted	23	15
Passes Completed	12	5
Had Intercepted	0	2
Fumbles	3	4
Fumbles Lost	1	1
Yards Penalized	91	22

Mogadore	0	14	7	7-	-28
Ayersville	14	0	10	5-	-29

AHS- Schlachter 1-yard run (PAT Schlachter kick)

AHS- Burket 22-yard fumble recovery (PAT Schlachter kick)

MHS- Ronald Pierce 10-yard Pass from Richard Pierce (PAT Adolph kick)

MHS- Sharpless 1-yard run (PAT Adolph kick)

AHS- Schlachter 27-yard field goal

MHS- Owens 20-yard interception return (PAT Adolph kick)

AHS- Groll 25-yard pass from Martin (PAT Schlachter kick)

MHS- Richard Pierce 7-yard interception return (PAT Adolph kick)

AHS- Safety: Richard Pierce ran out of end zone

AHS- Schlachter 30-yard field goal

NOVEMBER 29, 1986

- -

NEWARK CATHOLIC GREEN WAVE
OHIO STADIUM COLUMBUS, OHIO
DIVISION V STATE CHAMPIONSHIP
WEEK 14

Ever since the Hicksville game, we had been doing the 14 push-ups, 14 sit-ups and 14 squat thrusts. Unbelievably, they had not been done in vain. We were finally there and it was week 14, the one we had toiled so hard for all season.

No matter what, the week would be our final days of high school football.

A menacing adversary awaited our arrival at the end of the week inside Ohio State University's Ohio Stadium. Our foe would be a chiseled veteran and one that brought with it a treasure trove of accolades.

Looming on the horizon was the Newark Catholic Green Wave and they cast an immense shadow. The back-to-back defending Division V state champions, with an entire football tradition, rich in playoff appearances and championships would be our daunting adversaries.

Would the no-name Ayersville Pilots go unnoticed? Sure, we had a 22-game winning streak dating back to 1985, but that failed in comparison to the juggernaut we'd be facing from Licking County.

The Newark Catholic Green Wave came into the state finals with a 12-1 record. Their only loss of the season came at the hands of Watkins Memorial, 14-13.

If Mogadore had been a football powerhouse, what could Newark Catholic be called?

Take a look at these numbers and judge for yourself: State champions in 1978, 1982, 1984 and 1985. The years of 1975, 1980, 1981 and 1983 they were state runners-up. Plus, NC had made additional playoff showings in 1973, 1974 and 1976.

With 16-year veteran head coach J.D. Graham at the helm of the Greenie program, calling the Green Wave a "Football Championship Machine" might not have been giving them enough credit.

Watching them on film revealed that they weren't flashy; they just got the job done. To say the Ayersville Pilots were just a bunch of football players, I would have to say the Newark Catholic Green Wave had been a bunch of football players for a very long time. They featured a balanced offensive attack, they could run or they could throw. Defensively, they didn't give up the big play, and they made adjustments to their opponents very well.

In order to beat them, we had to play a near perfect game, because we knew on their side of the ball, they always executed their assignments flawlessly.

The week of practice was good for us and we did everything we needed to prepare for the state final game. The week of school, however, was a total mess. We got out of school early on Wednesday for Thanksgiving break and there was no school Thursday or Friday. I am sure it was the same for both teams, but the week just missed that school spirit atmosphere.

We still practiced hard and put all of the other distractions aside. We even traveled to The University of Toledo to practice on the artificial turf in preparation for the turf at Ohio Stadium. That time there were news crews there, and Coach McCord pulled me aside and handed me over to a news reporter. Apparently, Coach McCord hadn't figured out that I was terrible at that stuff. I took the microphone and muttered, "We have been keeping it real low key and concentrating on playing the game. We want to be prepared when we play the last game of the season."

Just a horrible statement once again, but that time, it was on the six-o-clock news. A few other guys were interviewed and they gave much better speeches. All in all, I could have done without all of that junk. I just wanted to play the game.

Thursday was Thanksgiving and I celebrated at my Grandma and Grandpa Dunbar's before taking off for the school and practice. My whole family was excited about the championship game and it was a nice feeling to have them wish me well before the game of my life.

On Friday, we left for Columbus. The game was scheduled to begin at 11 a.m. and it was necessary for us to drive down Friday and spend the night in a hotel. Coach McCord did not like that at all, but there was no other choice.

On Friday afternoon, we were once again sent off by our faithful fans and we boarded the charter bus for our trip southeast to Columbus. When we boarded, it wasn't like we were actually going to the game, so for some reason or another, someone other than Rob Giesige took the seat next to me. As Rob walked by, he gave me a look that would kill. He was very superstitious and even though we weren't actually going to the game, he didn't want to mess anything up. Right up to the present day, if this is mentioned to Rob Giesige, he will go off in a fit of rage because of it.

The bus ride was once again an oddity of the week and I do believe it took a toll on us. There we were getting on the bus for a game we wouldn't play until the next day. I think the conditioning of always preparing to play the game on the bus ride was immanent in all of our players' minds. To then arrive in Columbus, and have no game to play was a huge let down to our conditioned bodies.

Coach McCord had set up all of the rooming arrangements. I don't know how he selected who was going to be in a room together, but we all had assigned roommates. I was paired up with Chris Schlachter, and even though we talked about it, we did not go out squirrel hunting that night or in the early morning before the game, because after all, it was the state championship. If it was just a normal game, I am sure we would have found a way to go out hunting.

Instead, we sat in the room and talked like a couple of old women. We had all kinds of snacks and we just ate away while we shaved our ankles like a couple of girls. I can honestly say that once we checked into the room, we were completely oblivious to the outside world, until Coach McCord came by and told us it was lights out time.

Being away from home was the distraction I felt. I missed my parents saying their good-byes before I left for the game, and I especially missed my little brother Lynn's face of wonderment as I walked out the door of our house right before a game. As much as a big night in a hotel sounds fantastic for a bunch of high school kids, if you ever have the option, stick for familiarity and stay at home in your own beds. I know it was on Coach McCord's mind, but we just couldn't do anything about it.

> Others enjoyed the stay and what it enabled them to do. My brother Lynn has fond memories of the trip to Columbus for the game. "At state, I remember going into a K-Mart the night before the game and they had those Coke Icees. The cups they used had Chicago Bears' players' jerseys on them. Whoever else was with us all bought drinks so I could have each Bears' player they had in stock. That was the highlight of my year."[100]

The next morning we woke up and many guys had brought their pre-game meal from home. I know John Finn, Steve Deitrick, Mike Wilson and a few other guys had always stopped at Maag's Café before a game and ate hot beef sandwiches, which were considered the best in the area by many. The guys had purchased a bowl, or probably more likely, received a bowl free from Maag's Café. At the time, Maag's Cafe was the place to be after an Ayersville game.

> Steve Deitrick on the whole Maag's thing, "I'm not sure who or what the actual catalyst was behind that one honestly, but I'm thinking it was Finn ... he had to always have a side or two of cheese with extra mustard. We weren't about to break from tradition with that one. It was the best hot beef sandwich's I've ever eaten anywhere, bar none! I think it started out as me, John, Phil

and Harley Man, so naturally we had to keep it up even if it meant crock potting it out to Berea and Columbus! Besides Jeff, (Maag) was one of the coaches, so we had an in, and he wasn't about to let his family name be used as an excuse if we didn't eat the hot beef and lost the game."[101]

Coach Maag was definitely their "in". "Dad sent the beef along with me," explained Coach Maag. "Those guys came in every Friday before a game and he wanted to make sure they had it for the game. John Finn was the guy I remember starting it all."[102]

Other guys had brought a particular food with them, but I just ate what was catered to us there at the hotel. I indeed had my blue surfer dude half shirt with me and that was my main item of superstition. My Mom said I was superstitious right down to the short socks I wore and gave me a hard time about it, but she had no room to talk.

She said, "When we decorated the locker room, I would always leave you little notes. In past years I had quit writing 'Good-Luck' on them because it always seemed like you lost when I did. So I quit ending them with that and started using, 'Go get em.' You had always won after that."[103]

The team we would be facing was solid at every position. They had speed and size. They also had a tremendous amount of playoff experience, something we didn't. They also had been in the state finals an alarming eight times. To us, it was beyond our wildest dreams; to them, it was expected year in and year out.

Newark Catholic Green Wave starters on offense:

Quarterback: Co-Captain senior #15 Jeremy Montgomery (6-0, 180)

Tight End: Co-Captain senior #32 Bill Franks (6-0, 185)

Split End: senior #46 Tom Helms (5-10, 150)

Tailback: sophomore #42 Clay Shell (5-8, 160)

Fullback: junior #45 Scott Saad (5-10, 180)

Flanker: senior #34 Tom Parker (5-7, 145)

Guard: senior #65 Dale Backlund (5-10, 205)

Guard: junior #74 Jerry Oder (5-10, 185)
Tackle: senior #52 Jim Olson (6-1, 195)
Tackle: junior #73 Bill Keaser (6-2, 195)
Center: senior #70 Rich Walther (6-1, 200)
Defensively the Green Wave went with:
End: Jim Olson
End: senior #53 Jim Cross (6-3, 190)
Tackle: Bill Keaser
Tackle: senior #82 Wimberly Cook (6-2, 205)
Inside linebacker: Scott Saad
Inside linebacker: junior #41 Tim McKenna (5-10, 185)
Outside linebacker: Bill Franks
Outside linebacker: sophomore #22 Andy Helms (6-0, 160)
Safety: senior #33 Darby Riley (5-10, 160)
Defensive back: Tom Helms
Defensive back: junior #44 Damon Schumaker (5-7, 145)[104]

We boarded the bus after we ate our early morning breakfast/
lunch/dinner. That time, none other than Rob Giesige was sitting
next to me. We had a very short trip to Ohio Stadium, not even
enough time to really get into game mode. We took our walk in the
Horseshoe and noticed that the turf was in absolute perfect condition. To me it almost felt like natural grass. We were then directed to
the visitor locker room, where the victorious University of Michigan
Wolverines prepared for battle just a week before under legendary
coach Bo Schembechler. There were a couple of references made to
it; as the team was split between Ohio State and Michigan fans. Just
being there felt like we were involved in something bigger than just
high school football.

We all put on our equipment, and while some of us put on the
turf shoes our parents bought for us, others tried on pairs of loaners
they had made available to us.

> Jerry Carnahan related, "I remember walking out on the field at the
> Horseshoe like it was yesterday, wow, I still get chills! They told us
> they would have turf shoes for us, but they weighed about 15 lbs.
> I then went into the stands and got my brothers tennis shoes and
> played the game in them."[105]

Walking onto the field holding hands in our four class lines was a moving experience. Watching Coach McCord walk onto the field, is something I will never forget. We had done it; we had made it to the venerable Ohio Stadium, an arena where so many college legends had stood before. From the huge seating area, to the open end, and the big scoreboard, we were all in awe of actually warming up in such a place. We slowly realized, we better snap back to reality, the team we were going to be playing practically called the stadium their home field with their state championship lineage.

Since it was a chilly morning, Coach Ondrus, Coach Beef and Coach Beck weren't attired in their customary shorts just yet. Would they break tradition, or would they change before the game? The scoreboard showed 9:42 a.m. when we started our pre-game warm-ups. We were always the first team on the field.

> While we were stretching, we had two guys sneaking around according to Coach Beef. "While you guys were stretching, Coach Ondrus and I wanted to find the Presidents Suite. We rode an elevator all the way up to the press box and started looking around. We had quite a tour of the place, but we never found the Presidents Suite. Finally, we decided we better get back down there before somebody figured out that we were missing."[106]

Since it was a day game, Coach Ondrus had a tube of eye-black and he was going around applying it to the different players that needed it to keep the glare of the sun out of their eyes. It had been a very long time since I had played in a day game, all the way back to 1984 against National Trail. It was the first and only game I wore eye black.

Steve Deitrick and I were the chosen captains for the final game the seniors of 1986 would play in an Ayersville Pilot uniform. It was a great honor, and to get the opportunity to be game captain with Denny Martin in our first game against McComb, Rob Giesige in our first playoff game against Woodmore, and Steve Deitrick in our last game in Columbus at the state championship was something beyond my wildest dreams. Our eighth-grade year, I was standing on the sideline, wondering if I would ever be good enough to play the game I loved so much. With a record of 1-4 that year, nobody could have dreamed we would play for a state championship on such a grand stage as seniors.

I had always respected the way Steve Deitrick played the game. He was a leader by action. He never spoke negatively, never picked on anyone and he always played all out. He could have been concerned with all sorts of statistics, but none of them mattered to Steve, he was completely unselfish. He was just a pure football player and he liked to hit.

We made our way to midfield and then shook hands with the Green Wave captains' Bill Franks and Jeremy Montgomery, as we met for the coin toss. At that point in time, we were no longer in Ohio Stadium. My mind was on the glistening grass that smelled like fall, in some small stadium with fans crowded around a fence. To me that was football and that would always be the home for my heart when it came to the great game of blocking and tackling.

We won the toss and elected to receive the kickoff ... The scoreboard showed the temperature at 40 degrees. It was a great day for football. Deitrick and I headed for the locker room where we were treated to the assistant coaches in their customary shorts.

Believe it or not, I don't remember a whole lot about the locker room before the game. I do know Coach McCord made reference to the 14-14-14 we did all year. He was referring to the 14 push-ups, sit-ups and squat thrusts we did each week. He also spoke of it being the seniors last 48 minutes of football. He closed with the playing of "We Will Rock You" and "We Are the Champions". It was finally time to do battle with the ominous Green Wave.

As we took the field, all of our fans had finally arrived and it was a spectacle in itself. They let loose 100 blue and gold balloons as we ran onto the field. Our band was there, which was really nice because the playing of the fight songs always fired us up.

As we lined up to receive the kickoff, all of that stuff disappeared. I don't think I ever played a game where I was aware of anything going on outside of the game itself. It was like somebody turned on a switch. Once the game started it always felt like I was in the backyard playing.

Travis Lewis fielded the high kickoff at our 15-yard line and returned it eight yards to the 23. The Pilot offense made their way onto the field and set up on first down at our own 23.

Who would win out? Would the play be a 32 trap or a sweep? The 16 cross trap with Chris Schlachter carrying was our first play. It was a nice start as Shelby Dawson, Tim Boals and Tolly Hanna delivered excellent blocks springing Schlachter for 14 yards.

Next, Coach Ondrus called his beloved sweep play, and Schlachter picked up just one-yard on the left side. Denny Martin rolled out on second down and tried to connect with me in the right flat. The ball was under thrown and I couldn't make the reception. That brought us to third down with nine yards to go. Steve Deitrick carried on a 32 trap and picked up four yards, leaving us five yards shy of the first down. Carnahan dropped deep to punt and delivered a good punt down field that rolled dead on the Newark Catholic 27-yard line.

Jeremy Montgomery faded deep to pass on first down and threw a high wobbly pass down field on the right side. Tom Helms leaped, and hauled it in, while Phil Girlie and I hustled over to make the stop as he came down with it. The result was a 28-yard gain and a very angry Coach Ondrus. Newark Catholic decided to try it again on the next play. They switched sides and tried Todd Hanna, Todd slipped and fell, and Hans Schell got past him, but had to wait on another wobbly long pass, giving Girlie time to fly back and make the tackle.

"Since we couldn't wear our normal cleats on the turf, I was wearing a pair of the loaners that were dumped out on the locker room floor as we were getting dressed," responded Todd Hanna. "All of the shoes were worn and had little traction. The soles were hard rubber and slippery. I was having some serious trouble moving around on the turf. It felt like I was on ice. The receiver ran a down-out-and-up, while I just went (down), literally. I think just about everyone was having trouble with those loaner shoes."[107]

The Green Wave had the ball down on our 18-yard line thanks to a 27-yard pick up. What a simply terrible start to the biggest game of our lives because we hadn't really defended a play yet and they had the ball knocking on our doorstep.

Clay Shell got the first carry on an isolation right and I crashed hard to make the stop after just one-yard. On second-and-nine, Montgomery dropped back and hit Bill Franks on the right side for a pick up of nine.

A dive left by Scott Saad was stuffed by Scott Kolb and me after a gain of three yards. Newark Catholic then received a five-yard penalty for illegal procedure and had the ball moved back to our 10. An isolation right to Saad picked up two yards before Jeff Okuly could clog up the trenches and make the stop.

Montgomery then shuffled back to pass, I had the tight end Franks in man-to-man coverage. He came off of the line, took about three chop steps to make it appear like he was blocking, and then darted for the corner of the end zone on a tight end delay pass. I was right with him and thought there was no way Montgomery could get the ball in there. I even knew what brand of deodorant Franks was wearing. I jumped up, dove at the ball and it just skimmed across my fingertips, Bill Franks dove and hauled it in for an eight-yard touchdown. The ball was thrown absolutely perfectly. An inch either way and it would have been picked off or an incomplete pass. The kick by Matt Gase was good, making the score 7-0 early in the first quarter.

Travis Lewis fielded the kickoff and found some room to run making it out to our 34-yard line before he was stopped. Steve Deitrick got the call on a 32 trap and pounded ahead for two yards. Martin then faded back and tried to hit me on a long pass down the right sideline, but the ball was way out of my reach and we faced another third-and-long. Martin tried to hit Tolly Hanna on a waggle right but the pass was broken up, which forced the Pilots to once again punt on fourth down. Jerry Carnahan got off a good punt and booted the ball to the Newark Catholic 31-yard line where Eric Burket was waiting. Burket made the tackle for no return, and our defense went on the field to try and avenge our pathetic showing the last time we were out there.

J.D. Graham decided to continue to take long shots down the field. Montgomery again dropped back and heaved a jump ball down the right sideline. That time, Johnny Armes went up higher than Tom Helms to break it up. A sweep right on second down was then demolished by Eric Burket for a three-yard loss.

Montgomery faded back to pass and was forced to scramble when Jeff Okuly got free. Montgomery delivered the ball down field, but he was across the line of scrimmage when he threw the ball. The penalty was assessed and the Green Wave punt unit had to kick the ball to an awaiting Denny Martin.

Martin indeed caught the punt but the coverage was there, and he was dropped after a short three-yard return. The Pilot offense had the ball first-and-10 at our own 45-yard line.

Shelby Dawson got right up under the pads of outside linebacker Franks, and blew him off of the line of scrimmage, enabling Schlachter to pick up six yards on a sweep right. A 33 trap to Deitrick continued to move the ball down field for two yards and sat us up for a third-and-two. Schlachter then picked up just the yardage needed for the first down on a sweep left. The chain gang brought the marker onto the field and confirmed that it was indeed a Pilot first down.

I received the pitch from Martin on a blast right option but Tom Helms read it perfectly and was right there to make the stop after a two-yard pick up. I then went in motion right and kicked Franks out on a 16, enabling Schlachter to earn five yards. That ended the first quarter and I couldn't believe it. Quarter one of the state finals was the fastest quarter of football I had ever played in.

Denny Martin dashed back to pass to open in the second stanza and found some room to run. He took off and picked up 20 yards before he could be brought down, which sat us up first-and-10 on the Newark Catholic 26. Jaime Briseno and Aaron Roth cleared out a running lane for Deitrick on a 37 cross trap and he pushed forward for eight yards.

On the next play, Newark Catholic blitzed and we didn't pick it up at all. To make things worse, Schlachter was slow getting outside, but the play still picked up three yards. Martin then rolled out right on a waggle and found Deitrick wide open in the flat. Deitrick seized the leather and bounced to the one-yard line before he was stopped.

One play later, Chris Schlachter surged into the end zone and our offense had answered against the stiff Green Wave defense. Schlachter nailed the extra point and the score was even at 7-7 with 10:50 to play in the half.

Tolly Hanna, who was filling in for an injured Rob Giesige, got down the field in a hurry on the kickoff and made a nice tackle on Darby Riley at the Newark Catholic 28-yard line. I then knew Rob must have been very injured or there would be no way he would be on the sideline for a kickoff. He absolutely lived for the kickoff team. He had injured an ankle and could barely walk on it, which forced us to scramble for a defensive end. Chris Schlachter handled most of the task, he was a good defensive end, but Coach McCord really wanted him fresh to "tote the ball" as he always said.

On a cross right to Shell, Burket got driven inside and the pick up was 19 yards before Mike Wilson and I could drag him down. Another long out-pattern by Franks was successful when the Montgomery pass once again fluttered over my finger tips as I jumped and dove for the ball. Franks rumbled down the sideline for 25 yards before Todd Hanna and Girlie could make the stop. The pass set up the Newark Catholic offense for a first-and-10 at our 32-yard line.

Shell tried off tackle on the right side but a slanting Aaron Roth made the stop for no gain. A pass out in the left flat was in front of Hanna to Tom Helms for 12 yards and a first down, before Todd could make the stop. Coach McCord decided to blitz on first down, I blitzed on the outside, but just as I got to Montgomery, I got knocked off by a falling teammate. The Montgomery pass was delivered across the middle to an open Tom Helms for another six points. Dase once again kicked the extra point after the 20-yard touchdown. Mike Wilson almost got there to block the kick, but the Green Wave had it timed perfectly and we were down 14-7 with 8:59 to play in the half.

Lewis couldn't get anything going on the kickoff return team and was dropped at our own 19-yard line. Then the game went from bad to worse for the Pilots. Deitrick was hit and fumbled on a 32 trap after a short gain. The ball was recovered by Newark Catholic and we just couldn't seem to catch a break. That was the only fumble Steve Deitrick lost in 155 carries that year.

Montgomery rolled out left on first down, but Deitrick, Kolb and Roth were there for the sack and nine-yard loss. A pass left to Bill Franks was once again complete for 18 yards, before I could club him out of bounds. I say "club" because that's exactly what I did. I had seen enough of the Montgomery to Franks garbage, so as he was running down the sideline, I swung my right arm into his helmet to knock him out of bounds.

We then got a taste of Scott Saad off of right tackle. He went the distance from 12 yards out and it was starting to look like our defense was made of Swiss cheese. I felt like Saad was a pretty good runner, he seemed to have some good acceleration when he got into the hole. The Dase kick was again good and we were down 21-7 with 7:23 left to play in the second quarter.

Newark Catholic was scoring at will and unless we figured out a way to contain them promptly, the Green Wave was going to breeze to their third-straight state title.

Scott Kolb returned the high kick out to our 27-yard line before he was wrangled to the ground. Martin elected to pitch the ball on a 33 option to Schlachter and the Fat Boy took over. He made Darby Riley grasp for shoe laces when he put a nice juke on him. He then ran right over Damon Schumaker for an 18-yard gainer. Schlachter continued to pick up yardage on a sweep right for seven yards on the following play.

On second-and-three, Travis Lewis converted with a four-yard gain on a 17 cross trap. Scott Kolb checked in for Deitrick and couldn't get anything on a 32 trap to set up a second-and-10. Martin then hit Deitrick on a 16 cross trap pass for a pick up of four yards.

Coach Ondrus faced a fourth-and-four and he elected to go for it. Martin dropped back and tried to hit me in the right flat, but I couldn't dive forward far enough to make the catch. Our offense had to turn the ball over on downs. If we could have executed on that series, we would have been right back in the game.

Instead, the ball was back in the hands of Montgomery and a Newark Catholic offense that had been unstoppable.

Shell carried on first down and picked up just one-yard before Marv Andrews and Roth could cause the train-wreck. Bill Franks once again got open in our weak side flat and hauled in a Montgomery pass for 21 yards. The flat would definitely have to be addressed at halftime. The passes in our weak-side flat were just killing us. Hanna came up and made the stop on Franks at our 40-yard line.

On first down, Jeff Okuly decided he had seen enough of the passing attack and he got to Montgomery, sacking him for a seven-yard loss. An adjustment had already been made in our defense and Scott Kolb was there to break up a pass in our weak side flat on the second and 17. A counter with Tom Helms carrying was stuffed by Girlie for one-yard. The stop by Girlie forced the Newark Catholic punt team back onto the field. The Backlund punt rolled into the end zone, giving us little time and 80 yards of artificial turf between us and a score before the halftime break.

Aaron Roth delivered a crushing block on the right linebacker, Tim McKenna, which allowed Deitrick to run for eight yards on a 33 trap. A 33 trap option was then set up beautifully with Martin pulling the ball out, and getting some good yardage, before he then pitched to Schlachter for a gain of 13 yards. Martin then kept on a 32 option that gained four yards.

The yardage train rolled to a stop with Deitrick getting stuffed on a 33 trap for no gain. Martin then faded back to pass, Wimberly Cook came free without being blocked and forced Martin to scramble, the result was a hit and fumble. Jim Cross fell on the loose ball and Newark Catholic had the ball back on our 44-yard line with just 30 seconds remaining.

Montgomery dropped deep to pass, and Steve Deitrick slammed his hands to the turf in frustration, after the pass glided over his outstretched hands and into the hands of Franks for a 23-yard gain. Franks wisely got out of bounds to stop the clock which gave Backlund a chance to kick a 37-yard field goal. As time expired, the kick was short and wide left, sending us into halftime with a score of Newark Catholic 21, Ayersville 7.

> "I remember being so frustrated when they were throwing the ball all over us in the first half on that deep down and out to the tight end right between us LB's and the safeties. I was running my mouth yelling, who has the freaking tight end, who has the freaking tight end! on my way back to the huddle. The ref just looked at me and said, 'Which tight end would that be, son?' My response was to quickly shut up and get back to playing ball," related Steve Deitrick.[108]

At halftime, Coach McCord and Coach Ondrus addressed the problem we were having covering the weak side zones of the Green Wave passing attack. They remedied this by setting us up in a 5-3 defense. Phil Girlie and I would move up and play outside linebacker while Jerry Carnahan would get inserted as the middle safety. We had a three-deep zone and both flats covered. We of course would still be running our standard 5-2 and play some man coverage, while we tried to get after Montgomery with the blitz.

> "I felt at the half things were going too easy for us," recalled Graham. "They (Ayersville) were a much better team. I knew they would come back."[109]

While we were resting and making adjustments, the Ayersville Pilot Marching Band was performing on the field at Ohio Stadium. They even performed my personal favorite (The Smoking in the Boys Room skit). The band, directed by senior Melissa Barnes was very good and I did not realize it until I watched the tapes of our games. I was pretty much unaware of that kind of stuff while I was playing, but I sure did enjoy the sounds our marching band created when I watched them on tape. They were very good and it took me 23 years before I actually experienced it. They laid down an awesome halftime show in Columbus. It was just a great job by everyone. There were flags, rifles, drums, horns and all of the different musical instruments. I was very impressed with our bands performance. Thank you to the band for laying down some true football sounds!

Coach McCord told us to never give up, never quit, we had made it this far, and we had 24 minutes of football left. He concluded with, "Leave it all out there on the field."

That's what we would do.

We kicked off to begin the second half and we needed a defensive stop in a bad way. The Schlachter kick was fumbled around and once it was picked up, Jerry Carnahan and Don Andrews made the tackle. Chris Schlachter, who always got down the field in a hurry after his kickoffs, put a great hit on lead blocker Tom Parker.

An isolation left with Shell carrying picked up two yards before Marv Andrews and I could crush him to the turf. The Green Wave then faced a second-and-eight from their 28. The same play with Shell again carrying picked up three yards as Andrews made the tackle by himself. Scott Saad then picked up four yards, before Girlie could not only take on the lead blocker, but make one of his great no arm tackles as well.

The measurement revealed that the Newark Catholic offense was just inches short of the first down. They decided to go for it and gave the ball to Tim McKenna on the right side. Okuly, Wilson and Girlie were there to pile up the line of scrimmage, but McKenna lunged forward for a yard and the first down.

There was an injury timeout called so they could attend to an injured Newark Catholic player down on the field. When Wilson held his ground at the line of scrimmage, it looked like #73 Bill Keaser tweaked his neck. The injured player finally got carted off of the field and play was able to be resumed.

On a dive left, Saad picked up nine yards before Hanna and I could make the tackle. Unfortunately for the Green Wave, they received a holding penalty and lost five yards instead of gaining nine.

On first-and-15, Parker carried on a counter right. Girlie and Roth were right there to lay a hit on him and make the stop after a gain of two. Saad then carried on a dive left and I pasted him after another gain of two.

On third-and-11, we sensed the pass and dropped to our 5-3 defense. I covered Franks in the flat, and saw Montgomery release the ball. That time it wasn't over my finger tips. The precious pigskin was not out of reach and I made the interception like it was the last one I would ever make. I grabbed the ball like it was a cheeseburger on a plate and I was a starving man sitting in front of it. Franks slammed me to the turf in front of their bench after I caught the ball, but the ball was OURS!

Finally, one of those buzzing aerial assault footballs had been caught by one of guys in Blue and Gold.

With a first-and-10 in Newark Catholic territory, our offense went to work. Travis Lewis picked up five yards on a sweep left, then the other game captain stepped up. Steve Deitrick took it to the house on a 32 trap right up the middle. He shook off a tackler and outraced the Green Wave defenders for a 32-yard touchdown.

> Deitrick said it was one of his high points of the year. "One of my personal highlights from the 1986 season was scoring in the Horseshoe (twin's right, 32 trap)."[110]

The Schlachter kick was high, but good, making the score Newark Catholic 21, Ayersville 14.

On the kickoff, Scott Kolb hustled down the field and made the hit at the Green Wave 28-yard line. We were back in business. We were finally playing the kind of football we had played all year. Our defense would make a big stop and our offense would shove it right down the other team's throat.

A quick pitch right to Saad was busted up by Roth for no gain. Our other tackle, Okuly, then rushed Montgomery hard on second down and he got a hand on his arm as he was throwing the pass. The ball was incomplete, but Aaron Roth dove on it like he dove in the mud puddles that one rainy afternoon practice while we all watched. On third-and-10, Montgomery converted with a pass to Franks in the right flat for 11 yards. Girlie made the stop, but he too was feeling the frustration of the ball being just out of reach.

Montgomery was back to pass on first down, Eric Burket almost got to him, but he stepped up and evaded the sack. Montgomery let fly down the middle of the field but the ball was overthrown and Franks was on the receiving end of the ball being just out of reach. I was there, but couldn't come forward fast enough to corral the ball. On second-and-10, the Green Wave tried a screen left. Schlachter read it perfectly, and was in perfect position, forcing Montgomery to throw the ball away.

On third-and-10, Montgomery connected with Saad, but I was there to make the hit and wrap up, four yards short of the first down. The Green Wave had to bring on the punt team, the punt was good and Denny Martin decided to allow it to drop. Unfortunately for us, it was downed at the Pilot eight-yard line. The Ayersville offense had a long way to go, but we needed another score badly. A sweep left to Travis Lewis gained four yards before a 33 trap to Deitrick was stuffed for no gain.

Backed up close to our own end zone, we were in dire need of first down yardage on third down. The play called would turn out to be one of the most exciting plays in Ayersville Pilot history. Everyone on the field had a chance to participate, because it may have been the longest play in Ayersville history as well.

Enter Denny Martin, the third-and-six call was a waggle right. I had seen it run about a million times, but I had never seen it run quite like it was run that day. Martin faded back to pick up his guard escort around the right end. He faded all the way back to our one-yard line. He then decided to keep the ball. Slowly the offensive line took off down field as well. I was a decoy running a deep route on the left sideline and as I turned I saw the play developing. I watched Martin cutting across the field, and caught a glimpse of Scott Saad flying across the field on an angle to tackle Martin. I then circled around and decided to peel the chasing Saad off of Denny.

I remembered back to when I was a sophomore, and I got called for a clip, on the peel-off block that sprung Denny on the long punt return touchdown at Hicksville. I decided to just let Martin come to me. Denny set up the block perfectly and curled right around me. I then lowered my right shoulder and drove it up into the chasing Saad. He went sprawling over backwards and Denny continued down the sideline.

By then, John Finn and Tim Boals were down field as well. We had so many blockers down field that Denny ended up stiff arming one of his own teammates as he curled back to the other sideline. Our guys were everywhere. I had stayed on my feet but I couldn't catch up to the Martin caravan and I trailed behind as Denny made it into the end zone and collapsed in a heap, exhausted.

Denny Martin had ran backwards, forwards, and to both sides on his winding, dodging, start and stopping 88-yard touchdown scurry. I think Denny probably ran closer to 200 yards on the play. It was a marvelous run and broke a state championship game record for the longest run from scrimmage. The extra point however was blocked and Newark Catholic clung to a 21-20 lead.

The kickoff was fielded by Darby Riley and he was dropped by a charging Scott Kolb at the Newark Catholic 24. A hand back left to Shell picked up three yards before Marv Andrews could crush him to the ground. A pass left was caught by Helms and converted into a first down after a pick up of 12 yards. Shell then carried on an isolation right and he was met hard by Jeff Okuly after a pick up of just one-yard.

Another long, up-for-grabs Montgomery pass down the middle was thrown, but Girlie, Armes and Carnahan were all there to bat it away. Montgomery then dropped back to pass again on third down but his pass to Franks on the left side was covered well, and the ball fell incomplete, forcing a fourth-and-nine. The Newark Catholic punt team had to return to the field.

Martin began to get things rolling when he took off down the left sideline on a 15-yard punt return. The Pilot offense rolled to the line, but an off side's penalty on first down against the Green Wave defense tacked on another five yards before we could start our drive. A quick pitch right to Deitrick then gave us a first down when he picked up six yards. Lewis was then shut down for no gain on a 17 cross trap and the third quarter came to an end.

We had just 12 minutes left in the 1986 season. It would be the last 12 minutes of their entire high school football career for 16 seniors. We had already played for 660 minutes in 1986; the final 12 would be the most important of all.

A 33 option left found Martin flipping the ball back to Lewis for a gain of two yards. On third-and-eight, a Martin pass to Tolly

Hanna over the middle was ruled incomplete, much to the dismay of Hanna. Tolly went ballistic, jumped around and emphatically pleaded his case of catching the ball. Hanna was escorted to the sideline as our punt team took the field. Carnahan banged the punt into the end zone, giving Newark Catholic the ball at the 20.

> Tolly Hanna had this to say. "I caught that ball. I have never watched the film of the game, but all of the people that did, emphatically claim that I scooped that ball up before it touched the turf. I got up and handed to the ball to the ref thinking he was going to spot it right there for the first down. When he waved it off, I did go kind of crazy because it was clearly a catch. Mike Wilson kind of told me to let it go, and pulled me away before I got some sort of penalty.[111]

A dive by Shell was stuffed with Schlachter making the tackle after a one-yard gain. Montgomery then hit Hans Schell in the left flat for a pick up of 11 yards before Schell could be forced out of bounds. An isolation right with Shell carrying picked up two yards before Jaime Briseno could wrestle him to the ground. Briseno hurt a leg on the play and had to be walked off of the field.

A dive by Saad was totally blown up by Marv Andrews and Jeff Okuly for a loss of two. As if it never got old, Montgomery dropped back and floated a pass just over my outstretched hands and into the hands of Bill Franks. The gain was for 31 yards before Carnahan and I could chase him down.

Our defense continued to control the Green Wave run game as a counter by Parker on first down was demolished by Andrews and Burket for another two-yard loss. Newark Catholic tried the old halfback pass play on second down. Scott Saad took off and was ready to throw, but we were in a man defense and the receiver down field was covered. Saad kept the ball and picked up two yards on the play.

On third-and-10, Schlachter finally got to Montgomery for the sack with Andrews there as well. Our defense continued its dominant ways in the second half and forced another Green Wave punt. Martin fielded the punt and retreated back to our three-yard line to get around the end and to the wall. Denny raced down the sideline for 22 yards and we started our drive from our 31. It was another nice return by Martin and it was the last one of his career.

As we lined up for the play, Deitrick noticed he didn't have his mouthpiece and an equipment timeout was called. He retreated and found it lying on the turf and we were ready to get on with the action.

A 17 cross trap with Lewis carrying went for seven yards. Scott Kolb then picked up the first down with a four-yard run on a 33 trap.

Schlachter checked back in and picked up another nine yards on a sweep left. There was 5:51 showing on the clock, the drive we were on could be for the game. On second-and-one, Schlachter failed to pick up the first down, gaining absolutely nothing on a hand back trap.

The Newark Catholic defensive stop was short lived when Schlachter rumbled for nine yards on a sweep right. We had the ball first-and-10 on the Newark Catholic 40-yard line. A 17 cross trap, with Lewis carrying got us two yards closer. Once again we went to a waggle right; Deitrick was open and took the Martin pass down field for 21 yards. It was a great play and nice pick up with Deitrick slicing his way through the defense.

The Pilots were lurching toward the go-ahead score with a first-and-10 at the 17. Oh, how we wanted to hear the famous Ayersville touchdown bell ring. The call was a blast left reverse to me. Wimberly Cook blew the play up and I was dropped for a two-yard loss. Schlachter then gained only three yards on a 17 cross trap when the hole just wasn't there. We faced a third-and-nine and we needed a huge play to keep the drive alive. Shelby Dawson went real low and scraped the Martin pass right off the turf across the middle for eight yards. The official signaled a catch! The catch was a key play in the drive, and gave us a good shot at converting on fourth down.

Fourth-and-one at the Green Wave seven, I knew the play I wanted. It happened to be the same one Coach Ondrus called, combo right blast right. Deitrick and I would be leading Schlachter through the vacant hole left by our double-teaming Mike Wilson.

If there was a linebacker filling that hole, he would have Deitrick and I to contend with before the battering ram Schlachter hit the hole. I really felt like the combo blast play could never be stopped for less than two yards ever. The ball was snapped and everything happened according to plan. The Newark Catholic defense swarmed the hole but it did no good, we had created an explosion on the right side, the pick up was three yards.

We were teetering near the end zone at the four and it was time to see if Newark Catholic could stop our devastating tailback Chris "Fat Boy" Schlachter.

Phil Girlie checked in and we ran the same play to the left side. Phil and Deitrick blasted into the left side of the line. That time, Schlachter hammered ahead with second effort and struck up the renowned Pilot touchdown bell ring with a 4-yard plunge into the end zone.

Schlachter banged the kick through with 2:24 remaining in the game. We had the lead for the first time in the game, 27-21. All we had to do was get a stop or force a turnover and we would be STATE CHAMPS!

The kickoff was fielded by Darby Riley and he returned it out to the Green Wave 29-yard line. Phil Girlie had made the tackle, but I think he received a stinger on the play.

It all came down to stopping the passing attack, all we needed was to pick off one of the Montgomery passes or to hold them for four consecutive downs. Montgomery began his assault and hit Franks for 16 yards before he stepped out of bounds on the right side. A pass left from Montgomery to Shell gained only two yards. On second down, Hanna went up and broke up the long pass on the left sideline, setting us up to cover the pass.

It was third-and-eight, we needed a stop to force a fourth-down.

The Montgomery pass on the right side landed right into the arms of Tom Helms and he picked up 23 yards before Johnny Armes could bring him down. The Newark Catholic offense had just recovered for a fresh set of downs. The next play was a pass to

Saad on the left sideline and it was good for another 13 yards before Hanna and I could make the tackle.

The way things were going, we needed a stop immediately. Our defense seemed to be in chaos, and players were running in and out of the huddle the whole time.

Montgomery dropped back to pass and found Helms on the right side for a pick up of eight yards. Girlie and I made the stop, as Deitrick was shaken up on the play.

With 59 seconds left, the Newark Catholic offense had swiftly marched right down the field and they had the ball at our 12-yard line. Things had looked so good just a minute before, but there we were scrambling to stop a "Green Tidal Wave" that was rumbling towards our end zone.

We had all sorts of guys shaken up and it was a hodge-podge defense out there, but that was why we practiced. We had to have ourselves ready for that kind of situation. We had the players on the field and we had to dig deep and get the stop. Shelby Dawson was in at defensive end and we had a man defense called. Dawson had the tight end and I was set to cover the halfback on my side. Either that or I was supposed to blitz, either way, I failed to do my assignment.

I started to feel like everything was in slow motion. I knew what play they were going to run. It was going to be that tight end delay pass they ran against me for the first touchdown. I saw Dawson lining up to cover Franks. Everything moved in slow motion, the guy I had in man coverage stayed in to block, and I failed to blitz. Franks was taking those chop steps at the line of scrimmage, Dawson was there to cover him. I totally saw it coming. My instinct was to cover the tight end. I reacted too late; I just knew it was going to Franks.

Jaime Briseno was charging after Montgomery and he let the pass fly just before Briseno got there. It was indeed intended for Franks. It drifted right over Dawson and me and into Bill Franks' arms in the end zone.

"I thought we (Ayersville) were there," said McCord of the TD pass. If he (Montgomery) throws it a little bit one way it's an interception or incomplete."[112]

333

I felt like there was something telling me where the ball was going, I felt like I should have listened and covered Franks better. The way Montgomery was throwing passes that day; it may not have mattered if I was on Bill Franks back. It had been that kind of frustrating day.

I do think about that play often, I know it was just one play in the game, but it was a big play that I could have made a difference on. At the time, it was chaos on the field and it all happened so quickly. I should have called a timeout so our team could have regrouped. I should have stuck closer to Franks. I knew the ball was going there. I take full responsibility for that play, and it will always haunt me.

"The last drive was the greatest drive in our history," said Graham who owns a 167-17-1 record at NC. "I've been here 18 years. Maybe our tradition helped us."[113]

The Newark Catholic team had executed, we had not. We couldn't take anything away from them; they did the job when they had to. It was extremely frustrating, but they were well coached and they knew what they had to do, and they did it.

The game was only tied; we still had a chance, if we could force them to miss the extra point. I am sure J.D. Graham had practiced extra points over and over with his team and he had great confidence they would execute flawlessly. That was the Newark Catholic way; they did things the correct way, each and every time.

Our fans held their breath for the second week in a row. Some wished, some prayed, while others chanted, "Miss it, miss it." The snap was made, and there was no overachieving Pilot there to block the kick. The foot of Matt Dase struck the ball and it flew toward the pipes. There was only silence, no outside force intervened and caused the kick to go off target. On that day there would be no miracle. The kick was good, and the Green Wave faithful erupted, the score was Newark Catholic 28, Ayersville 27.

I was not ready to call it a game, we had 47 seconds left and anything could happen. We had found that out the previous week. We did not get the same start as the week before when the kickoff bounced past Lewis and he made it back out to our 19-yard line. To make things worse, we received a penalty that backed us up to our own four-yard line. It wasn't looking good, but we still had a chance.

Martin dropped back on first down and couldn't find anybody to throw the ball to. He was sacked and barely made it out of the end zone. When we didn't think things could get any worse, things got a whole lot worse, time was running out and we had just lost another two yards, when we only had four to spare in the first place

We had to take our final timeout to stop the clock after the sack. Coach Ondrus came onto the field and he designed a hook and lateral for Carnahan and me. Carnahan was to catch the ball on the hook pattern and then flip the ball to me as I ran by. Martin dropped back to pass, and the ball was delivered off target, the play didn't work but at least the clock wasn't running anymore.

It was on to plan B, or by that time it was plan F, a pass down the sideline. It was one of the most exciting plays in football, the Hail Mary. Martin again dropped back to pass, and as he threw the ball, his arm was hit and the ball fluttered harmlessly to the turf.

It was fourth down and we had only 17 seconds left on the clock. We could only try another Hail Mary pass down the right sideline. I had seen so many of them where the ball was tipped and then caught by somebody away from the actual play. I decided that was my only chance at a miracle.

Martin dropped back and had the time to throw. He unloaded with all he had and the ball was coming down in the middle of a bunch of different players. It was tipped and it went flopping past the entire pile five yards further down field.

That was the place I had positioned myself, the ball came right into my awaiting arms. Was this the miracle?

I took three steps after hauling in the pass, and got tripped up immediately at the midfield stripe. I wanted one more shot as our offense hustled to the line because we were out of timeouts.

The clock began to run again as soon as the ball was spotted and the first-down chains were in place. Denny had to throw the ball away to stop the clock and give us one more Hail Mary heave to the end zone, but the clock struck zeroes as Denny took the snap and threw the ball away.

The Green Wave side erupted in jubilation, and our dream season ended on a somber note.

I then ran that final play through my head. *Was there a lane I could have escaped through? How could I have escaped, could I have lifted my legs higher to avoid being tripped up? Could I have lateraled the ball to somebody else? I didn't see anybody on our team, maybe I should have just flipped it backwards. There had to be an escape route, what if I would have stutter stepped and went for the other side of the field? What did the scoreboard say? One stinking point, you have to be kidding me, it was definitely the "Point of Sorrow".*

I think our whole team was in a state of shock, we hadn't lost in so long, we had forgotten what it felt like. We finally made our way to shake the victor's hands. We had done battle with a great team. There wasn't a whole lot of handshaking going on at the end of the line. It was hugging, the gracious winners did not gloat over us. They were humble and gave many of us hugs instead of simple handshakes.

The Newark Catholic Green Wave was also a class organization. Some champions can be chumps, but that was not the case with Newark Catholic. They were winners, and I am sure they worked very hard day in and day out to achieve all of the success they had on the football field.

Coach J.D. Graham knew a little about football. He went on to coach the Green Wave through the 1991 season and accumulated an astounding record of 220-30-1 while he captured seven state titles.

After acknowledging the Newark Catholic state champions, I made my way to the sideline with the rest of the team. I remember the team receiving a standing ovation from our fans, but after that I don't remember too much about that afternoon. I don't remember anything that happened in the locker room. I don't remember anything about the bus ride home. I don't even know if we rode the bus home, that's how out of it I was.

Manager Amy (Shinabery) Snyder explained the scene. "What a crushing blow to lose by one point. It was on every one of the players' faces. It was awful to see the tears on some of my best friends' faces. We all cried for our guys."[114]

The next thing I remember was walking into our packed gymnasium back at Ayersville.

The band was playing and everyone was cheering. Walking into that gymnasium was a very difficult thing to do. When I watched it later on, Coach McCord seemed to have the hardest time of us all.

He walked in holding son Jonathan's hand and had to take a deep breath every few steps. At the end of the welcome home, Coach McCord wanted somebody to say something. I flat out told him I couldn't say anything. I hadn't said 10 words since the game.

Thankfully, Mike Wilson stepped forward, and instead of a touchdown saving tackle, he delivered a fine thank you to our fans. When it was all over, I took off for the locker room and found my place in front of my locker.

Manager Kristen (Bell) Warren was surprised by the reception. "When we were coming back I kept thinking that everyone would be mad because we didn't win. Then, when we got back and saw the cars lined up with the fans waving their support, I was astonished."[115]

Offensively, Denny Martin played a great game. He picked up 116 yards rushing and had the record-breaking run. Chris Schlachter picked up another 82 yards on the ground, with Deitrick adding his 67 hard-fought yards.

Defensively, I had 10 tackles and an interception to end my career. Jeff Okuly ended his reign at tackle with seven tackles and a quarterback sack. Steve Deitrick wrapped up his fine tenure with six tackles and one sack.

Defensively, we had made the necessary adjustments at halftime and kept the Green Wave offense at bay until that fateful final possession. The Newark Catholic passing attack racked up some huge numbers that day. Jeremy Montgomery and Bill Franks were just plain unstoppable. Jeremy Montgomery had a game of a lifetime passing the ball.

> "WE KNEW WE had to throw the ball to win this game," said Newark Catholic head coach J.D. Graham, whose team won its third straight Division V football championship. "In order to win a state championship game, you have to have some kid play beyond his limits. Nobody is that good except once."[116]

> "He's (Montgomery) a good one," praised McCord. "We could not get any pass rush on him. We weren't able to cover their deep outs."[117]

It was such a frustrating game, we were so close. We got off to a horrible start, but then picked it up in the second half to lose it at the end. There were so many plays and instances that could have changed the outcome of the game. I believe that after the game, every one of us thought about what we could have done as an individual to change the outcome of that fateful score. To all of us, that would be attributed to the "Point Of Sorrow".

The title of the book actually goes deeper than the reference made to a one-point loss. The word (point) can also mean a definite moment in time. That is where the actual title comes from. It refers to more than just a person directly involved in the game. It can refer to a spectator of the high school game, college game or even the pro game. When the last play of the year or career is in the history books, anyone that truly loves the great game of football, experiences a "Point Of Sorrow".

STATISTICS

	NCHS	AHS
First Downs	15	15
Rushing Yards	44	301
Passing Yards	326	78
Total Offense	370	379
Passes Attempted	30	14
Passes Completed	21	6
Had Intercepted	1	0
Fumbles	1	2
Fumbles Lost	0	2
Yards Penalized	35	15

Newark Catholic	7	14	0	7-	-28
Ayersville	0	7	13	7-	-27

NCHS- Franks 8-yard pass from Montgomery (PAT Dase kick)

AHS- Schlachter 1-yard run (PAT Schlachter kick)

NCHS- Helms 20-yard pass from Montgomery (PAT Dase kick)

NCHS- Saad 12-yard run (PAT Dase kick)

AHS- Deitrick 32-yard run (PAT Schlachter kick)

AHS- Martin 88-yard run (PAT kick blocked)

AHS- Schlachter 4-yard run (PAT Schlachter kick)

NCHS- Franks 12-yd pass from Montgomery (PAT Dase kick)

EPILOGUE

We had just walked out of the locker room for the final time as an Ayersville football player. Our final game had been in a losing effort. I had made the journey to the parking lot after a varsity game 42 times before. Of those walks, 37 had been after victories and only five had been after a loss. There were many jubilant walks from a big victory, and there were the few silent walks from a heart wrenching loss. The final walk would be the hardest of them all. Only one week earlier, there was the walk of a lifetime. The walk from when we beat Mogadore in a miraculous way and knew we were heading to the state championship. It was late and we were battered and tired from an incredibly long day, but that walk was a walk to be remembered. There was the walk after we beat Edgerton, finishing with a perfect 10-0 regular season. That was the walk of knowing our season was still alive, and we would be fighting to keep it alive in the playoffs. After each one of those walks, we knew there would be another.

I was on the last one, there could be no other. We had made it to the final game, and even if we had won, it was that fateful final walk. It was amazing at how insignificant those walks had been at the time. Why hadn't I performed some sort of ritual after all of those walks? I could have picked up a loose stone each time and started a pile somewhere, so that on the last walk, I could have looked at it and seen all that had been accomplished. I could have scratched a mark on the pavement while I was on those walks. Then I could have knelt down and looked at the faded marks from before and scratched the final mark. At that moment in time, those walks meant so much to me, but they had all been taken for granted prior to my final walk.

Jeff Okuly walked with me in silence. I was in deep thought, and he must have been as well. We stood there by our cars for awhile, him by his Cutlass, and me by my trusty rusty Monza. It was dark, incredibly peaceful, and by moonlight, we looked out over the practice fields to the football stadium in the distance. The landscape had not changed much since the first varsity season in 1976. I thought back to 1977 when a nine-year-old boy had tagged along with his sister. He was standing in the grass, watching as four lines of players in fabulous matching uniforms, held hands, and made their way to the battlefield. That nine-year-old boy had made the entire journey and now it had come to an end.

As I looked out over the dimly lit grass, with the football stadium looming in the background like a billboard, I saw 11 lines of seniors; 10 lines were from each class that had already graduated. The 11th line was a group of 16 that played for a state championship. Briefly, they huddled together one last time, and then took their place in line as well. A guy in brown coveralls was walking from player to player and slapping them on their backs. As my mind drifted, slowly the silhouette of hundreds of young boys appeared around them, watching and longing for their chance to play.

Jeff and I gave each other a nod, started our cars, and drove off, with Coach McCord's voice echoing in my mind:

This is the beginning of a new day

God has given us this day to use as we will

We can waste it or use it for good

What we do today is important

Because we are exchanging a

Day out of our lives for it

When tomorrow comes, this day

Will be gone forever, leaving

In its place something that

We have traded

We want it to be gained not lost,

Good not evil, success not failure

Amen

BANQUET

On December 6, 1986 at 5:00 p.m. all 16 seniors said their final good byes as an Ayersville Football player in the crowded Ayersville cafeteria. In the years past, the end of the year banquet was an exciting affair, and we had the realization that we would come back next year, and be another step up the ladder in the playing pecking order.

There were some smiles and laughter, overall it was a joyous event, but there were also a lot of tense moments. The state final game had been played only seven days prior. I still had a bad taste in my mouth, and it was quite evident I wasn't alone.

There can be all kinds of things said about what a great year it was, how we had nothing to feel bad about, it was a fabulous year, state runners-up was a great accomplishment. I couldn't seem to buy into any of that. I may have been wrong, and maybe I had too much of a competitive nature, but being runners-up gave me no sense of relief from the one-point loss we suffered. I will be honest and say, at the time, I was still completely torn up inside. I had finally come to the realization that I would no longer suit up in the Blue & Gold, but at that point all I could focus on were the what ifs. What if I or anybody else could have got their hands on one of those final drive passes? That would have meant game over. What if on that final Hail Mary pass from Denny Martin, I could have found a seam and stayed on my feet?

I will have to tell you, the what ifs drove me crazy. I came to a realization that it was pointless to think about all of the things that could have changed the outcome of the game. For anything that could have changed the outcome in our favor, there was something equal on the other side that could have changed it in the other direction.

It was in the past, it was history, and it could not be changed. Quite frankly, it was what it was. It did take me awhile to realize all of that, and I still can't say I am not disappointed about the loss, but I have learnt to accept it.

On that night, a week after the loss, it was still too recent in my mind for me to totally enjoy the banquet. The food didn't taste as good, I didn't look forward to the awards and gift presentations, and I especially didn't look forward to my farewell speech.

Coach Ondrus opened the banquet with some dinner instructions. Everyone was hungry and couldn't wait to fill their plates from the huge buffet tables set up. It was a pot-luck dinner and every family brought a dish. I think some may have brought even more than one dish.

Coach Ondrus closed his dinner instructions with, "I think we should probably let the girls go first." It was as if he sensed the swarming heard of boys, wreaking havoc with those buffet tables. Without his instruction, I would have hoped we all would have had the correct sense to let the girls go first.

Coach Norman Beck then took center stage and delivered the pre-meal prayer. Then it was time to eat. While players, managers, cheerleaders, coaches and parents waited their turns, they turned their attention to the many displays laid out in the room. There were awards, scrapbooks, pictures and endless statistics provided by Coach McCord.

Once we had all finished eating, Coach Ondrus once again stepped forward and performed the introductions. When our Athletic Director Richard Baldwin was introduced, he stepped forward and said, "I would just like to say a few words," as he pulled a stack of papers out of his pocket. Everyone laughed, and hoped he was joking, but I wouldn't have cared, I always enjoyed listening to Mr. Baldwin.

He made the remark about how far we had come, how as eighth-graders we were 1-4. He then proceeded to tell us all about his experience dealing with our playoff run as athletic director. He loved every minute of it, but he hated the motel situation. He went on to say, "Our biggest battle wasn't going to be our opponent, it was going to be the motel. We had to keep everyone separated, make sure we got a good night of sleep in a foreign atmosphere, and in general, make it go as smoothly as possible." He closed out his time at the podium with his story about buying us pizza if we shut Tinora out, and how much trouble it got him in. I had known Mr. Baldwin from the time I was a little boy, I would surely miss him after I graduated.

Next to take the spot behind the microphone was statistician Larry Green. He not only did all of our stat work, but he had the glamorous job of driving the yellow Turbo Van. He talked about how for 12 weeks, he limped the Turbo Van filled with our equipment to the away games. Then for the final two games when we traveled so far away, the Turbo Van had to stay behind. He gave thanks to managers Kristen Bell, Kim McCord and Amy Shinaberry for riding along with him. They were in fact the ones that came up with the whole Turbo Van legacy in the first place. His remarks were, "I got to drive the Turbo Van to the away games. I am sure most of you saw the big yellow van with the cardboard signs with Turbo Van written on them and taped to the sides. I just want to thank Kristen Bell, Kim McCord and Amy Shinaberry for holding the doors shut and wiping the windows on our trips to and from the away games."

It was astonishing that three high school girls could make something so positive out of a trying situation. They didn't complain about the terrible condition of the van, they did the exact opposite, they anointed it the Turbo Van, and it became a legacy in Ayersville football folklore.

Head Coach Craig McCord then made his way to the podium. He thanked everyone, and didn't leave anyone out. Coach McCord was one of the finest speakers I have ever listened to. His presence behind the microphone commanded the attention of anyone within earshot. He was that good at public speaking. His speech flowed freely and eloquently at all times, he was a great motivator, and I could listen to him for hours.

He introduced his assistant coaches, and gave them the recognition they deserved. He then turned it over to the senior players. The senior class presented all of our parents a plaque. On the plaque was a picture of us standing with our parents on Parents' Night.

Cheerleading advisor Denise Knicely then gave all of the cheerleaders their recognition. Coach McCord followed by honoring the team managers. He made reference to all of the hard work they put in. He remarked, "They even washed all of the game jerseys and pants, I am sure they enjoyed it a lot more after the last two games though." (Referring to the games played on artificial turf, where grass and dirt wouldn't be present) The 16 seniors then again came forward and Mike Wilson took the microphone. He stressed, we all appreciate all that you did for us, and "You are a part of the team." The seniors then presented the senior managers (Kim McCord, Kristen Bell and Amy Shinaberry) a small gift thanking them for all of the hard work they did.

> Amy (Shinabery) Snyder remembered this. "All the managers received a wooden keepsake box from a senior player(s). John Finn presented my box to me. It was so sweet and we felt that we were appreciated for the support that we had given through the season."[118]

Coach Beck and Coach Hammersmith then proceeded to introduce the underclassmen of the team. Once that was finished, Coach McCord once again took center stage. He addressed the underclassmen as the future of Ayersville football. He then said, "As I was looking through the entire seniors' scrapbooks, I noticed that in many of them, the seniors had written to each other. I guess all of this was worth it when we were on the scout team as freshmen. That was where it all started, and look what can be accomplished."

Coach McCord then proceeded to call each player that earned a varsity letter up front. He then said a few words about each player before handing them their varsity letter. I was the last person called, and I had to bite my lip the entire time, to keep from tearing up. It would be the last time I was addressed by Coach McCord as an Ayersville football player and it was an emotional time for me.

Once that was finished, Coach McCord went into the various awards. The first award was for our Physical Fitness Champ. Whoever scored the most points in the contest we held in the spring before the season, would be the recipient of the award. We all knew who the person was ahead of time because we had received the results in the mail prior to the season.

Physical Fitness Award

Chris Schlachter

Next was the blooper of the year. Coach said that it was really hard to come up with one that year. In the years past a kicker would miss the ball on a kickoff or somebody would fall down, but that year we didn't have any of that. He gave the award to the player that was tackled in the huge mud puddle during the Hicksville game.

Blooper of the Year

Travis Lewis

The Block of the Year, was just as it stated, a great block that went above and beyond performing one's assignment. The block was performed during Denny Martin's touchdown run in the Fairview game.

Block of the Year

Jaime Briseno

The Tackle of the Year applied the same as the Block of the Year. It was also performed in the Fairview game, to stuff a fourth-and-one.

Tackle of the Year

Eric Burket

The Top Scout Award went to the player that performed day in and day out on the scout team. This player worked hard and forced those playing against him to work hard. The coaches couldn't decide on one, so they gave two players the honor.

Top Scout

Corey Ankney

Don Andrews

The Outstanding Freshman Award went to the freshman that put forth an outstanding effort.

Outstanding freshman

Matt Lloyd

The Crescent-News Player of the Week was also public knowledge. Each week the local newspaper chose an outstanding performer in the area for the week. For his performance in the Holgate and Edgerton Games, this player was a two-time recipient.

***The Crescent-News* Player of the Week**

Chris Schlachter

The Most Improved Player was the player that had improved the most from the end of last season to the end of the current season. Again the coaches couldn't decide on just one.

Most Improved Player

Marv Andrews

Shelby Dawson

The Team Champ Award had been voted on at the beginning of two-a-days.

Team Champ

Andy Groll

Next were the Most Valuable Awards, the awards could have gone to any of the players. I think we had OUTSTANDING PLAYERS at every position

Offensive Lineman- Mike Wilson

Offensive Back- Denny Martin

Defensive Lineman- Jeff Okuly

Defensive Back- Andy Groll

The Iron Man Trophy was something new. It was a mess of metal welded into a giant "A" and it was the most rudimentary award, but also looked the coolest. It was given to the player spending the most time on the field. Probably the most coveted award, this was the player that rarely came off of the field, even for special teams.

Iron Man Award

Steve Deitrick

The Perseverance Award went to the players exemplifying a never-say-die spirit. They always hung in there and they played hard. They were also a good team leader.

Perseverance Award

Marv Andrews

George Schaffer

A Pilot Award was given to a defensive player if they accumulated enough points for tackles, fumbles caused and recovered, sacks, interceptions and blocks. It was difficult for a defensive lineman to accumulate enough points for a Pilot Award because Coach McCord's defense was set up for them to take on most of the blockers, so the linebackers and rotators could make the tackles. The safeties being concerned with pass coverage were also hard pressed to accumulate enough points. Coach McCord made reference to this, "Getting a Pilot Award is very difficult for a lineman, they are required to do their assignment, while the linebackers and rotators are free to make the tackle. Coach Beef will tell you, because he got one his senior year and he was a defensive tackle."

Pilot Awards

Jeff Okuly

Aaron Roth

Phil Girlie

Steve Deitrick (Second year receiving award)

Andy Groll (Third year receiving award)

All Green Meadows Conference performers were next. The head coaches nominate their own players. Then all of the head coaches in the conference do the voting. A coach can't vote for his own player.

Honorable Mention

Phil Girlie: Defensive Back

Aaron Roth: Defensive Tackle

Second-Team Offense

Jerry Carnahan: Split End

John Finn: Center

Tim Boals: Offensive Tackle

Second-Team Defense

Marv Andrews: Middle Guard

First-Team Offense

Jeff Okuly: Offensive Tackle

Mike Wilson: Guard

Denny Martin: Quarterback (Second year on first-team)

First-Team Defense

Rob Giesige: Defensive End

Jeff Okuly: Defensive Tackle (First-team both sides of the ball)

Steve Deitrick: Linebacker

Andy Groll: Defensive Back (Second year on first-team)

The AP All-District Team was nominated by the area sports-casters.

AP All-District Nominees

John Finn Center

Andy Groll Defensive Back

Eric Burket Defensive End

The AP All-Ohio awards were done the same way.

AP All-Ohio Nominees

John Finn Center

Andy Groll Defensive Back

Eric Burket Defensive End

The UPI All-Ohio Team was voted on by the other coaches in the state. This was not broken down in the five divisions. Instead there were only the class (A, AA, AAA) All-Ohio Teams. This meant we would be pitted against the division IV schools as well as the division V.

UPI All-Ohio

Jeff Okuly Defensive Tackle

Steve Deitrick Linebacker

Chris Schlachter Tailback

Andy Groll Defensive Back

The final award was for the elected Captains

Captains

Steve Deitrick

Andy Groll

All of the seniors then received their scrapbooks. The scrapbooks were put together by managers, cheerleaders and classmates. The scrapbooks were all done in a professional manner. Missy McCord did mine, and it was just awesome. Thanks to all of her hard work, I had almost every resource I needed for this book at my fingertips. I know they all had to put a lot of hard work into them, and we all surely appreciated it.

We then presented Coach McCord with a few things to express our gratitude to him. We all looked up to Coach McCord and he was the main reason we were so successful. We all respected him at a level where it was out of the question to disappoint him. He did not achieve this by striking fear into us. He could be hard when he needed to be, but he truly cared about us on and off the field. We all had so much respect for Coach McCord because he truly taught us how to play football the right way.

The senior farewell speeches were last on the evening's agenda. One-by-one all 16 seniors hesitantly approached the microphone and said a few parting words. Some were inspirational, some were humorous, and some were serious, while a few were somber.

"Our senior year was one of the greatest times of our lives. From going 10-0 and winning the GMC outright, to qualifying for the playoffs for the first time ever and being the top seed in Division V Region 18 was a great ride! It kind of ended on a sour note with the one point loss to Newark Catholic in the State Championship Game ... although most of us don't think we lost the game, we just ran out of time," related Denny Martin. "That team and the group of guys on that team will always be remembered in my heart as the greatest team and greatest group of guys I have ever played any sport with. Every one of them means the world to me, and I only wish them well and I hope 50 years from now we can still talk about that team!"[119]

We had all suffered a great loss and not just in the final game of the year. Our time was over. We would never be together on the football field again as fellow warriors. We were 16 players holding hands in matching uniforms, working together for a common goal, laughing together, encouraging each other during the bad times and enjoying the good times. Being together through an entire football season and seeing it come to an end, was a great loss.

Being together on the snow-covered playground when we were little kids in grade school, to the final seconds in the Ohio Stadium, you could say we were a bunch of football players. Not being able to play football together again, was the greatest loss of all.

CONCLUSION

To say I enjoyed writing this book would be an understatement. Through the countless hours and constant research, I trudged on, finally completing the task at hand. Writing this book was almost an identical duplicate of my high school football career. I started off thinking, *there is no way I will be able to accomplish anything here. I may not be good enough.* Then as the work piled up, and my efforts increased, I saw a book taking shape. There were times when I didn't want to go on because I felt exhausted, and there were other times I couldn't stop working. When I started to put the finishing touches to my work, I began to dread the day it would be over. What would I do when I pushed that last key on the keyboard? Once again there would be silence, and I would be left with the memories of doing something I truly enjoyed and didn't want to end.

Through it all, I realized that football had affected my life in a much more powerful way than just in the time I spent on the field. There were life lessons learned; if you want something bad enough you can achieve it. You are in control of your own destiny. When tomorrow comes, this day will be gone forever, leaving in its place something that we have traded. Stick together, play hard and give it all you got.

All of those things stick with me in my everyday life. Coach McCord and all of the other Coaches spent many sunny afternoons getting us prepared for football, but at the same time they were getting us ready for life. Winners do things losers don't like to do. How many times did I hear Coach McCord say this? Hundreds, but he was exactly right. If I can take one quote from him and use it to sum up my time playing for him that would be the one. Winners do things losers don't like to do.

This brings me to something that has been on my mind since I started to write this book. This has actually been on my mind for 23 years. What if we would have came out of that state championship game victorious. How would it have changed our lives? What is the real difference between victory and defeat? Mogadore felt the same kind of defeat just a week before we felt it. How did it affect them? One stinking point in both games was the difference between cheers or tears. Was winning better than losing? I can say without a doubt that it was. However, I did not play for trophies, awards or accolades … I played because I loved the game. If I could trade all of the wins, for a chance to play in one more game, I would without hesitation. So the question to answer would be if I had my choice of winning a state championship in my final game or the chance to go back and play in one more game, what would I choose?

What made the game so great to me was that during victory or defeat, I still didn't want the game to be over. There would have been no amount of winning that could have cured my thirst for looking through that face mask. The thing that mattered, even more than winning or losing was that there were no more games to be played. What we would take from this game wasn't the wins or losses, but the memories of getting to play the game.

With all of that being said, I have come to realize, that 16 seniors, would no longer play in a high school football game after the state championship game. It was the end of the line, and we were at the pinnacle of all we had worked for. Would have a win in the state championship game and culmination of a perfect 14-0 season been a fitting end to our high school football careers? I think it would have. We would have made it to the end of the line, and there would have been nothing left for us to accomplish. That would have been the perfect way to say good-bye.

APPENDIX A

- -

STATISTICS AND RECORDS

Individual Passing

Player	Att	Comp	Yards	Int	TD
Martin	156	77	1134	9	15
Groll	1	1	20	0	0
Hanna	1	1	7	0	0
Florence	1	1	10	0	0

Rushing

Player	Att	Yards	Avg	Fum.	Lost	TD
Schlachter	205	1156	5.6	6	3	15
Deitrick	155	982	6.3	2	1	7
Lewis	84	313	3.7	2	2	4
Groll	39	298	7.6	0	0	6
Martin	55	201	3.7	17	4	6
Kolb	28	138	4.9	0	0	1
Ankney	28	113	4.0	3	0	1
Girlie	17	85	5.0	1	1	0
Td. Hanna	6	39	6.5	1	0	0
Guilford	7	32	4.6	1	1	0
Delano	7	29	4.1	0	0	0
DeWolf	1	16	16	0	0	0
Briseno	2	11	5.5	0	0	0

Schlosser	3	3	1	0	0	0
Giesige	3	-3	-1	1	1	0
Florence	3	-7	-2.3	2	1	0

Punt Returns

Player	Ret	Yards	Avg	TD
Martin	21	248	11.8	2
Carnahan	9	52	5.7	0
Groll	2	26	13.0	0
Girlie	1	4	4.0	0

Receiving

Player	Rec	Yards	Avg	TD
Deitrick	24	188	7.8	3
Carnahan	14	177	12.6	0
Dawson	12	206	17.2	6
Groll	9	284	31.6	4
Giesige	8	93	11.6	0
To Hanna	5	83	16.6	0
Girlie	3	89	29.6	2
Schlachter	2	26	13	0
Richard	2	13	6.5	0
Askins	1	10	10.0	0

KickOff Returns

Player	Ret.	Yards	Avg	TD
Lewis	17	238	14.0	0
Kolb	6	112	18.6	0
Girlie	3	42	14.0	0
Groll	1	22	22.0	0
Carnahan	1	16	16.0	0
Deitrick	1	8	8.0	0
Giesige	1	7	7.0	0
Dawson	1	5	5.0	0

Punting

Player	Punts	Yards	Avg	Long
Carnahan	30	922	30.7	52
Giesige	6	182	30.3	36
Leatherman	4	82	20.5	31

Kicking

Player	Extra Point		Field Goal		
	Att	Made	Att	Made	Long
Schlachter	55	43	5	3	34
Dearth	3	2	0	0	-

Defensive Statistics

Player	Tkl	Ast	Int	Fumble Rec	Caus	Sack	Block
Deitrick	66	27	0	2	1	1	0
Groll	53	28	4	1	1	0	2 Pass
Girlie	45	50	2	1	1	2	1 Pass
Okuly	46	26	0	2	0	3	5 Pass
Roth	35	29	0	2	1	3	2 Pass
Kolb	32	21	0	1	1	5	1 Pass
Giesige	30	20	0	2	1	5	0
Burket	24	18	0	1	1	3	0
M. Andrews	21	16	0	0	0	1	0
Wilson	21	21	0	1	0	3	1 FG
Td. Hanna	29	13	3	2	0	0	1 Pass
Armes	20	13	6	1	0	0	1 Pass
Carnahan	24	19	1	0	0	0	0
J. Briseno	10	10	1	0	0	5	0
Schlachter	20	7	0	0	0	2	0
Guilford	3	1	0	0	0	0	0
Richard	3	1	0	0	0	2	1 Pass
D. Andrews	3	6	0	0	0	0	1 Punt
Dawson	12	6	0	0	0	0	0
S. Briseno	0	0	1	0	0	0	0
Gerschutz	1	0	0	0	0	0	0
Brown	1	1	0	0	0	0	0
Finn	1	1	0	0	0	0	0
Boals	0	0	0	1	0	0	0
Martin	0	1	0	0	0	0	0
Lloyd	1	0	0	0	0	0	0
A. Giesige	0	1	0	0	0	0	0
Ankney	0	1	0	0	0	0	0
Stark	1	0	0	0	0	0	0

Team Stats

Stat	AHS	Opp	Stat	AHS	Opp
Run Plays	643	445	Pen. 1st D	11	3
Yds Gain R	3616	1527	Run 1st D	142	67
Yds Loss R	210	440	Pass 1st D	41	49
Net Yds R	3406	1087	Tot 1st D	194	119
Avg Yd Run	5.3	2.4	Punts	40	69
Pass Att	159	230	Punt Long	52	48
Pass Comp	80	90	Punt Short	1	7
Int Thrown	9	18	Punt Avg	29.7	30.7
Pass Yds	1169	1230	Fumbles	41	35
Penalty Yd	487	468	Fum Lost	15	14
Pts Scored	418	115			

Scoring by Quarter

Ayersville	102	107	111	98-	-418
Opponents	20	55	13	27-	-115

Individual Records

Denny Martin
Longest run 88 yds. (1986 Newark Catholic)
Pass Completions/Year 77 (1986)
TD Passes/Year 15 (1986) TD Passes/Career 18 (1985-1986)
Longest Pass 67 yds. to Andy Groll (1986 Edgerton)
Longest Punt Return 87 yds. (1984 National Trail)

Andy Groll
Avg. yds. Per Catch/Year 31.6 Career 27.1 (1985-1986)
Longest Reception 67 yds. From Denny Martin (1986 Edgerton)
Pass Interceptions Career 13 (1983-1986

Steve Deitrick
Rush avg./Game 18.0 Year 11.1 (1985) Career 8.1 (1983-1986)
Pass Rec./Year 24 (1986) Career 31 (1985-1986)

Individual Records Continued

Chris Schlachter
Rushing Attempts/Year 205 (1986)
Ex Pts/Game 6 (1986 Hilltop) Year 43 (1986) Career 64
Field Goals/Game 2 Mogadore (1986)

Johnny Armes
Pass Interceptions/Year 6 (1986)

Jaime Briseno
Sacks/Game tied 4 (1986 Tinora)

Shelby Dawson
TD Pass Rec./Year tied 6 (1986) Career 7

Team Records

Running Plays 643
Rushing Yards 3616
Passing Yards 1169
Total Offense 4785
Total Points 418
Pass Interceptions 18
QB Sacks 36
1st Downs 194
Points given up/ Regular season 59
Total defense against run/ Game -9 (Tiffin Calvert)
Total Defense against pass/ Game -2 (Hicksville)

APPENDIX B:

1986 ALL-AYERSVILLE OPPONENT TEAM

During the year I had the chance to play against some great players. I thought it would be fun to pick an All-Ayersville Opponent Team. Some players may be left off that may have been a better selection overall, but for the game I played against them that year, these were the guys I felt deserved the honor.

I could not do this alone, and many of my teammates added their input. Some of the linemen remembered some real battles with their opponents.

Offense

Quarterback- Jeremy Montgomery (Newark Catholic): He picked us apart with his long drop backs and accurate passes. I have never seen a quarterback have such a great day passing the football. He received the nod over Richard Pierce (Mogadore) and Scott Davis (McComb)

Fullback- Bob Siebenaler (Edon): Of all the runners we faced that year, he was the most bruising of them all. He came through the line like a truck and was extremely hard to bring down. Brian Buck (McComb), Doug Sharpless (Mogadore) and Scott Saad (Newark Catholic) should be mentioned as well.

Halfback- Joe Radabaugh (Edgerton): He was an exceptional running back. He hit the hole hard and had the speed to run through it. He could even power his way through the line of scrimmage if he had to.

Halfback- Todd Rothert (Woodmore): He was almost the mirror image of Radabaugh in every way. At one point in the Woodmore game, I wondered if Radabaugh had been recruited for the playoff game. They ran the ball that much alike. I will also have to mention Todd Tadsen (Fairview) and Chris Sanderson (Wayne Trace)

Tight End- Bill Franks (Newark Catholic): A phenomenal football player. He caught some tough passes that day and didn't drop a one. He was hard nosed and played the game with everything he had, a true leader on the field.

Split End- Ronald Pierce (Mogadore): He ran his routes hard and fought to get open. Great hands and precision routes were also why he made the team.

Center- Rich Walther (Newark Catholic): I never saw much of the center during a game, but I know this guy kept our two nose guards in check during the game. We even had a few guys beat up in the middle, so he must have been a good one.

Guard- Dale Backlund (Newark Catholic): We couldn't get a good pass rush on the quarterback. He was always there in protection.

Guard- Ron Krill (Edgerton): He opened the holes for the Edgerton backs. He was quick enough to get up field and strong enough to hold his ground.

Tackle- Keith Traver (Woodmore): Early in the game, they were controlling the line of scrimmage. He stayed low and was able to create some nice holes.

Tackle- Jim Olson (Newark Catholic): He provided great protection and could drive block as well.

Defense

End- Dave Maugel (Edgerton) Just a beast when we tried to hook him or kick him out. He would hold his ground and was very difficult to block.

End- Buffard Butler (Holgate): He almost ended my season with that hit on the goalline. That wasn't the main reason he is on the team. He was equally difficult to block and he flew to the ball.

Tackle- Wimberly Cook (Newark Catholic): Controlled the line of scrimmage and could disrupt the passing game as well.

Tackle- Ron Hesselschwardt (Fairview) Strong in the middle and kept us from gaining much ground with the running game.

Nose guard- Jamie Herman (Edgerton): He was quick and had good strength, that's a deadly combination for a nose guard.

Linebacker- Doug Sharpless (Mogadore): A great football player that was always around the ball, he made some great tackles in the semifinal game.

Linebacker- Tim McKenna (Newark Catholic): Another great football player, he liked to hit and he played hard. He was in at fullback for a play, and I had to meet him in the hole. The result was a nice crack of the pads and he didn't give any ground.

Linebacker- Rob Breininger (Fairview): We couldn't run the ball very well against them. It all started with a good linebacker and he did the job well.

Defensive back- Eric Barker (Mogadore): Great competitor and was tough to shake on a pass route. He was a sure tackler as well.

Defensive back- Darby Riley (Newark Catholic): Played great in coverage and could come up in run support.

Defensive back- Shawn Kroeckel (Tinora): Played well against us, and kept us from getting any big plays.

Kicker- Matt Dase (Newark Catholic): Every point counts and he was perfect against us.

Punter- Jeff Davis (Edgerton): He could really bomb his punts out there.

Head Coach- J.D. Graham (Newark Catholic): Did whatever it took to beat us, had a complete gameplan and executed it well.

Appendix C: Alignment and Plays

Standard 5-2 Defense

5-2 Defense basic right showing pass coverage (Roger call) right

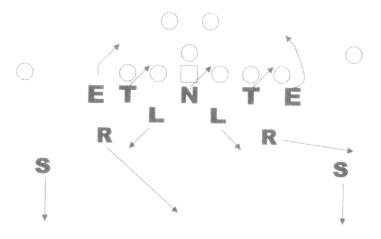

5-3 Defense

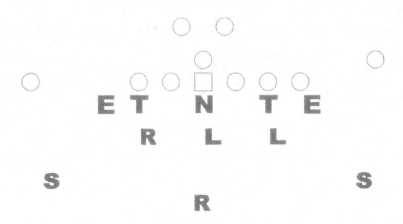

5-3 Defense Pinch showing pass coverage

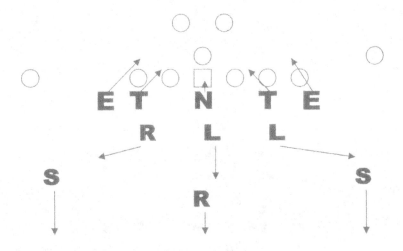

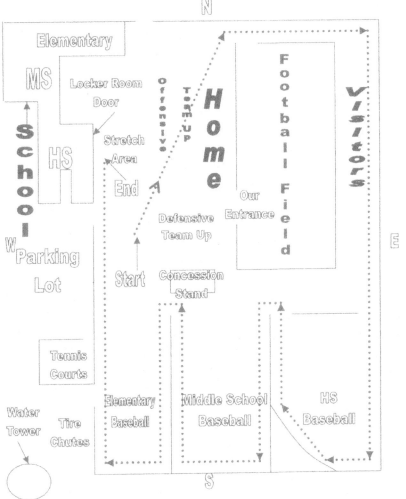

Diagram of the School grounds

The dotted line is the route of the dreaded
Cross Country

Offensive Plays

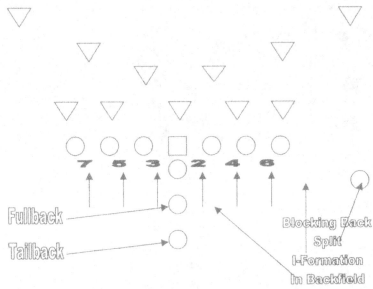

Diagram showing the numbered gaps

The first number in a plays sequence was for the designated ball carrier

1-Tailback
2- Blocking Back
3- Fullback

The second number was for what gap the play was ran through

Even numbers- Right
Odd numbers- Left

A 32 trap would be the fullback carrying through the 2 hole.

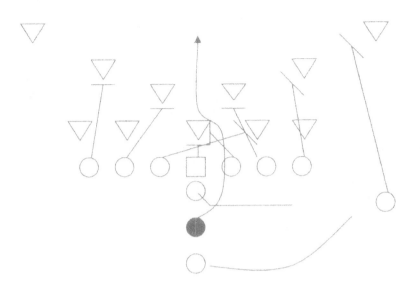

Flanker Right Tight 32 Trap

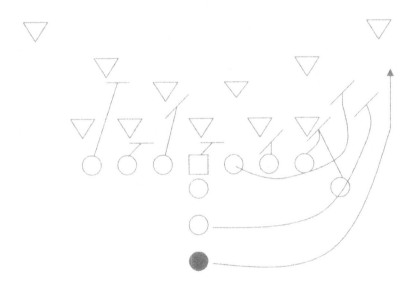

I-Right Tight Sweep Right

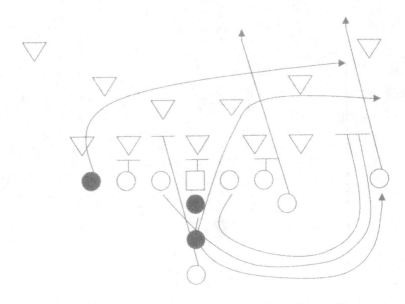

I-Right Waggle Right (Run first Pass second)

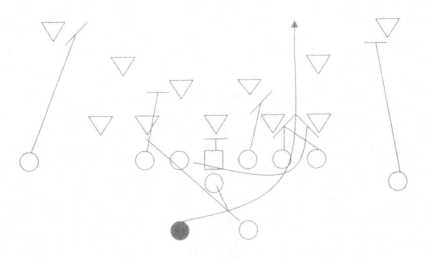

Pro-Right 16 Cross Trap

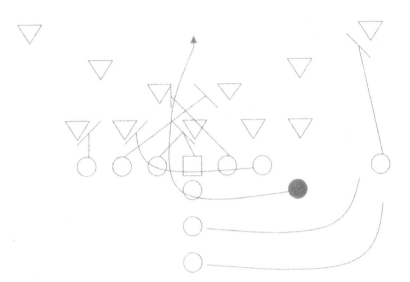

I-Right 23 Counter

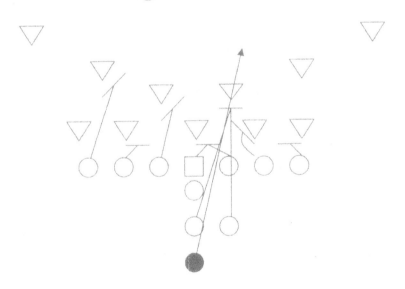

Combo-Right Blast Right

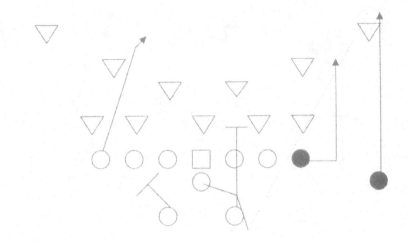

Pro-Right Purdue

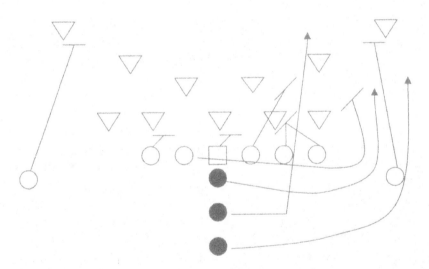

Flanker Right 36 Option (Triple option)

THE TEAM TODAY

#25 Steve (Deek) Deitrick joined the US Army for four years after he graduated. He was stationed in Georgia, and then spent some time in Italy where his passion for football resurfaced. Steve actually had the opportunity of playing professionally in the Italian American Pro Football League. He then took a Defense Contractor position overseas in Greenland for two and a half years. Steve currently resides in Colorado Springs, Colorado with his wonderful wife of 15 years, Leslie, and their two teenage daughters. Steve currently works as the Corporate Security Architect for Oracle.

Steve Deitrick had this to say about his Ayersville football experience. "There are always those special people in your life that when you look back, you realize played a key part as a mentor in shaping your character and the person you are today. For me, the entire 1986 team is on that list, along with Coach McCord, and Coach Ondrus at the top. I didn't just learn how to play football from those experiences, I learned teamwork, character, leadership traits, integrity, camaraderie, humility and sportsmanship, all combined, which have guided my life and career ever since. The ending result, which matters the most, was my experience. It was a true life's blessing."[120]

#63 Mike (Harley Man) Wilson took a job with Sauder Manufacturing after graduating in 1987. He recently accepted a severance package that allowed him to start his own business, Wilson Woodworking. By being self-employed, he can continue the skills he applied even back in high school when he made the covers for all of our scrapbooks. Mike was an assistant wrestling coach under Coach

Ondrus for a few years at Ayersville, while also participating in the other sport he enjoyed (baseball) as an umpire. Mike was a high school baseball umpire for 15 years and even achieved the pinnacle of that profession by being selected to umpire in the state tournament. Mike currently resides in Archbold, Ohio. He lives in a home he built with his own hands, with his wife Lisa, daughter Alexa, and son Austin.[121]

#87 Rob Giesige committed to the Army National Guard for six years before he graduated. He then attended the Bowling Green State University, where he met his wife Karen, and received a degree in Accounting. Rob is currently the Director of Finance and Administration for the Four County Alcohol Drug & Mental Health Services Board. Rob lives in Defiance, Ohio with his wife Karen and their two sons. Going against everything he stood for in high school, Rob lives on the other side of the Maumee River and is now associated with the Tinora Rams. Becoming a member of "That team across the river" is something Rob receives, and will continue to receive, an endless amount of torment for.

Rob Giesige had this to say. "The thing I learned from Coach McCord was teaching technique. I coach both of my boys in baseball. I find myself teaching technique every practice.[122]

#44 Chris (Fat Boy) Schlachter was a heavily recruited football player before he finished his senior year and graduated in 1988. He ended his fine career at Ayersville as the all-time rushing leader and was named AP Division V Co-Back of the Year as a senior. He elected to attend the University of Toledo as a walk-on and was given a football scholarship after his first season. Chris was red-shirted his first year and then went on to letter four years with the Rockets at tight end, special teams and was a starting defensive tackle his last two years. Chris received a degree in Electrical Engineering, and applies that trade today working for Johnson Controls as an Engineering Manager. Chris currently resides in Toledo, Ohio with his wife of 16 years Tammy, daughter Hannah, and son Harrison.[123]

#88 Jerry (Jear Bear) Carnahan returned to Ayersville for his senior year. The team once again went undefeated during the regular season, but lost to Delphos Jefferson in the first round of the playoffs. Jerry Carnahan enjoyed a fine all around athletic career at Ayersville. Jerry is currently a Supervisor for the Water Department of the County of Sacramento. He currently resides in Sacramento, California with his wife of 20 years, Kim, and two sons.[124]

#60 John Finn after graduating from Ayersville, went into law enforcement, where he worked for 15 years. After 9-11, John went into federal service and then took a job overseas as an International Police Advisor in Afghanistan for 15 months. John performed the task of teaching and mentoring a newly stood up Afghan Police Force. John currently resides in Charlottesville, Virginia where he is a Biometric Forensic Technician. John has two children, Jacob 13, and Abbey 12.

John remembered this about his playing days. "There are so many memories out there on that field and I'm sure you heard 'gee fer socks' in more than one response. Of course, there's always the clipboard to the face mask, Welty's 53 stack, the infamous liniment in the jock, countless cross countries, the walk in holding hands as unity, the fourth quarter four on the hand, two-a-days, film room, senior kill drills, the senior ceremony the last week of practice, the state title game and kill blocks on punt returns. Football to me was always about the family of it. You don't go through all the time we spent together and not have a common interest. Family is always about tradition. The things we learned on the field have carried over into our personal lives. We received traits of perseverance, pride, discipline, education, logical thinking, self control, but most of all, carrying out an assignment which led to everyone's success. Most of the people we played with have had great success both personally and professionally. A lot of the decisions we chose to make, or not make on the field, affect us today."[125]

#71 Marv (Marvelous) Andrews attended Defiance College after graduation for one year. He then transferred to the University of

Toledo for his final three years. Marv has been raising and selling Christmas tree's for the past 15 years, while working at Defiance Metal Products. He currently resides in Defiance with his wife Cathy. Marv and Cathy are expecting their first child in January of 2010.[126]

#61 Tim Boals joined the Army out of high school. He became a medic stationed out of the Pentagon. After that, he was a pediatric Allergy Technician/Lab Manager. Upon graduation from George Mason University, he joined his current biotech firm as an Associate Scientist, now as a Project Manager. Tim resides in Maryland with his wife Liz and son Thomas.[127]

#64 Eric Burket signed up for the Army before graduation. After leaving the Army, he worked as a Mill Right at General Motors for 10 years. Eric currently lives in Woodburn, Indiana with his wife Mary and son Jacob. He is currently a Mechanic at B.F. Goodrich.[128]

Coach Norman Beck only coached the 1986 season at Ayersville. He then moved to Avon Lake, Ohio. Shortly after that, he made his way back to Archbold, Ohio. We all knew he was loyal to Archbold, but for that year in 1986, he was one of us. Coach Beck resumed his passion for football and coached all the way through the ranks at Archbold. He is currently the eighth-grade football coach and a sixth-grade math teacher. Coach Beck lives in Archbold with his wife Karen and son Andrew.[129]

Coach Bill (O) Ondrus continued to coach alongside Coach McCord for another 10 years. He then took a break from football and concentrated on the other sport he loved, wrestling. Coach Ondrus will be coaching his 30th year of wrestling in 2009. He did resume coaching football for a few years after 2004, but for now, he concentrates on his wrestling team. Coach Ondrus was the athletic director at Ayersville for a number of years, but he has given that up as well, and now teaches high school History. He and his wife Char (also an Ayersville High School History teacher) still live in the Ayersville school district. They are the parents of two daughters, Keri and Kylee.[130]

#77 George Schaffer after graduation, he went to auto mechanic school in Lima, Ohio. He then worked as an auto mechanic until 1994. George then took a job at General Motors as a Mill Right, where he still works today. George lives in Hicksville, Ohio with his wife Ronda, two daughters Amanda and Courtney, and son Dylan. He still applies his auto mechanic trade working on cars in his spare time. George still regrets getting rid of the 1968 Cadillac ambulance[131]

#75 Aaron Roth also went to school in Lima, Ohio. He specialized in auto and diesel mechanics. Aaron then went into the Army until 1991, after that, he worked for John Deere for a few years. He then revisited Lima and became an Ag diesel welding instructor, and also an instructor in high performance welding, and tractor and combine mechanics. Positions he still holds today. Aaron currently resides just outside of Ayersville in Continental, Ohio with his wife Paula and two daughters, Taylor and Allison.[132]

#12 Denny Martin is a Controller at Defiance Metal Products. His passion for the Ayersville School continues, with him being the Vice President of the Ayersville School Board. Denny lives in the Ayersville School District with his wife Sheila and children, Kaleigh, Brayton and Ryan.[133]

The 1986 Ayersville Pilots football team imbedded its name in the history books of one of the greatest teams to ever play football for Ayersville. To say that our team started the tradition at Ayersville though would not be a true statement, as that foundation was put down with the first football team ever to play the game for Ayersville and the teams that played up until we took the field. What we all did as a team in 1986 would never have been possible, had the teams from the mid to late 70s all the way through the mid 80s, not provided that foundation. During that time, those of us on the 1986 team were in middle school playing football at recess pretending to be the next Dave Temple. During the seasons of 1983, 1984 and 1985 we all saw a lot of playing time and we got better and better the more we played. None of it would have been possible without the awesome coaching staff we had led by Coach Craig McCord. That guy was a second Dad to all of us. We would have done anything for him and we did anything for him. We believed in him and his system. Our assistant coaches were awesome too. Guys like Bill Ondrus, Don Hammersmith, Bob Luderman, Norm Beck, Mike Anderson and Jeff Maag made sure we were all prepared for every game. They were great coaches to play for and made practice fun.[134]

Manager Kim (McCord) Engel went to Ashland College after graduation. She then received a degree in Elementary Education from Defiance College and her Masters degree from Bowling Green State University. She resides in the Ayersville School District with her husband Bob. Kim is currently a stay-at-home-mom taking care of their three daughters, Elizabeth, Meghan and Allison.

Kim related what it all meant to her. "As I look back on all this, I got to experience it from two angles. The first angle was as a manager, whose classmates achieved one of the greatest moments in football history at Ayersville. The second, and most sentimental - at least now that I'm older - is that my dad did that. Not alone of course, but when we came here, he was supposed to start a program from nothing, and look at what was accomplished. He was able to accomplish all of that because of his coaches and the players. All of you respected him, and you also respected each other. Even today, after dad's retirement, they still look up to him, and that makes me so happy to see that he has touched so many lives. I want you to know (and I'm sure you do) that he would do anything for any one of you, then and now. I am so lucky, because I get to say my dad, and my classmates went to State."[135]

Manager Missy (McCord) Weyrich attended The Ohio State University upon her graduation. She received degrees in Massage Therapy and Education. Missy and her husband Tony live in London,

Ohio with their two sons, Stuart and Nick. Missy is also currently a stay-at-home-mom.[136]

Coach Don (Beef) Hammersmith continued to coach with Coach McCord through the 1989 season. He then took his talents to Centerville, Ohio and coached the freshman team from 1990-1994. He proceeded to then coach the offensive and defensive line at Bellbrook High School in 1995. Ayersville High School then called the legendary Coach Beef back home, where he is the Vocational Agriculture teacher and FFA advisor. Coach Hammersmith is also the junior high wrestling coach. He resides in the Ayersville school district with his wife Anne and three daughters.[137]

#21 Andy Groll upon graduation, I attended Ashland College for one year and became a member of the Ashland Eagles' football team as a defensive back. After the one year, I decided to join the work force and took a job with my Dad at Hudson Feeds. I then took a job with the United States Postal Service, and currently work as the Postmaster of Montgomery, Michigan. In the summer of 1999, my job allowed me to take an assistant football coaching position. It was another dream fulfilled, as I once again joined the Ayersville football program under Coach McCord. Due to a change in work hours, I was only able to coach for the one year. I reside in Camden, Michigan with my wife Lana and five children, Brie, Carly, Greg, Billy and Austin.

Playing for Coach McCord, Coach Ondrus, Coach Hammersmith, Coach Beck and Coach Maag was an honor. I consider them the role models of my youth. They were great leaders, and they not only taught us how to be winners, they made the time we spent with all of them incredibly enjoyable. I have many fond memories involving each of them. Coach McCord was a true leader that made us all feel special. Anyone that played for him realizes that he takes the statement "I will never forget you, for I have carved you on the palm of my hand," with the utmost sincerity. The other 18 seniors on the team were not only my classmates, they were my fellow warriors. Yes, I am including you Kim, Kristen and Amy, because you were right there with us every step of the way. I have a great respect for each and every one of the 1986 seniors, because we all came together and had an unforgettable season in the fall of 1986.

#76 Jeff (Oak) Okuly upon graduation, he worked a few odd jobs before enrolling at Wilmington College in 1988. Jeff played defensive tackle on the Wilmington College football team. He is currently working in Production at General Motors in Defiance, Ohio. Ever the Ayersville football player, Jeff resides right across the fence from where we did battle on Friday nights with his wife Hope and their girls, Cassie, Danielle and Samantha.[138]

Coach Jeff Maag continued to coach with Coach McCord until 1990. He is currently the Data Base Administrator at Chase Copper and Brass in Montpelier, Ohio. He continues to live near Ayersville in Defiance, Ohio with his wife Teresa, and three children, Jenni, Nick and Michelle.[139]

#18 Shelby Dawson returned for his senior year and was an instrumental piece of the team's success in 1987. After graduation he dove right into the family pool and spa business. Shelby has taken multiple business courses on his way to his current position as President of Defiance Water Recreation. Shelby currently resides in Defiance, Ohio with his wife Christa and their two children, Will and Macy.[140]

Manager Kristen (Bell) Warren was the lone four-year letter winner of our class. Upon graduation, she attended The Ohio State University and received a bachelor's degree in Psychology. Kristen then continued her education and picked up her Masters Degree in Social Work. She currently works as a Mental Health Therapist for the Marion Area Counseling Center. Kristen resides in Cardington, Ohio with her husband Malcolm and two boys, Mac and Liam.[141]

Manager Amy (Shinabery) Snyder enrolled at the University of Toledo and received her Masters Degree in Higher Education Administration. Amy has been employed with Private School Aid Service as the Director of Human Resources and Customer

Relations for the last 10 years. Amy resides in Lakewood, Ohio with her husband Craig and two daughters, Logan and Elliott.

Amy shared this about her experience in the fall of 1986. "Being a part of the football family was wonderful. I had played volleyball for as long as I could remember, and then I had to have major knee surgery the summer before my senior year and couldn't play. Being a football manager was a great experience and really made my senior year stand out with fantastic memories. I think I became so much closer to many of the senior guys due to all of those evenings spent "In the trenches" being a support to them."[142]

#85 Johnny Armes after graduation, joined the Air Force where he went to basic training at Lackland Air Force Base, Texas. He then went on to Grissom Air Force Base in Indiana. He was sent to Saudi Arabia twice during his four years in active duty among other temporary duties. He met his wife, Corie, while in the military and has been married for almost 19 years. After getting out of the service, Johnny and Corie moved to Richmond, Virginia for three years and then back to Ohio. After 9-11, he rejoined the Reserves which led him into a civilian job with the government back in Peru, Indiana where he still resides today. Johnny and Corie have two children, Trevor and Makinsey, who he states are both awesome kids.[143]

#84 Tolly Hanna took off for the Air Force just two weeks after graduation to become an Electromechanical Technician. When the program he was working on disbanded, his squadron was offered an early-out incentive. He accepted this incentive and left the military with an honorable discharge. Tolly, with the GI Bill in hand, then attended the University of Toledo and received a Bachelors degree in Industrial Relations. He then applied that trade working for a few different corporations while continuing his education earning his MBA (Master of Business Administration) from the University of Findlay. Tolly is currently the Division Human Resource Manager for Parker Hannifin Corporation and resides in Waterville, Ohio. Tolly gives credit where credit is due, and credits his wife, Debbie, for all of the support she has given him. Tolly and Debbie are the proud parents of two sons, Joshua and Nathan, and daughter, Allison.[144]

#10 Todd Hanna returned for his senior season and took over the helm of the "Pilot" ship as Coach McCord's signal caller. After graduation, Todd attended Kent State University and earned his BA (Bachelor of Arts) degree in Political Science. He then returned to Defiance, Ohio and worked for General Motors before transferring to the General Motors plant in Parma, Ohio. In 2006, Todd accepted the early buy-out offered by General Motors and pursued another career with TCI (Tire Centers LLC) as the Director for the Commercial Division. A position he currently holds today while residing in sunny Ormond Beach, Florida.[145]

#56 Jaime Briseno is currently living in Ann Arbor, Michigan and is The System Administrator for The University of Michigan Health System.

Living in Ann Arbor and working at the football tradition-rich University of Michigan has many similarities with our days at football-crazy Ayersville. By this I mean the way campus and the whole town are electrified for the home games, especially the rivalry games. It provides plenty of excuses to reminisce. Probably the best example of how valuable my/our football experience is to me now, is in how I approach work activities. Some projects require coordination and cooperation between several departments. A teamwork atmosphere is conductive to the success of the project. When I notice there are individuals on the assignment with poor team working skills, when they don't realize the whole is greater than the sum of its parts, I feel sorry for them that they didn't get to experience what we did. This makes it that much more valuable to me.[146]

Coach Craig McCord was named *The Crescent News* Coach of the Year for his outstanding effort in our 1986 campaign. Even though it was the first time he won the award, it would not be his last, as he would go on to win the award two more times. Coach McCord would stay in the Pilots' seat for another 17 years as the head coach. The initial GMC crown in 1985 was just the beginning of a decade of dominance for the Ayersville Pilots football program. Coach McCord etched the Ayersville name on the conference title an astounding 10 straight years from 1985-1994. During his tenure, he made seven other trips to the state playoffs following the state final appearance in 1986. When the 2003 Ayersville football season came to an end, so did the reign of the man that started the program from complete scratch in the autumn of 1974. Coach McCord said good-bye after touching the hearts of countless players, parents and fans. During his tenure as the varsity head coach of Ayersville football, he compiled a record of 209 wins, 80 losses and two ties. On April 21, 2006, Coach McCord was honored for all of the hard work he put into the Ayersville football program. The coach we all loved in the small community of Ayersville, became a legendary figure in the state of Ohio when he was inducted into The Ohio High School Football Coaches' Association Hall of Fame. Coach McCord was also a three-time Jennings Foundation Scholar and received the 200-victory award from The Ohio High School Football Coaches' Association. Even though our great coach isn't patrolling the sidelines at Ayersville, he can still be found on the sidelines at Defiance College football games. Coach McCord took his coaching skills to the next level and joined the college ranks after he retired from Ayersville. He is currently the special teams coordinator and linebackers coach for Defiance College. Coach McCord and his wife, Patti, still reside in Ayersville. They are the parents of grown children: Kim (Engel), Missy (Weyrich) and Jonathan. They are also the grandparents of eight.

Since Coach McCord was the cornerstone of the Ayersville foot-ball program and touched so many players, parents and fans lives, I asked him to sum up what it all meant to him. This is what he had to say.

When I was a freshman in high school, our freshman team didn't have a good season. My Dad told me that you had to work hard and persevere through the tough times to achieve your goals. I tried to take that advice about working hard and put it to practical use throughout my coaching career. Coach Jim Bowlus, my high school coach, whom I also coached with four years, was a big influence on my life as a person and coach. Much of what I tried to instill in young men's lives comes from the teachings of Coach Bowlus, my mentor.

Football taught me so many things about life, football is more than a game; team work, loyalty, hard work, sacrifice, perseverance, courage, love, to name a few. I always tried to coach and teach the game as I would want my own son to be coached. I tried to instill these same characteristics into my players knowing they may not understand what I was trying to do until many years later. One of the greatest rewards for a coach is to have a player come back after several years and tell you he now understands what I was trying to teach and for him to say thank you. By teaching these basic principles that players could use their entire life along with the basic fundamentals of football - blocking and tackling - the winning side of things just seemed to fall in place.

Obviously, I was very blessed to have been surrounded with great players and loyal assistant coaches who were superb teachers of the game. I tried to involve the parents of our team and the hundreds of loyal Ayersville fans of the community in our program. It gave us all a strong sense of family pride in what we were trying to accomplish. I was also blessed to have had my children be a part of the Ayersville program over the years. My daughters, Kimberly and Melissa, were managers and my son, Jonathan, has been by my side from the time he was in the second grade going to summer workouts, as a player, and an assistant coach. The pride and joy I felt to have had them by my side through all the years can't be measured in words. Patti and I have reaped so many rewards over the years, including the countless friendships that we have developed. Friends are friends forever. In good times and bad times, that's what friends are for.

As I enter the twilight of my coaching career, I just feel that I need to pay back what football has meant to me. I love working with young people. Whatever I can do as a coach to help them achieve their goals, on and off the field, is well worth the effort. It is awesome to see a young freshman (who many coaches might write off) mature and develop over a four-year period to become a productive and integral part of your program. They just need a chance, and as a coach, it is your job to "coach them up" and give them every opportunity to be successful. I know that the ones who hang in there and develop a great work ethic will be productive citizens one day. They in turn might be able to pass it on to the next generation. I am very proud of the tradition that developed over the 30 years I coached at Ayersville. That tradition, which all of the players and coaches are part of, can never be taken away. I cherish all of the memories I have of my coaching days at Ayersville. I will never forget you - players and coaches - for I have carved you in my heart."

My wife, Patti, was the glue that held everything together for us as a family. When I was gone so much, she was always there to take care of our children and handle any crisis that might arise. She was and has always been my biggest fan. Coach Jim Tressel (Head Coach at Ohio State) and I were talking at the Hall of Fame Banquet about why there should be a Hall of Fame for coaches' wives. They are the ones who sit through all kinds of weather, listen to the fans in the stands, and they always have to listen to your concerns when coming home from practice. Many times Patti has had to sacrifice for the benefit of my coaching career. She has been a loyal supporter of Ayersville football and what it stands for. Patti has been by my side through it all. She is my best friend.[147]

ENDNOTES

----

[1]   Teresa Weddelman phone conversation with author 10/27/2009
[2]   Gary Groll phone conversation with author 10/27/2009
[3]   Gary Groll phone conversation with author 10/27/2009
[4]   Kim Engel e-mail to author 10/30/2009
[5]   Teresa Weddelman phone conversation with author 10/27/2009
[6]   Denny Martin e-mail to author 11/13/2009
[7]   Denny Martin e-mail to author 11/13/2009
[8]   Jeff Okuly conversation with author 10/25/2009
[9]   Rob Giesige conversation with author 10/25/2009
[10] Steve Deitrick e-mail to author 10/21/2009
[11] Steve Deitrick e-mail to author 10/21/2009
[12] Kristen Warren phone conversation with author 11/01/2009
[13] Jeff Okuly conversation with author 10/25/2009
[14] Rob Giesige e-mail to author 10/19/2009
[15] Steve Deitrick e-mail to author 10/21/2009
[16] Rob Giesige phone conversation with author 10/18/2009
[17] Tolly Hanna e-mail to author 11/07/2009
[18] Steve Deitrick e-mail to author 10/21/2009
[19] Gary Groll phone conversation with author 10/27/2009
[20] Denny Martin phone conversation with author 11/10/2009
[21] Jeff Okuly conversation with author 10/25/2009
[22] Rob Giesige e-mail to author 10/19/2009
[23] Coach McCord conversation with author 10/25/2009
[24] Kim Engel phone conversation with author 10/28/2009
[25] Coach McCord conversation with author 10/25/2009
[26] Coach Don Hammersmith phone conversation with author 10/28/2009
[27] Coach Bill Ondrus phone conversation with author 10/21/2009

[28] Steve Deitrick e-mail to author 10/21/2009

[29] Coach McCord conversation with author 10/25/2009

[30] Todd Helberg, "Multi-faceted offense has been Pilots' key", (*The Crescent News*) November 5, 1986

[31] Pat Groll phone conversation with author 10/27/2009

[32] Steve Deitrick e-mail to author 10/21/2009

[33] Steve Deitrick e-mail to author 10/21/2009

[34] Amy Snyder e-mail to author 11/04/2009

[35] Todd Helberg, "Second half lifts Ayersville, 21-12", (*The Crescent News*) August 30, 1986

[36] Todd Helberg, "Second half lifts Ayersville, 21-12", (*The Crescent News*) August 30, 1986

[37] Coach Don Hammersmith phone conversation with author 10/28/2009

[38] Todd Helberg, "Pilots survive in mistake-filled game", (*The Crescent News*) September 6, 1986

[39] Todd Helberg, "Pilots survive in mistake-filled game", (*The Crescent News*) September 6, 1986

[40] Rob Giesige e-mail to author 10/19/2009

[41] Coach Norman Beck phone conversation with author 10/20/2009

[42] George Schaffer phone conversation with author 10/24/2009

[43] Rob Giesige phone conversation with author 10/18/2009

[44] Jeff Okuly conversation with author 10/25/2009

[45] Marv Andrews email to author 10/21/2009

[46] Amy Snyder e-mail to author 11/04/2009

[47] Amy Snyder e-mail to author 11/04/2009

[48] Coach Jeff Maag phone conversation with author 10/27/2009

[49] Rob Giesige e-mail to author 10/19/2009

[50] Coach McCord conversation with author 10/25/2009

[51] Steve Deitrick e-mail to author 10/22/2009

[52] Lynn Groll e-mail to author 10/28/2009

[53] Todd Helberg, "Ayersville scores early and often", (*The Crescent News*) October 4, 1986

[54] Marv Andrews phone conversation with author 10/20/2009

[55] Todd Helberg, "Ayersville scores early and often", (*The Crescent News*) October 4, 1986

[56] Kim Engel e-mail to author 10/30/2009
[57] Rob Giesige e-mail to author 10/19/2009
[58] Tolly Hanna phone conversation with author 11/06/2009
[59] Lynn Groll e-mail to author 10/28/2009
[60] George Schaffer phone conversation with author 10/24/2009
[61] Steve Deitrick e-mail to author 10/22/2009
[62] Shelby Gerken, "Rushing game keys Pilots", 20-7 (*The Crescent News*) October 25, 1986
[63] Shelby Gerken, "Rushing game keys Pilots", 20-7 (*The Crescent News*) October 25, 1986
[64] Todd Helberg, "GMC title and playoff berth await the winner", (*The Crescent News*) October 28, 1986
[65] 1986 Ayersville High School Fall Sports Program
[66] Coach McCord conversation with author 10/25/2009
[67] Gary Groll phone conversation with author 10/27/2009
[68] Todd Helberg, "Interception key as Pilots go perfect", (*The Crescent News*) November 1, 1986
[69] Jerry Carnahan e-mail to author 10/09/09
[70] Todd Helberg, "Interception key as Pilots go perfect", (*The Crescent News*) November 1, 1986
[71] Marv Andrews e-mail to author 10/21/2009
[72] Mark Froelich, "Schlachter rebounded from sprained ankle", (*The Crescent News*) November 4, 1986
[73] Kim Engel phone conversation with author 10/28/2009
[74] OHSAA 1986 Regional Football Tournament Official Program
[75] Teresa Weddelman phone conversation with author 10/27/2009
[76] Doug Johnston conversation with author 10/25/2009
[77] Coach Don Hammersmith phone conversation with author 10/28/2009
[78] Tolly Hanna e-mail to author 11/07/2009
[79] Tolly Hanna e-mail to author 11/08/2009
[80] OHSAA 1986 Regional Football Tournament Official Program
[81] Coach Norman Beck phone conversation with author 10/20/2009
[82] Jeff Okuly conversation with author 10/25/2009
[83] George Schaffer phone conversation with author 10/24/2009
[84] Jeff Okuly conversation with author 10/25/2009

85 Mark Weddelman phone conversation with author 10/27/2009
86 Todd Helberg, "Pilots defense stuffed Calvert", (*The Crescent News*) November 17, 1986
87 Todd Helberg, "Pilots may be leery on pass defense", (*The Crescent News*) November 19, 1986
88 Gary Groll phone conversation with author 10/27/2009
89 OHSAA Boys Football Tournament State Semifinals Official Program 1986
90 Steve Deitrick e-mail to author 10/22/2009
91 Tolly Hanna phone conversation with author 11/06/2009
92 Steve Deitrick e-mail to author 10/21/2009
93 Shelby Dawson phone conversation with author 11/01/2009
94 Denny Martin e-mail to author 11/13/2009
95 Todd Helberg, "Pilots overcome adversity", (*The Crescent News*) November 24, 1986
96 Coach Norman Beck phone conversation with author 10/20/2009
97 Teresa Weddelman phone conversation with author 10/27/2009
98 Todd Helberg, "Pilots overcome adversity", (*The Crescent News*) November 24, 1986
99 Lynn Groll e-mail to author 10/28/2009
100 Lynn Groll e-mail to author 10/28/2009
101 Steve Deitrick e-mail to author 10/21/2009
102 Coach Jeff Maag phone conversation with author 10/27/2009
103 Pat Groll phone conversation with author 10/27/2009
104 OHSAA Football Championship Games Official Game Program 1986
105 Jerry Carnahan e-mail to author 10/09/2009
106 Coach Don Hammersmith phone conversation with author 10/28/2009
107 Todd Hanna phone conversation with author 11/09/2009
108 Steve Deitrick e-mail to author 10/21/2009
109 Todd Helberg, "Pilots couldn't survive aerial bombardment," (*The Crescent News*) December 1, 1986
110 Steve Deitrick e-mail to author 10/10/2009
111 Tolly Hanna phone conversation with author 11/6/2009

[112] Todd Helberg, "Pilots couldn't survive aerial bombardment," (*The Crescent News*) December 1, 1986

[113] Todd Helberg, "Pilots couldn't survive aerial bombardment," (*The Crescent News*) December 1, 1986

[114] Amy Snyder e-mail to author 11/04/2009

[115] Kristen Warren phone conversation with author 11/01/2009

[116] Todd Helberg, "Pilots couldn't survive aerial bombardment," (*The Crescent News*) December 1, 1986

[117] Todd Helberg, "Pilots couldn't survive aerial bombardment," (*The Crescent News*) December 1, 1986

[118] Amy Snyder e-mail to author 11/04/2009

[119] Denny Martin e-mail to author 11/13/2009

[120] Steve Deitrick e-mail to author 10/10/2009

[121] Mike Wilson phone conversation with author 10/15/2009

[122] Rob Giesige e-mail to author 10/19/2009

[123] Chris Schlachter e-mail to author 11/02/2009

[124] Jerry Carnahan e-mail to author 10/8/2009

[125] John Finn e-mail to author 10/10 2009

[126] Marv Andrews phone conversation with author 10/20/2009

[127] Tim Boals e-mail to author 10/23/2009

[128] Eric Burket phone conversation with author 10/24/2009

[129] Coach Norman Beck phone conversation with author 10/20/2009

[130] Coach Bill Ondrus phone conversation with author 10/21/2009

[131] George Schaffer phone conversation with author 10/24/2009

[132] Aaron Roth phone conversation with author 10/24/2009

[133] Denny Martin phone conversation with author 10/28/2009

[134] Denny Martin e-mail to author 11/13/2009

[135] Kim Engel e-mail to author 10/30/2009

[136] Kim Engel phone conversation with author 10/28/2009

[137] Coach Don Hammersmith phone conversation with author 10/28/2009

[138] Jeff Okuly conversation with author 10/24/2009

[139] Coach Jeff Maag phone conversation with author 10/27/2009

[140] Shelby Dawson phone conversation with author 11/01/2009

[141] Kristen Warren phone conversation with author 11/01/2009

[142] Amy Snyder e-mail to author 11/04/2009

[143] Johnny Armes e-mail to author 11/08/2009

144 Tolly Hanna e-mail to author 11/07/2009
145 Todd Hanna phone conversation with author 11/09/2009
146 Jaime Briseno e-mail to author 11/15/2009